"Frank and his students have worked with my Public Service Innovation Branch at the Division for Public Institutions and Digital Government of the United Nations Department of Economic and Social Affairs (UN DESA) over the last decade. Frank is uniquely qualified to talk about SDG implementation, especially at the local level. He has brought some innovative concepts and best practices to the UN to implement SDGs. I am familiar and impressed with most of the research highlighted in this book as I listened to him, and his students present at the UN over these last ten years. I had shared the results of the research with my colleagues at UN DESA and in these findings we found much inspirational thinking".

Juwang Zhu, *Director of the Division for Public Institutions and Digital Government*

ADVANCING AND NEGOTIATING SUSTAINABLE DEVELOPMENT GOALS (SDGS)

Advancing and Negotiating Sustainable Development Goals (*SDGs*) presents a negotiation framework based on the principles of network/collaborative governance in implementing UN Sustainable Development Goals (SDGs). Trialed in the classroom and workplace, the practical toolkit gives you the tools necessary for facilitating future collaboration and knowledge transfer to all those working to strengthen the formulation, implementation, and achievement of SDG-oriented policies. *Advancing and Negotiating Sustainable Development Goals (SDGs)* is essential reading for those interested in a better and more sustainable future for all.

Frank V. Zerunyan is Professor of the Practice of Governance at the University of Southern California (USC) Sol Price School of Public Policy (USC Price) and Director of Executive Education, USC's Reserve Officers' Training Corps (ROTC) for the U.S. Air Force, Army, Naval Reserves ROTC, and Nautical Science Programs. Professor Zerunyan lectures locally and globally as part of building capacity and fostering leadership among public executives worldwide. He is the author of books, book chapters, and many short articles published nationally, internationally, and on his blog page. He has worked with the United Nations' Innovation Branch as an expert on public administration since 2013.

Yann Duzert is Professor at Rennes School of Business and Visiting Professor at various universities across the globe. Yann has authored or co-authored more than 30 books published in several languages. He has been a mediator for the Brazilian Presidency and coach for Brazilian government leaders. He has also done training and coaching for many international organizations and corporations. He is the inventor of Newgotiation and board member of the MIT Technology Review in Brazil.

ADVANCING AND NEGOTIATING SUSTAINABLE DEVELOPMENT GOALS (SDGS)

A Practical Toolkit

Frank V. Zerunyan and Yann Duzert

Routledge
Taylor & Francis Group
LONDON AND NEW YORK

Designed cover image: ©Getty Images/FG Trade Latin

First published 2025
by Routledge
605 Third Avenue, New York, NY 10158

and by Routledge
4 Park Square, Milton Park, Abingdon, Oxon, OX14 4RN

Routledge is an imprint of the Taylor & Francis Group, an informa business

Library of Congress Cataloging-in-Publication Data
Names: Zerunyan, Frank V., author. | Duzert, Yann, author.
Title: Advancing and negotiating Sustainable Development Goals (SDGs): a practical toolkit/Frank V. Zerunyan and Yann Duzert.
Description: New York, NY: Routledge, 2024. | Includes bibliographical references and index. |
Identifiers: LCCN 2024005900 (print) | LCCN 2024005901 (ebook) | ISBN 9781032804927 (hardback) | ISBN 9781032769134 (paperback) | ISBN 9781003497097 (ebook)
Subjects: LCSH: Sustainable Development Goals. | Sustainable Development Goals–Case studies. | Sustainable development–Government policy. | Sustainable development–Government policy–Case studies.
Classification: LCC HC79.E5 Z4434 2024 (print) | LCC HC79.E5 (ebook) | DDC 338.9/27–dc23/eng/20240407
LC record available at https://lccn.loc.gov/2024005900
LC ebook record available at https://lccn.loc.gov/2024005901

ISBN: 978-1-032-80492-7 (hbk)
ISBN: 978-1-032-76913-4 (pbk)
ISBN: 978-1-003-49709-7 (ebk)

DOI: 10.4324/9781003497097

Typeset in Times New Roman
by Deanta Global Publishing Services, Chennai, India

To my remarkable graduate students at the University of Southern California Sol Price School of Public Policy and a dedicated group of friends and public servants led by Director Juwang Zhu, retired Director Dr. John-Mary Kauzya, Gary Manukyan (ret.), Elida Reci, and Tiblet Tesfaye Kelemwork at the United Nations in New York. This book would not have been possible without your collaboration. Fight on!

Frank Vram Zerunyan, J.D. LL.D. (hc)

CONTENTS

Preface *xiii*
Prologue *xvii*
Introduction and Acknowledgments *xx*
List of Tables *xxiii*
List of Figures *xxiv*
List of Acronyms and Terms *xxvi*

1 Background and Motivation 1

2 Collaboration and Co-Creation in Governance 9

3 Effective Institutions—Research and Cases 18

Methodology 18
Phase 1: Literature Review, Interviews, and Instructive Case Studies 19
Phase 2: Random Selection 20
Phase 3: Case Analysis 23
Case Studies: Overview 23
Armenia: Elimination of Mother-to-Child Transmission of HIV 24
Australia: Cape York Region Project 26
Chile: Port Works Management 27
India: SAKALA Mission 28
Palestine: Establishment of the Palestine Public Finance Institute 29
Rwanda: Automated Passenger Clearance System 31

Spain: Decide Madrid 32
Thailand: Sa Kaeo Shelter for Children and Families 33

4 Effective Institutions—Applied Conceptual Framework 35

Overview of Framework Elements 35
Values and Ethics 35
Values and Ethics in Addressing Corruption 36
Values and Ethics as Seen in the Case Studies 40
Transformational Leadership 43
Individualized Consideration: Mentor or Coach with Empathy and Support 44
Intellectual Stimulation: Encourage Creativity and Innovation 44
Inspirational Motivation: Motivates Associates 44
Idealized Influence: Role Model 45
Transformational Leadership as Seen in the Case Studies 46
Strategic Planning 48
Components of a Strategic Plan 48
Comprehensive Environmental Assessment 49
Strategic Planning Best Practices 51
Planning as Seen in the Case Studies 52
Innovation and Co-Creation 54
Forms of Innovation 54
Innovation by Co-Creation 55
Innovation and Co-creation, as Seen in the Case Studies 56
Applied Conceptual Framework 59
Best Practices for Framework Application 60
Limitations 65
Conclusion 67

5 Newgotiation—An Ethical and Methodic Process 69

6 Newgotiation of SDGs—The 4-10-10 Technique 76

Context 76
Interest 78
Options 80
Power 81
Self-centered Motivations 81
Tactics that Misfire because They Damage Relationships 82
Qualities that Lubricate Negotiations because They Improve Relationships 83
Communication 87
Relationship 89
Concessions 92

Conformity to the Rule of Law 93
Standards 94
Time 96
Evaluation of the Completed Newgotiation—the Last Ten of the 4-10-10 97

7 Newgotiation Applied—Research and Cases 101

Methodology 101
Phase 1: Qualitative Method—Literature Review 102
Phase 2: Qualitative Framework—Survey 102
Phase 3: Qualitative Method 3: Case Study Analysis 102
Qualitative Method 4: Interviews 103
Strengths and Weaknesses 104
Characteristics of Negotiations in the Literature 104
Establishing Common Spaces for Negotiation 105
Establishing a Workable Consensus from Individual Interests 105
Establishing an Equitable Negotiation Space for Disadvantaged Stakeholders 106
Context of this Chapter and Research 106
Steps of a Negotiation Process 107
The Public Institutions Context—Institutionalizing Effective Negotiation 109
Survey Insight 113
Case Studies 114
Overview 114
Case Study Insight Summary 115
Introducing the Five Case Studies and What We Learned 118
Case 1: Smart City Platform for Mayor, Republic of Korea 118
The Application of Our Four Newgotiation Steps to the Seoul Case Study 120
Case 2: Decentralized Cooperation to Democratize Cities, Brazil and Mozambique 121
The Application of Our Four Newgotiation Steps to the Brazil–Mozambique Case Study 125
Case 3: Careers by Design LA, United States 127
The Application of Our Four Newgotiation Steps to the CDLA Case Study 132
Case 4: Shanghai “One Net Office,” People’s Republic of China 135
The Application of Our Four Newgotiation Steps to Shanghai’s “One Net Office” Case Study 139
Case 5: Endearing Homes for Our Silver Generation, Singapore 141

A Successful Blueprint: Kampung Admiralty 143
The Application of Our Four Newgotiation Steps to the Singapore Case Study 143

8 Final Newgotiation Framework and Recommendations 148

Recommendations for Practitioners 152
Governance and UN Principles of Effective Governance for Sustainable Development 154

Appendix A: Subject Matter Expert Interview Summaries *157*
Appendix B: Subject Matter Expert Interview Questions *160*
Appendix C: Selected Qualtrics Survey Results *161*
Appendix D: Official Interview Questions *171*
Appendix E: Principles of Effective Governance for Sustainable Development *173*
Bibliography *177*
Index *188*

PREFACE

By Dr John-Mary Kauzya, Chief, Public Service Innovation Branch, UNDESA (ret.)

World leaders met at the Headquarters of the United Nations (UN) in New York in September 2015. They adopted the 2030 Agenda for Sustainable Development (2030 Agenda or Agenda) with its 17 Sustainable Development Goals (SDGs).

The 2030 Agenda was adopted to protect the planet from degradation, ensure prosperity for all, foster peaceful, just, and inclusive societies, and mobilize global partnerships to ensure effective and timely implementation. It has been under implementation since January 2016. Its operational execution presents a determination from world leaders to protect the planet from degradation, a resolve to ensure prosperity for all, foster peaceful, just, and inclusive societies, and mobilize global partnerships to ensure that the Agenda is operating effectively and timely.

The Agenda is based on a transformational vision of a world free of poverty, hunger, disease, and want, with equitable and universal access to quality education, health care, and social protection, where physical, mental, and social well-being are assured. This vision is for an equitable, open, and inclusive world in which the needs of the most vulnerable are met. If it succeeds, people will be well off, the planet will be saved, peace will be assured, all lives will be profoundly improved, and the world will be transformed for the better. With the implementation of this vision, we will have learned that collaboration and partnerships constitute the strength that will sustain its existence and prosperity.

The 2030 Agenda is the culmination of intensive and extensive negotiations among multiple intersectoral actors. These actors include governments, the private sector, civil society, and local governments worldwide. Most importantly, implementing the Agenda is a process of constant negotiations in an ever-ongoing search for optimal solutions to the "wicked problems" facing societies, communities, and individuals at different levels.

To begin with, public administration, whether at the central government or local level, cannot approach the implementation of the Agenda in the "usual way." The Agenda calls for transformation instead of reform, which has been the buzzword for changes in public sector management.

In the socio-politico-economic development of many countries, the process of change in public administration has been driven by reforms aiming at optimization. The negotiations that resulted in the 2030 Agenda and the SDGs brought about significant values and principles that have accentuated the need for public administration reforms and transformation. These include integration, leaving no one behind, partnerships, equity, equality, justice, ethics, the rule of law, inclusive and accountable institutions, and the transformation itself, among many others.

Achieving all 17 goals necessitates capable public administration in all countries, including at the international level. Moreover, Goal 16 commits Member States of the UN to build effective, inclusive, and accountable institutions. Public administration can only ensure these with significant qualitative transformation in its capacities, including ideological orientation, institutions, organization, systems, processes and procedures, practices, behavior, methods, and many aspects that improve public administration outcomes.

The whole Agenda is the bold and transformative steps urgently needed to shift the world to a sustainable and resilient path. In the Agenda, Member States of the UN set out a supremely ambitious and transformational vision for the world. In negotiating the implementation of this vision, "transformation" needs to replace "reform" as the driving buzzword for profound change.

In many countries, public administration institutions, systems, structures, practices, and other capacities at central and local government levels must be transformed, even if change or reform may still be part of the appropriate terminologies in some countries. This change alone is a point of negotiation, and in many circumstances, replacing reforms with transformation is not an easy negotiation process, mainly because it concerns shifting emphasis from the values of optimization (efficiency and economy) to matters of transformation such as equity, inclusion, integration, leaving no one behind, ethics), and others.

The emphasis that the 2030 Agenda puts on "integration" necessitates negotiations that will transform public administration to enable it to pay particular value-based governance and leadership at all levels. Such negotiations will be complex because some of the values in question are far-reaching in their implementation. For example, we must understand the "integration" value in a broader, fuller, and deeper meaning to include:

(i) Integration of the three pillars of sustainable development (economic, social, and ecological).
(ii) Integration in coordination and coherence of various institutional components, policies, strategies, and programs that governance and public administration put in place to implement the 2030 Agenda effectively.
(iii) Integration of the various sectors and development activities to collaborate their inputs and outputs and create a mutually complementally collective impact.
(iv) Integration in terms of current and future policies and strategies, collaborating in the way current policies will impact the needs of future generations.
(v) Vertical integration of the different levels of government (central government and local government (or local authorities as they are called in some countries).
(vi) Integrating modern state/government institutions with traditional institutions so that the two join forces to cause sustainable development, especially in grassroots communities.
(vii) Integration of government, private sector, and civil society in terms of all the three sectors working in collaborative governance in the same direction of achieving sustainable development.

Because of the collaboration and partnerships central to implementing the 2030 Agenda to achieve the SDGs, leaving no one behind, negotiation is a critical feature and an essential competence in public administration at all levels of government in all societies.

Transforming public administration concerns makes it future-oriented, proactive rather than reactive, more dynamic, and innovative. A future-oriented public administration will promote the spirit of innovation and change readiness in the public sector, transforming mindsets and creating a different organizational culture in terms of principles, norms, and values.

The significant difference between optimization (as in reform) and transformation is that while optimization is about making the most of existing resources, change is about innovation, creative thinking, and trying out new ideas and ways of doing things. In the short term, some items may look inefficient in terms of using resources. Still, in the long term, they are most useful in terms of cherished values such as inclusiveness, equity, responsiveness, and leaving no one behind in development.

For developing the capacities and competencies of a transformational public administration, universities, management development institutes, and all tertiary institutions need to be fully on board to include negotiation and collaborative governance in their priority capacities for effective and equitable implementation of the 2030 Agenda. In this light, this book on advancing and negotiating SDGs constitutes an enormous and welcome contribution to the ongoing global, regional, national, and local efforts to implement the 2030 Agenda.

Capacities and competencies for negotiation become inevitably critical when one bears in mind that, as indicated in the Report of the Eighth Meeting of the Group of Experts on Public Administration and Finance of the United Nations, no matter how just and desirable it may appear to the majority of the UN Member States, "no single model or set of recommendations applied in the same manner or sequence to all developing or least developed countries." Transformation in implementing the 2030 Agenda to achieve the SDGs is a process highly engaged in negotiation.

PROLOGUE

As I begin my 16th year of academic service at one of the best research universities and highly ranked public affairs schools in the United States, I want to reflect on the value of local municipalities as the antidote to many wicked challenges we face today. This book is dedicated to those resilient cities, towns, and boroughs that make sustainability and development the critical component of their ethos.

Several years ago, I shared the podium at Fordham Law School, New York, with Professor Benjamin Barber, who wrote a book entitled, *If Mayors Ruled the World*."At Fordham, I spoke about my then-forthcoming journal article, "The Evolution of the Municipal Corporation and the Innovations of Local Governance in California to Preserve Home Rule and Local Control.[1]" Professor Barber then observed in his book, "We have come full circle in the city's epic history. Humankind began its march to politics and civilization in the *polis*—the township ... The city, always the human habitat of first resort, has in today's globalizing world once again become democracy's best hope." I want to add that it is also sustainability's best hope.

The former mayor of Denver, Wellington E. Webb, said, "The 19th century was a century of empires, the 20th century was a century of nation-states. The 21st century will be a century of cities." This perception is accurate today, as a coalition of business, government, and academic colleagues has joined in surveying cities with diverse populations and economies to design an evidence-based roadmap to post-pandemic urban resilience and sustainability. As a member of the board of advisors for this worldwide endeavor, I see and appreciate the value of local public service and leadership. In this book, we cite and describe some of the findings of this research.

I always tell my students there is no greater joy or honor than serving humanity. In my case, this is my fourth time as Mayor of Rolling Hills Estates, California, during my 25th year of serving my local community and 21st year as an elected policymaker, which includes several leadership roles as president of California Contract Cities representing over 7 million Californians and vice president of the California Medical Board as a gubernatorial appointee representing 38 million medical consumers of the state.

Public service is not about collecting a paycheck from the government. Helping humanity is an activity beyond self-interest. For over eight years, I have had the pleasure of collaborating with the United Nations Department of Economic and Social Affairs and, specifically, the Public Service Innovation Branch. I have taught in every urban continent, except Australia.

My primary function has been to explain the value of local public service and collaboration in typically centralized governments where hierarchical bureaucracies tend to create public bureaucrats rather than servants.

In a world of constant competition for power and influence, we govern through values of collaboration and compassion. These values are more focused at the local level, where we are the closest to the people we serve. We serve to facilitate neighbors, helping neighbors without the divisions imposed on us by political interests and the media, which thrive on accentuating differences. Professor Barber's confidence in mayors and cities is not misplaced.

Focusing on our shortcomings at the national levels, we are losing sight of our progress and what we do exceptionally well in local communities. Mayor Bloomberg accurately reflected that while the American government is "just unable to do anything … the mayors of this country still have to deal with the real world." Some political scientists and politicians pontificate and agitate, "Mayors pick up the garbage." I presume he meant this literally and figuratively. In this book, we hope to guide those local officials to have a framework and a common language to "Newgotiate" the most wicked problems facing our communities across the globe.

As competitive as we are, humanity's impulse to lend a helping hand is second to none. This impulse exhibits itself at the local level, often during disasters. Recently, I wrote an article on disaster management planning, published in Apolitical.co, highlighting the importance of a local "facilitative platform for a limitless number of actors coming together for the greater good.[2]" This collaboration is not just a theory but a reality we witnessed in Florida and Texas in the aftermath of hurricanes, where neighborly acts of human kindness were displayed for all to see and experience.

I am not naïve about observing bad actors in local governments. Sadly, there will be evil while there are living and breathing humans in this world. Local governments are not immune. We must collectively fight this evil in all forms. But let us not confuse this small number of evildoers with the overwhelming majority of those who seek to do good.

President Kennedy once said, "If a free society cannot help the many who are poor, it cannot save the few who are rich." Martin Luther King alluded to a "promissory note to which every American was to fall heir." These calls to unity and values are what we generally practice at the local level. We serve our communities for the greater good without regard to divisions or differences. I say generally because, sadly, some people continue to push the political ideology of division to my colleagues in local governance today. Some even practice it, causing more harm than good.

Today's ideological and less-tolerant narratives and fights simply do not work at the implementation level. They erase a sense of unity in communities and complicate governance, delivering much less than the quality products and services our residents deserve.

I predict that the love of local public service, the local reality, and the importance of delivering results will promote collaboration in governance. As we begin 2025, let us focus on the good and what unites us. In the early 18th century, which remains applicable today, Montesquieu wrote, "Le mieux est le mortel ennemi du bien" (The best is the mortal enemy of the good). If cities succumb to the hatred exhibited by the ideologues and political classes, we will truly see the end of hope for democracy.

Frank Vram Zerunyan, J.D. LL.D. (hc)

Notes

1 Frank Vram Zerunyan, The Evolution of the Municipal Corporation and the Innovations of Local Governance in California to Preserve Home Rule and Local Control, 44 Fordham Urb. L.J. 217 (2017).

2 https://apolitical.co/solution-articles/en/why-you-need-a-strong-disaster-management-plan-in-governance

INTRODUCTION AND ACKNOWLEDGMENTS

Some of the significant challenges of our era include "wicked" problems, which the United Nations (UN) describes and categorizes as Sustainable Development Goals (SDGs). SDGs, also known as the "blueprint to humanity's highest aspirations," span general disciplines in law, medicine, technology, economic development, public policy, and administration, public–private partnerships, and ethics. These challenges require a renewed sense of governance among sectors instead of just government. The former term implies that the development and implementation of public policy and administration are increasingly shared among a plurality of actors.

We use this topic of governance, and more importantly, "collaborative governance," to frame our subject matter in addressing the advancement and negotiation of SDGs. Governance requires a different mindset and collaborative effort to search for the common good. Successful governance is about the quest for the win–win, which mirrors the negotiation process we explored in our book *Newgotiation for Public Administration Professionals* and our various student-led research projects on effective institutions and negotiation frameworks.

Advancing and Newgotiating SDGs: A Practical Toolkit is our newest book. This readable book compiles the remarkable work of our graduate students at the University of Southern California, Sol Price School of Public Policy (USC Price), third-party research, and the standard "Newgotiation" language and framework we created in our previous book.

As we approach 2030, the UN's deadline for realizing SDGs, this book highlights the importance of effective institutions and negotiation skills for implementation. This book comes when citizens locally, nationally, and globally demand better governance, equity and inclusion, greater sectoral participation in public affairs, and enhanced integrity and accountability of their leaders in all institutions and organizations. We write this book intending to orient all those leaders and managers in charge of delivering this ambitious set of goals for global development. This orientation we describe is a new frame-based perspective on normative theory but suggestive of areas for empirical analysis written for all disciplines covered by the SDGs. Most of our research points to the needs at the local level for better education, support, mentoring, best practices, and leadership. The UN is uniquely positioned to provide this general education and support.

We are not naïve enough to think that this book somehow produces magic or provides a "silver bullet" to deal with the challenges of SDGs. We simply attempt to help leaders and managers strengthen institutions, find the collaborative frame, and achieve the often-desired but hardly-obtained win–win result. We hope to guide all to better governance, management, and public service. The most elusive commonality between all sectors dealing with SDGs is exploring the ethical implementation of the public interest. Other commonalities impeding the progress of SDGs include impatience, lack of tolerance, and misalignment of values and interests. We tackle these topics in our applied conceptual framework about effective institutions and Newgotiation.

This book is rooted in research, literature, theory, analysis, and practice, as reflected by our original work in governance and negotiation. Thus, this book provides theoretical and practical insight to all involved in delivering the UN 2030 Agenda (2030 Agenda) and generally addressing "wicked" problems worldwide.

We want to acknowledge that we chose not to make this book highly scholarly in documenting sources used in great bibliographic detail. However, we provide extensive references on relevant authors, book titles, and journal articles, making it possible for our readers to readily search for these sources when more detail or information is desired.

Moreover, we made every effort to compress our discussion to make this book short and to the point yet rich in real-life examples. We aim to use this book and other training materials to build capacity among our students and professionals to deliver SDGs. In this regard, we acknowledge our friends and colleagues in academia, the UN Department of Economic and Social Affairs (DESA), and public and private executives for their assistance and encouragement in writing this book.

Finally, we wish to acknowledge our students who researched, wrote, presented, and provided us with a great laboratory to test our subject matters. I thank my former doctoral student, Dr Michael D. Falkow, for his peer review and help in editing this book. Michael's contributions to the field of public administration are remarkable and is the subject of another book we are editing. As professors in preeminent research universities, we know that the quality of our students directly correlates to our ability to research, write, and educate. We, therefore, thank them for their extraordinary contributions.

For seven years now, I have had the honor of leading the best and brightest graduate students in their practicum projects. We are known as Team UN at USC Price. In 2019 and 2021, Team UN's work has focused on SDGs. Now-graduated students Hannah, Umesh, Lorraine, and Dong researched and developed an applied conceptual framework of an effective public institution to be used as a teaching tool for local entities working to advance SDGs. The framework highlights values, ethics, transformational leadership, strategic planning, innovation, co-creation, and best application practices. These concepts are applicable in our Newgotiation framework, which we also discuss in this book.

The framework's outcomes include good governance through increased transparency, accountability, and responsiveness. The framework is for a more efficient public institution where the provision and delivery of services are predictable, timely, and consistent. In this context, we learned from our research that increased public trust, where constituents are satisfied with services and confident that they will continue to receive them, and increased public participation, aid in prioritizing equity and co-creation. In addition, we found resilient institutions where the institution's capacities are safeguarded, especially in the face of crisis and changing circumstances. The most significant impact is the advancement of the SDGs through the development of effective, accountable, and transparent public institutions.

Team UN 2021, Lewei, Siyi, Kim, Gregory, and Alex, building on the work of prior teams, including Team UN 2019, researched, developed, and presented a negotiation framework based on our Newgotiation model in our book *Newgotiation for Public Administration Professionals*[1] through case study analysis of exemplary projects across the globe. In addition, they highlighted the pressing need to teach more robust policymaking processes at the local and grassroots levels to ensure that the 2030 Agenda can be achieved on time. Finally, Team UN 2021 and the UN discussants identified the aspect of negotiations, more specifically, collaborative negotiations, as an essential toolkit to strengthen the formulation and implementation of SDG-oriented policies. The recommendations that followed incorporate insights gained from the research to educate and inform future collaborations to facilitate the achievement of the 2030 Agenda.

Note

1 Duzert, Y & Zerunyan, F.V. Newgotiation for Public Adminsitration Professionals. Vandeplas Publishing (2019).

TABLES

3.1	Research Questions and Methodology	19
3.2	Evaluation Criteria	21
3.3	Statistics of Cases by UN Region and HDI Level	21
3.4	Results of Random Selection	22
3.5	Eight Selected Cases for Case Analysis	24
7.1	Case Study Analysis and Identification	103
7.2	UNPSA Cases Reviewed	103
7.3	Relevant Table for Stakeholdership	108
7.4	Initiatives for Case Analysis	114
7.5	Smart City Platform, Seoul, Republic of Korea	118
7.6	Cooperation of Brazil and Mozambique	122
7.7	Collaboration of Cities	122
7.8	Collaboration among Sectoral Stakeholders	124
7.9	Careers by Design in the City of Los Angeles	127
7.10	Shanghai "One Net Office" (People's Republic of China)	135
7.11	Stakeholder Analysis	138
7.12	Singapore Housing and Development Board	141

FIGURES

1.1	Sustainable Development Goals	1
3.1	World Map with Highlighted Selected Cases	24
3.2	Elimination of Mother-to-Child Transmission of HIV	25
3.3	Cape York Region Package [infrastructure]	26
3.4	Port Works Management	28
3.5	SAKALA Mission [e-governance]	29
3.6	Establishment of the Palestine Public Finance Institute	30
3.7	Automated Passenger Clearance System [border crossing]	31
3.8	Citizen Participation Project	33
3.9	Sa Kaeo Shelter for Children and Families	33
4.1	Interdependent, Interrelated, Interconnected Elements of Institutional Effectiveness	36
4.2	Transformational Leadership	43
4.3	Strategic Planning Components	49
4.4	Factors of Co-Creation	53
4.5	Applied Conceptual Framework	59
4.6	Overview of Application Best Practices	61
4.7	Levels of Capacity-Building	62
6.1	Newgotiation 4 Steps and 10 Elements	77
6.2	Proper Communications	89
6.3	Treating Time as an Essential Element	97
7.1	Distributive and Integrative Negotiation	111
7.2	Negotiation Framework	111
7.3	Dual Concern Model of Strategic Preferences	112

7.4	Selected Cases for Case Analysis	115
7.5	Effective Collaboration	116
7.6	Los Angeles Demographic Breakdown; Diversity	128
7.7	Ratio of Disparities in Los Angeles	129
7.8	Map of South Los Angeles shown with SLATE-Z	129
7.9	Los Angeles Census Statistics (2015–2019)	130
7.10	Careers by Design LA Program Model	132
7.11	Shanghai "One Net Office" (People's Republic of China)	136
7.12	Shanghai's "One Net Office" System Framework	137
8.1	Newgotiation Framework	149
8.2	Toolkits for Success	151

LIST OF ACRONYMS AND TERMS

ACA	Affordable Care Act [United States]
AEC	architecture, engineering, and construction
AI	artificial intelligence
ANAMM	National Association of Municipalities of Mozambique
APCS	Automated Passenger Clearance System [Rwanda]
ARV	antiretroviral
ASME	American Society of Mechanical Engineers
BATNA	Best Alternative to a Negotiated Agreement
C2C	city-to-city
CCM	Country Coordination Mechanism
CDLA	Careers by Design LA
CEA	Careers Excellence Academy [Los Angeles, CA]
CEPA	Committee of Experts on Public Administration [UN]
CfA	Code for America
CSO	Civil Society Organization
CYRP	Cape York Region Package [Australia]
DESA	Department of Economic and Social Affairs
DGIE	Directorate General of Immigration and Emigration [Rwanda]
DPIDG	Division of Public Institutions and Digital Governance
DRC	Democratic Republic of Congo
EASE	Enhancement for Active Seniors [Singapore]
ESI	ESI Thought Lab
FNP	National Front of Mayors of Brazil
GAAP	Generally Accepted Accounting Principles
GSC	Guarantee of Service to Citizen

HBR	Harvard Business Review
HDB	Housing and Development Board [Singapore]
HDI	Human Development Index
ICA	Institutional and Context Analysis [UN]
ICTs	Information and Communication Technologies
IEPP	Indigenous Economic Participation Plan [Australia]
IMD	International Institute for Management Development [Switzerland]
IoT	Internet of Things
ITSA	interrupted time-series analysis
KRAs	Key Result Areas
LAC	Los Angeles County
LATTC	Los Angeles Trade and Technical College
LBS	Lease Buyback Scheme [Singapore]
LDCs	Least Developed Countries
MDGs	Millennium Development Goals
MINALOC	Ministry of Local Government [Rwanda]
MND	Ministry of National Development [Singapore]
MOH	Ministry of Health [Singapore]
MOT	Ministry of Transport [Singapore]
MP	Members of Parliament [Singapore]
MPS sessions	meet-the-people sessions [Singapore]
NAP	National AIDS Programme [Armenia]
NCAP	National Center of AIDS Prevention [Armenia]
NFP	Not-For-Profit
NGO	Non-Governmental Organizations
NIDA	National Identification Agency [Rwanda]
NTNU	Norwegian University of Science and Technology
PDR	Peninsula Development Road [Australia]
PPFI	Palestine Public Finance Institute
PMTCT	preventive mother-to-child transmission of HIV
PPA	Peninsula Development Road Priority Agreement [Australia]
PSAI	Public Service Award Initiatives
PSIB	Public Service Innovation Branch
RDB	Rwanda Development Board
ROK	Republic of Korea
RPA	Robotic Process Automation
SAKALA	Karnataka Guarantee of Services to Citizens Act of 2011
SCAG	Southern California Association of Governments
SCP	Smart City Platform [Seoul, Korea]
SDGs	Sustainable Development Goals
SIAC	Integral Information and Citizen Assistance System [Chile]
SICP	Seoul Information Communication Plaza

SLATE-Z	South LA Transit Empowerment Zone
SMEs	Small-to-Medium-sized Enterprises
SMG	Seoul Metropolitan Government
SODP	Seoul Open Data Plaza
TMR	Queensland Department of Transport and Main Roads [Australia]
UCLG	United Cities and Local Governments
UCLG	United Cities and Local Governments
UNDP	United Nations Development Program
UNPSA	United Nations Public Service Awards
USC Price	University of Southern California Sol Price School of Public Policy
WeGO	World Government Organization of Cities and Local Governments
WFC	Workforce Connections, Inc. [Los Angeles, CA]
ZOPA	Zone of Possible Agreement

1

BACKGROUND AND MOTIVATION

The 2030 Agenda for Sustainable Development has defined the trajectory of the UN since its inception in 2015. This 2030 Agenda was established to build on the Millennium Development Goals (MDGs), focusing the efforts of the UN Member States on alleviating global poverty, inequality, and injustice. It comprises 169 targets for 17 Sustainable Development Goals (SDGs) (See Figure 1.1), each to be achieved through local implementation.

FIGURE 1.1 Sustainable Development Goals

DOI: 10.4324/9781003497097-1

No Poverty
Zero Hunger
Good Health and Well-being
Quality Education
Gender Equality
Clean Water and Sanitation
Affordable and Clean Energy
Decent Work and Economic Growth
Industry Innovation and Infrastructure
Reduced Inequalities
Sustainable Cities and Communities
Responsible Consumption and Production
Climate Action
Life below Water
Life on Land
Peace, Justice, and Strong Institutions
Partnerships for the Goals

In implementing local development objectives, cities must overcome various challenges and resolve concerns pertinent to their communities. The UN constantly seeks to support these local organizations by equipping them with the knowledge and skills to achieve their objectives effectively. In partnership with these local entities, the Public Service Innovation Branch of the Division of Public Institutions and Digital Governance (DPIDG) of the UN Department of Economic and Social Affairs (PSIB/DESA) aims to transfer the "SDG Mindset" through education and training. By mobilizing knowledge transfer and exchange, PSIB/DESA strengthens public sector institution-based systems, structures, and processes to provide services to their constituents better.

Cities are the most networked and interconnected of our political organizations. Of the global population, 55% lives in cities, and 75% of global CO_2 emissions comes from cities. According to the most recent Voluntary National Review Synthesis Report of UN DESA, implementation of SDGs heavily relies on policies and programs at the local level. In countries like Argentina, Austria, Burundi, India, Morocco, Panama, and Uganda, local governments integrated the 2030 Agenda into local planning and encouraged vertical and horizontal collaboration strategies for implementation.

Recently, we participated as advisors in a worldwide ESI Thought Lab (ESI) research project. The project surveyed 167 global cities with diverse populations, economies, and geographic locations. The project aimed to understand how cities cope with the SDGs' social, environmental, and economic goals. The project also focused on what the UN categorizes as the five "Ps," including people, planet, prosperity, peace, and partnerships. We dedicate several pages in this chapter to this remarkable data set to reemphasize the importance of effective institutions and negotiation at the local level. One of our case studies in our Newgotiation framework features Los Angeles, which is ranked second in the 167 cities surveyed in SDGs leadership.

These goals and aspirations are bold; the 15-year timeline to achieve them globally added a layer of challenge and ambition. The 2030 Agenda requires strong political will, innovative strategies, and international collaboration for the global community to achieve. The year 2020 marked the completion of the first one-third of the Agenda's timeline. After assessing the progress, the UN Member States recognized that global efforts were insufficient to accomplish their goals by 2030.

The UN reported in a pre-COVID-19 assessment that most targets are 10% outside of their desired range. Most targets on a projected, negative, long-term trend are environmental-related (Goals 12–15). The onset of COVID-19 has made the ability to remedy and accomplish these goals substantially more arduous for UN Member States. Estimates indicate that the global economy is experiencing its most significant and extreme contraction since the Great Depression. Furthermore, the global poverty headcount is estimated to increase by approximately 100 million people. This surge reverses the global trend of declining poverty realized over the past 20–30 years.

The most recent United Nations (UN) Sustainable Development Goals (SDGs) Progress Report 2023 ("Report")[1] is grim. This Report is a systemic survey of UN Member States at the national level. According to the Report, halfway to the deadline of 2030, we are leaving more than half the world behind. More importantly, 30% of member states have regressed. The climate crisis, the lingering effects of COVID-19, war, and geopolitical conflicts are cited as among the reasons seriously threatening the implementation of SDGs by 2030.[2]

The Report finds that global temperature is already 1.1°C above pre-industrial levels. We continue to experience catastrophic and intensifying heat waves, droughts, floods, and wildfires. Rising sea levels are threatening hundreds of millions of people in coastal communities. In addition, the world is facing the most significant species extinction event since the dinosaur age. Oceans were burdened with over 17 million metric tons of plastic pollution in 2021.

By 2023, the devastation of war, geopolitical conflicts, and coups orchestrated by unchecked authoritarians have displaced over 110 million people, of which 35 million are refugees—the highest figures ever recorded. War crimes, threats to commit genocide, military coups, and related human rights violations, even sanctioned by the International Court of Justice, threaten SDG 16, which seeks peace, justice, and strong institutions. SDG 16 is critically important for the implementation of the remaining 16 SDGs.

The breadth of the SDGs lends itself to a comprehensive policy approach. However, a primary criticism of this goal structure is that it generates obscurity regarding how to carry out the 2030 Agenda. Our book addresses this issue by identifying overarching impediments to implementing the SDGs in institutions and local government negotiations with relevant stakeholders.

In its call to advance a sustainable and resilient future, the 2030 Agenda requires transparent, effective, inclusive, and accountable institutions. Institutions contribute to and determine resource allocation and services that establish equity and access, among other process-oriented functions and outcomes. As such, institutions play a significant role in ensuring the achievement of the SDGs. This role is captured in the language of SDG 16, whose aim is to "promote peaceful and inclusive societies for sustainable development, provide access to justice for all, and build effective, accountable, and inclusive institutions at all levels."

To accomplish this goal, SDG 16 identifies four focus areas: (1) conflict prevention and peacebuilding, (2) responsive and accountable institutions, (3) inclusive political processes, and (4) the rule of law, justice, security, and human rights. While building accountable and inclusive institutions is the primary objective of these focus areas, SDG 16's goal of producing effective institutions also advances all other SDGs and promotes locally led development efforts. Thus, progress toward the SDGs relies not only on progress toward SDG 16 but also on identifying best institutional practices.

With this need in mind, based on Team UN 2019's work, we recognize that education is a critical component of building capable, SDG-focused institutions. Moreover, educating local leaders, public servants, and constituents about best institutional practices is essential to improving their communities. In this context, our conceptual framework of an effective public sector institution will offer teaching tools that can be used to transfer knowledge to local entities working to advance the SDGs.

Our applied conceptual framework for effective institutions highlights the complementarity of institutional capacity, ethics and values, leadership competencies, and strategic planning, among other relevant characteristics. Specifically, our findings are contingent on current and relevant academic research and literature and the institutional aspects of award-winning, local-level programs, as seen in the Knowledge Base of UN Public Service Award Initiatives (PSAI). Furthermore, applying the conceptual framework relies upon understanding the varying local contexts in which public institutions operate. These contexts offer socially, economically, and politically diverse scenarios that must be considered when designing a framework for institutional effectiveness. Considering these varying environmental factors, the framework must adapt to local contexts and equip institutional leaders with best practices for combating barriers and constraints to effectiveness.

Team UN 2021 built on the previous research by proposing a conceptual framework for policy negotiations at the local government level. This framework aims to enhance SDG achievement through effective and collaborative policy negotiations. This new conceptual framework combines policy negotiation theory and insights gained from the team's in-depth analysis and qualitative evaluation of case studies across different continents. In summary, the framework consists of four steps of negotiation combined with three underlying critical elements based on insights gained from five case studies, each from a different country.

Sustainable Development Goal 16

> Promote peaceful and inclusive societies for sustainable development, provide access to justice for all and build effective, accountable, and inclusive institutions at all levels.
>
> United Nation, 2015

We derive the four steps of negotiation from our Newgotiation framework. The Newgotiation framework focuses on the following four steps to negotiation: (1) Preparation, (2) Value Creation, (3) Value Distribution, and (4) Implementation. Adapting the Newgotiation framework to evaluate our chosen SDG-oriented case studies, research revealed that three critical elements were essential to good collaborative negotiations across all the case studies. These elements are (1) Leadership, (2) Toolkits, and (3) Trust. The case studies identified in our research have promoted at least one of the UN's SDGs. In addition, the team evaluated each case to have performed well in its public policy negotiation process for that initiative. These case studies originate in developed and developing countries across multiple continents.

In the past seven years, our UN Teams have researched and presented on Millennium Development Goals (MDGs) and, more recently, SDGs, as discussed in this book. The common characteristics and reoccurring topics have been collaborative governance, community engagement and involvement, the public interest, values, ethics, innovation, co-creation, strategy, and transformational leadership. While there are other sub-topics worthy of recognition, in this book, we discuss all these reoccurring topics through our research of case studies, third-party research, and survey of global cities, literature review, and our Newgotiation paradigm, which UN Team 2021 applied to various case studies across the globe.

The importance of having cities advance SDG policies cannot be understated. Prepared and more innovative cities will lay the groundwork for collaborative governance mechanisms to deal with the world's most wicked problems.

A global coalition of academics, government, and business joined to create an evidence-based road map for SDG planning, leadership, and implementation. The Project headed by ESI Thought Lab (ESI) explored, surveyed, and interviewed 167 cities with diverse demographics and economies (Project).[3] The survey, to which we provided input, reached 167 cities in 82 countries, representing over 500 million residents, nearly 7% of the world's population.

Using the SDGs as the framework, the Project helped us understand how cities achieve their social, environmental, and economic goals in the face of many contemporary challenges. The Project revealed that most cities include SDGs in their urban plans, focusing mainly on people: 91% on poverty, 89% on good health and wellness, 86% on education, and 77% on gender equality. We discovered that cities also plan for economic development, including decent work and wages 86% of the time and incorporating sustainability principles 78% of the time.

Cities have made the most progress in SDGs related to people and prosperity, a natural focus of local governments, and minor progress in topics like hunger and climate. Cities with more manageable populations are typically ahead in SDG planning and implementation by about 6% (64–58%). On average, 74% of cities in advanced economies progressed on SDGs compared to half that percentage in emerging markets. European and North American cities lead the way, while African cities trail behind by relatively wide margins (e.g., Europe with 77%, North America with 71%, and Africa with 33% on average).

The Project revealed that the most progressive cities ensure success through a methodical approach to monitoring progress, gaining public support, appointing a leader, and creating accountability measures. This systematic technique is a potent recipe for effective public institutions, which we discuss in later chapters.

On average, 81% of cities reported that COVID-19 was the most significant disruptor they faced recently. Its effect will most likely persist well beyond any new normalization. Over 75% of cities said they would reconsider their urban plan, including 54% by rethinking mobility. All this will change how people live in cities, including SDG planning, support, and implementation.

Post-pandemic, the imperative for SDG implementation has gained priority in cities, prompting 43% of European cities to refocus on social good. While the pandemic forced people to work differently, it underscored the importance of cross-sectoral collaborations.

Almost half the SDG-leading cities valued the need to collaborate with various sectors, particularly the private sector. SDG leaders work with a range of partners to achieve the desired results. They are twice as likely as other more developing cities to collaborate with various sectors, focusing on the necessary strengths to deliver the desired outcomes. Approximately 25% of the cities said that creating an ecosystem for collaboration was vital for their success. Along with the private sector, higher education research institutions remain typically untapped.

The Norwegian University of Science and Technology (NTNU) recruited volunteers and students to conduct research and suggest innovative solutions for sustainability for the city of Trondheim. In a city of 200,000 residents, 4,000 students typically work on these solutions.

At the University of Southern California Sol Price School of Public Policy (USC Price), we offer an executive program for local leaders to teach, discuss, and collaborate on innovative research in policy and administration. In return, these participative cities, rich repositories and sources of data and information, enhance our research quality. These types of partnerships are blazing the trail for cities to achieve SDGs. Accessing, analyzing, and extracting value from data are critical to any SDG implementation success.

Of the cities surveyed, 83% want their partners to offer real solutions and innovate. This innovative concept is critical in our Newgotiation paradigm because we value the "why" more than the cost. The most advanced cities reported that cost is on their mind only 21% of the time during their SDG negotiations. The more challenged cities, including 47% of African cities, responded at higher percentages. While we do not discount the importance of cost, some cities have become creative in various forms of funding to implement SDGs.

SDG funding remains challenging for all cities, as they bear a substantial portion of the financial burden. However, innovative cities rely on private and philanthropic support. Others focus on government borrowing, national governments, user fees, and taxes to plan and deliver SDGs. Concepts from our Newgotiation paradigm for shared values and interests make philanthropy a viable funding source for like-minded businesses that embrace more SDGs.

Leading cities, also referred to as Cities 4.0, are making significant investments in cloud computing, the Internet of Things (IoT), mobile applications, biometrics, blockchain, Artificial Intelligence (AI), and Robotic Process Automation (RPA). The Project found that 66% of cities in 2022 and 80% by 2024 will invest heavily in AI. One such example is in the city of Philadelphia, where a low-cost imaging start-up company scans 1,200 miles of pavement 30 feet at a time to determine the quality of the concrete to detect early deterioration. Regular pavement repair lowers the long-term maintenance cost and contributes to social equity and quality of life. The win–win possibilities with AI are limitless. However, it is also fair to mention that AI presents policy and ethical challenges for cities. We discussed some of these challenges in a book titled, *Next Generations Ethics*[4], particularly in a chapter, "Techno Innovations: the role of ethical standards, law, regulation, and the public interest."

The use of technology and data are critical to cities. However, cities must have a practical governance framework to achieve their SDG objectives. In the next chapter and throughout the book, we discuss the critical elements of good governance, developed with engagement, leadership, and collaboration. We also discuss institution-building resilience to sustain the long-term plan to implement SDGs.

Finally, cities need to consider economic and social benefits to achieve SDGs. The goal is to generate a valuable return on all investments based on long-term city goals. One of our colleagues from the Project advisory board summarized it best: "The first tool cities should leverage is a culture of collaboration. If the pandemic has taught us anything, it has revealed that no one person, stakeholder, or department in government has all the answers to solve all the community's needs." We agree and, therefore, discuss collaboration and co-creation in governance in our next chapter and beyond.

Notes

1 https://unstats.un.org/sdgs/report/2023/The-Sustainable-Development-Goals-Report-2023.pdf
2 https://sdgs.un.org/goals
3 The full ESI research and survey results can be found at https://econsultsolutions.com/wp-content/uploads/2021/03/ESITL-Smart-City-Solutions-eBook-Final.pdf
4 Zerunyan FV. Techno Innovations: The Role of Ethical Standards, Law and Regulation, and the Public Interest. In: Abbas AE, ed. *Next-Generation Ethics: Engineering a Better Society*. Cambridge University Press; 2019:328–342.

2

COLLABORATION AND CO-CREATION IN GOVERNANCE

We previously wrote and suggested that the field of public administration is experiencing a paradigm shift in the "steering of society" from "government" to "governance." The latter term implies that the development and implementation of public policy are increasingly distributed or shared among a plurality of actors and sectors. Today, public, private, Not-For-Profit (NFP), or Non-Governmental Organizations (NGO) and citizens (sometimes called the 4th sector) are much more connected and predisposed to collaborate than ever before. As a result, these sectors, organizations, or persons, each with unique interests, motivations, resources, and capabilities, provide unprecedented opportunities to restructure governments to govern better.

Collaborative arrangements today, especially between the sectors, provide novel approaches to organizing public administration. For over a century, the public, private, and not-for-profit sectors developed intrasectorally but exploited and consumed intersectorally. The hierarchical "silos" each of them created generally ignored the other, creating long-lasting tensions and breaches of trust. While all three sectors often serve the same constituency (the public), their motivations and intentions differ and are inconsistent in the framework.

The public sector remains the steward and guardian of the rule of law, social justice, the public interest, and the provision of "public goods." On the other hand, the private sector primarily focuses on profits, personal interest, and "private goods." These interests and goods compete, and at times, to the detriment of the other. Ironically, neither can exist without the other. Wall Street is untamed without rules and regulations. History is littered with decades of examples that illustrate this point. The irresponsible (at worst) and less thoughtful (at best), lack of laws and deregulation of savings and loans in the

DOI: 10.4324/9781003497097-2

late 1980s, the energy sector during the Enron era, and the recent mortgage-backed securities crisis of 2008 brought the private and public marketplaces to their knees. While regulation and deregulation are debated in the political context, their effects on public administration are apparent. Without a well-balanced and fair rule of law, these sectors are incapable of functioning, much less collaborating. The following pages discuss collaboration as a topic leading to sustainable results.

Our former colleague Warren Bennis clearly articulated that "in a global society where timely information is the most important commodity, collaboration is not simply desirable; it is inevitable." Historically, collaborations have brought us unique innovations and projects. In the private sector, alliances of innovators and skill sets created Apple, Disney, Hewlett Packard, and even the movie Star Wars.

In the public sector, collaborations facilitated the Lakewood Plan of 1954 in California, allowing municipalities to contract with other governments and sectors to deliver special municipal services. These collaborations provided statutorily defined special municipal services in finance, economics, accounting, engineering, administration, and law, creating an efficient system for public administration. For example, waste is collected by Waste Management, a private company in Rolling Hills Estates, California, a city in Los Angeles County of a little over 8,000 residents. The private sector also delivers city traffic engineering and legal services. The Los Angeles County Sheriff Department and the Los Angeles County Fire Department are the first responders of the city of Rolling Hills Estates. The city employs only 21 people, who primarily manage and remain accountable for all these contracts with other governments and the private sector to deliver all the needed municipal services in Rolling Hills Estates.

In the NFP or NGO sector, the product RED, conceived by U2's Bono and Robert Shriver, focuses on eradicating AIDS from Africa by connecting governments, international organizations, and private companies to the mission. For example, Apple, The Gap, Starbucks, and others produce "RED" products to donate portions of the proceeds to the mission. Also, a global collaboration sparked by former Ambassador Morgenthau in 1919 created the Near East Relief Foundation to help the orphans of the first genocide of the 20th century. The Near East Relief Foundation raised more than $117 million in 1919 for the "starving Armenians."

Today, collaborations require new skills and knowledge. According to the *Harvard Business Review* (HBR), these new skills require a "far deeper appreciation of societal needs, a greater understanding of the true bases of company productivity, and the ability to collaborate across profit/non-profit boundaries." Furthermore, HBR suggests that "government must learn how to regulate in ways that enable shared value rather than work against it." HBR explains:

> The solution lies in the principle of shared value, which involves creating economic value in a way that also creates value for society by addressing its needs and challenges. Businesses must reconnect company success with social progress. Shared value is not social responsibility, philanthropy, or even sustainability, but a new way to achieve economic success.

Aligning this shared value through good decisions and motivations provides our frame for collaborative governance, effective institutions, and what we call Newgotiation.

The competitive frame (fight or war) of the last century that brought about breaches of trust is in flux. Tensions built to create winners and losers, also known as "hard power," are reconsidered and replaced with "smart power." We discuss "smart power" in later chapters. The 21st-century necessities and the global media-dominated context help ease these tensions and provide a better understanding of each sector vis-a-vis the other, facilitating collaborations not necessarily to feel good but to improve productivity. The demographic changes and preferences of millennials, the largest buying cohort in 2017, refocused our attention to a smaller footprint through a shared economy and convenience through the Internet of Things (IoT). These observations are essential in advancing and negotiating SDGs.

Over a billion people have smartphones to connect, share, and collaborate. As the financial security of cities weakens and the complexity of public administration-based problems intensifies, the need to collaborate with partners who can bring fresh perspectives and resources to public administration has magnified. Heightened interest among the tech-savvy millennials improves engagement and leverages change. Public agencies are beginning to see the benefit of aligning themselves with mission-driven, high-tech nonprofits, innovative for-profit organizations, and engaged citizens to create the tools that enable better governance. Co-creation and crowdsourcing are new ways to engage stakeholders to develop internal and external credibility, resulting in relationships and trust.

Increasingly, creative innovations provide valuable solutions to the public sector by creating simple mobile applications. Code for America (CfA) is a nonprofit committed to bringing high-tech programmers together with local governments to solve real-world problems. Companies such as Google, ESRI, and O'Reilly Media have joined forces to sponsor these innovations and provide some of the needed human capital to do this good work.

The City of New Orleans partnered with CfA in 2012 to help resolve the slow identification of blighted properties. After Hurricane Katrina, the City of New Orleans assisted developers in identifying 35,000 abandoned properties. As a result, CfA launched Blight Status, an application that scoured through digital data layers and offered real-time information on blighted properties. This project has since been celebrated as an example of how innovation created and implemented by nongovernment actors can result in better governance.

Products like Waze for Cities, a collaboration among ordinary citizens, facilitate transportation policy. Nest, Home Kit, Siri, and Amazon's Alexa address energy challenges in homes, where 40% of all energy is used. Civic Insights, a private sector company, designed a new way to visualize the City of Palo Alto's permit process to make it easier and more transparent for applicants. Standby Taskforce, an NGO, was created by Patrick Meier to combat violence. Anyone in Kenya with access to a cell phone reported human rights violations via a text message. These messages were mapped and updated in real-time, giving complete coverage of Kenya. By clustering the number of calls by location, the Standby Taskforce generated a "heat map" that showed areas of concentration with the most reported violence. This innovation of heat mapping was used in Haiti when a devastating earthquake struck the island nation. A live map of human distress calls, updated in real-time, guided the United States Marine Corps teams for strategic deployment. In Colorado, the app Adopt-a-Hydrant allows community members to take responsibility for clearing snow off specific hydrants in their neighborhoods. The work of just a few minutes by citizens proves to be vital in case of a fire. Aligning interests, motivations, and values in these collaboration examples is the key to their success, facilitating today's governance. All sectors participate for efficiency, effectiveness, and mutual benefit.

Mission-driven, high-tech nonprofits have the networks to put this highly skilled and technically savvy workforce in touch with meaningful causes to solve complex civic problems. Public agencies need only provide access to their single-largest asset, which is the data. More than any other asset, public agencies produce a wealth of publicly available data. This data can be used to design practical applications, create predictive analytics, find patterns, and add significant value to the agencies that produce it. This form of data, both transparent and accessible, has been termed Open Data Systems and is part of a new Open Government movement. Open Data enables citizens to access collective knowledge and information to create new services, suggest innovative ideas, and identify critical bugs in the infrastructure and flaws in the services they receive. Such a concept has led to creative, third-party solutions to complex problems that cities may not have the means or ability to pursue, given the nature of their seriously tight budgets, heavily restricted resources, or inadequate technical capabilities.

In the hands of the right people, civic innovation is now possible with a notebook computer, a mobile device, and an Internet connection to access available public municipal data. Gone are the days when public and private partnerships were a virtue of proximity. Collaborative efforts between the sectors are now boundaryless. Collaborative governance with civic innovation at its core can scale quickly and on multiple levels. Not only can an idea develop and scale swiftly, but the number of innovations in one agency is limited by the bandwidth of the public administrators orchestrating the creation. This idea starts to challenge the traditional model of government, from public administrators providing a service to that of governance, where administrators become more of managers, facilitators, and enablers of many actors working together to offer and find solutions to real-life public administration challenges.

We, therefore, have entered an age where there is no limit on the number of actors and collaborators who can engage with a local agency. Rather than delivering solutions, governments act as the platform for various actors to offer solutions. Innovation is limited only by the imagination of the developers and the public data available for use. We encountered these innovations in public administration across the globe.

In India, we came across an outstanding and capable public administrator who described a fascinating public service initiative she had implemented in Karnataka. The law is known as the Karnataka Guarantee of Services to Citizens Act of 2011 or SAKALA, which guarantees services to citizens in Karnataka within a stipulated time limit. Under the Act, when a request for a state service is made, a citizen is given an acknowledgment receipt with a SAKALA number (equivalent to a tracking number). This tracking number ensures that the request is processed within the specified days. With the SAKALA number, citizens can monitor their applications online with real-time status. A citizen can even send an SMS from a mobile phone. Furthermore, if delayed, a citizen can appeal to the next level of management directly and, per the requirements of the Act, demand a "compensatory cost" at a daily rate for the period of the delay subject to a maximum penalty per application, in aggregate from the designated offending government officer.

Today, in Karnataka, 668 state services under 50 departments provide transparency, accountability, efficiency, and results, demonstrating almost everything we know good governance to be. Interest and motivation-based sectoral alignment allow Karnataka to deliver better public administrative services or govern with private-sector technological innovations. The SAKALA impact was so effective that 96% of services were delivered ahead of time with 100% transparency in workflow and accountability for officials. Additionally, the program reduced the human interface, reducing the number of application process follow-up visits and saving citizens' and government officials' valuable time and resources.

These sectors (public–private and NGO) have never been so interdependent and predisposed to collaborate, creating unprecedented opportunities for inter-sectoral and intra-sectoral negotiated relationships or collaborations. These collaborations deliver essential government functions, public goods, and infrastructure systems while addressing and solving socioeconomic problems.

Collaborative governance as a practice has many different definitions and usages. Our colleagues Chris Ansell and Alison Gash from the University of California, Berkley, provide a helpful working definition; they suggest that collaborative governance is "a governing arrangement where one or more public agencies directly engage non-state stakeholders in a collective decision-making process that is formal, consensus-oriented, and deliberative and that aims to make or implement public policy or manage public programs or assets." Other scholars expand this definition to include private sector areas and not-for-profit organizations. The private sector, the public sector, and the not-for-profit/civil society organization/non-governmental (NFP/CSO/NGO) sector complement each other with increasing complexity and contain prominent levels of foundational overlap. As a result, the distinctions between sectors are increasingly difficult to distinguish.

Ansell and Gash identify critical variables that influence whether successful collaboration can be achieved in the existing literature on collaborative governance. These variables include the prior history of conflict or cooperation, the incentives for stakeholders to participate, power and resource imbalances, leadership, and institutional design. Similarly, several factors within the collaborative process are helpful, including face-to-face dialogue, trust-building (social capital), and developing commitment and shared understanding. Various cycles of collaboration tend to develop when forums, networks, or organizations focus on "small wins" that deepen trust, loyalty, relationships, and shared understanding. Trust and relationship are core principles discussed throughout this book, especially for effective institutions and Newgotiation.

Groups, practicing intersectoral collaboration, work to redistribute power and control from a central authority to many vested actors who are individuals or organizations. This power-sharing leads to innovation, cooperation, coordination, and partnership on a higher level than typical hierarchical or bureaucratic systems. These collaborations address issues as diverse as HIV/AIDS, labor standards, obesity, corruption, and delivery of public services from education, water, planning, engineering, trash hauling, development, and public infrastructure construction. We have seen and studied many case studies at the UN dealing with these topics.

Collaboration, however, requires more than just working together. There must be a joint mission and commitment to shared resources, power, and talent where no single individual or organization's point of view dominates. Dominance undermines collaboration while assessing the success of the collaborative efforts regularly and systematically can build trust, relationships, and shared commitment. The success that we define as efficiency, quality, price, or delivery, building upon positive feedback loops and forward momentum, can be a powerful driving force. Finally, we describe collaborative governance as good governance, the purposeful interaction of these three-plus sectors to effectively and efficiently advance large and small communities. While the defining features of good governance are not universal or one-size-fits-all, several significant characteristics observed by the UN and the World Bank include transparency, efficiency, effectiveness, participation, accountability, and results.

In one of our earlier UN Team projects, we worked with the UN PSIB/DESA to study governance in the Least Developed Countries (LDCs). Examining over 200 collaborative projects sponsored by the UN, we found that high-quality governance, characterized by stakeholder collaboration, effective communication, elevated levels of accountability and transparency, and strong human and institutional capacity, is critical to improving human development indicators for vulnerable populations in LDCs. On the other hand, poor stakeholder collaboration, ineffective communication and information-sharing systems, low levels of transparency and accountability, and weak human and institutional capacity have all hindered progress toward sustainable development in many LDCs.

The literature supports these findings. Two recognized scholars in this field, Kania and Kramer, suggest that individual organizations operating in isolation typically cannot create systemic change. Cross-sector partnerships have been initiated in response to this restraint and to address complex social problems better. Osborne, another scholar, writes that these partnerships are viewed as "efficient and effective mechanisms for developing inclusive communities; providing public goods and services; meeting the needs of target populations; and implementing public policy." Because coordinated stakeholder collaboration is integral to the success of all partnerships, poor collaboration can hinder progress toward a shared goal. Poor stakeholder collaboration can occur at any point during the partnership and almost always leads to reduced outcomes. The same is true in negotiation outcomes when parties forego effective collaboration and instead resort to a high degree of competition that creates winners and losers. We discuss this in the later chapters of this book.

Based on our UN work and experience, effective communication and information sharing in governance are essential for collecting divergent resources, eliminating misunderstanding, and establishing public support. It is also a critical step of innovation transfer, which requires matching the interests of one party with the offerings. In later chapters, we discuss a similar process in our Newgotiation steps of value creation and value distribution. Lack of communication and information sharing discovered in public administration within LDCs impedes the flow of ideas, creates mistrust and disapproval, and hinders consensus.

When addressing a public policy problem, the policy formulation and implementation stages need communication to get various stakeholders to recognize the problem and agree on the implementation methods. Poor communication and limited shared information create obstacles to implementing policy, identifying shared solutions, and engaging various stakeholders. The similarities here in governance, institutions, and negotiation are remarkable again. Lack of communication and mistrust will hinder any negotiation process, yielding poor outcomes.

Professor Rothstein writes, "Accountability and transparency in the public sector is a cornerstone in ensuring economic and social stability." Distrust undermines the social contract between the people and those who govern and detracts from the process of poverty eradication in LDCs, for example. Greater levels of accountability and transparency in public institutions make the private sector and civil society more willing to partner in delivering public services. Furthermore, openness and transparency in government encourage valuable civic input and participation in decision-making processes. Community ownership is the difference between "done-to" and "done in collaboration with." It is essential for instigating political will where it does not exist organically from the top down.

Given that collaboration is a voluntary act, it is critical to understand the motivations and intentions of the sectors to forge the necessary bonds to act in cooperation with one another. The concept in Newgotiation is the same. Understanding the motivations and preferences of the other party is critical to creating and distributing value to cut a deal.

We briefly examine each sector here, identifying challenges and looking for collaboration opportunities. We seek collaboration to promote better public administration and, more importantly, to encourage "governance" today and tomorrow. The global pandemic, financial crises, constrictions of markets, formation of complex networks, competition, growing fears of unemployment, and substantial infrastructure deficits present significant challenges for the public, private, and not-for-profit sectors today. On the other hand, such significant challenges represent opportunities to collaborate through effective institutions, negotiation methods, and skills to forge win–win opportunities of more significant proportions for these three sectors. The evolution of the public sector mitigates these challenges through decentralization and using nonprofit or for-profit contractors to perform service tasks associated with a particular skill and effective public administration. As our readers note throughout this book, we borrow extensively from this collaboration and collaborative governance literature to create and distribute value in our Newgotiation paradigm.

Today more than ever, our leaders must master the art and science of Newgotiation to avoid polarization and instead forge collaborations among sectors to deliver effective governance. Seeking the public interest requires that we be willing to become informed, listen empathetically to various viewpoints, collaborate, tolerate, network, share, build relationships, and take responsibility for not only ourselves but, more importantly, our constituents. Fortunately, this leadership brand is still practiced at most local levels of government. The more politically motivated and ideologically positioned government organizations at the state and federal levels remain polarized and static.

The evolutionary continuum in public administration views citizens as constituents, voters, customers, owners, partners, and agents for change. The same evolution considers public administrators as public servants, trustees, managers, partners, facilitators, and leaders. The main challenge is to create norms and standard best practices among all these actors to advance society and establish a new public administration that does not exist in a hierarchical silo but rather is open to service with standards of legitimacy, transparency, inclusion, and efficiency across sectors.

By all accounts, the pandemic has "heightened the SDGs imperative." During the ESI project, a Deloitte leader, Michael Flynn, said:

> The pandemic will upturn traditional urban development models and compel cities to reimagine mobility, health infrastructure, housing, education, energy consumption, and more. It has laid bare the inequities in access and has impacted traditionally disadvantaged communities more. Along with inclusion, hacking at these systemic inequities in the current urban development model will be critical for cities.

The ESI research confirms our prior writings and the general collaboration literature. Kevin Taylor of Axis Communications said:

> The first tool cities should leverage is a culture of collaboration. If the pandemic has taught us anything, it has revealed that no one person, stakeholder, or department in government has all the answers to solve all the community's needs.

We agree.

In simple terms, collaborative governance in practice means integrating the voices of stakeholders in all decision-making processes of a given organization. This collaboration is a common thread between our research on effective institutions and the Newgotiation paradigm discussed in the chapters that follow.

3

EFFECTIVE INSTITUTIONS—RESEARCH AND CASES

In this chapter, we share the impactful research of the UN Team 2019, which developed an applied conceptual framework of an effective public institution that highlights the complementarity of ethics and values, transformational leadership, strategic planning, and innovation and co-creation. This framework aims to strengthen and support local public entities working to advance the Sustainable Development Goals (SDGs).

We outline project objectives, research methods, selection criteria, and case analyses that led to the development of the applied conceptual framework and best practices for its application. Guiding this inquiry were three research questions that assessed the necessary qualities and mechanisms for institutional effectiveness and analyzed best practices for localized framework application while considering barriers and constraints. The first research phase included conducting a literature review. The team then interviewed subject matter experts assessing the two instructive case studies to create selection criteria that enabled the team to choose six other cases from the Knowledge Base of UN PSAI. Finally, along with the two instructive cases, we analyzed these six case studies to understand better the elements required for an effective public institution and their application in various local contexts. This chapter concludes with a discussion of the framework's application, limitations, recommendations for further research, and conclusions.

Methodology

As a foundation for our analysis, we identified three research questions to guide our inquiry into institutional effectiveness. Drawing upon several research

DOI: 10.4324/9781003497097-3

methods, we executed a three-part research strategy that ultimately led to the creation of our applied conceptual framework. Our research began with an extensive literature review, subject matter expert interviews, and analyses of two instructive cases recommended by UN PSIB/DESA, through which we identified our initial framework elements and evaluation criteria. This first research phase laid the foundation for the second phase, culminating in the random selection of 27 cases from UN PSAI. The third phase used the evaluation criteria to select six meaningful cases from the random sample. Along with two cases recommended by UN PSIB/DESA, these six cases served as case studies to deepen our understanding of the elements of institutional effectiveness, the relationships among the elements, and best practices for application. Finally, we used these methods to answer the specified research questions as given in Table 3.1.

Phase 1: Literature Review, Interviews, and Instructive Case Studies

Literature Review

To identify critical elements of effective public institutions, we examined several academic papers, case studies, and open sources of information. Through this process, we began to identify common characteristics among effective public institutions that could serve as elements in our framework. Based on the UN PSIB/DESA's interests, we focused on values and ethics, leadership,

TABLE 3.1 Research Questions and Methodology

Research Question	*Methods*
What qualities and mechanisms make a public institution effective in attaining the SDGs? To what extent can these qualities and mechanisms be represented in an applied conceptual framework?	Literature review, subject matter expert interviews, sample instructive cases, randomly selected case studies
How are values, ethics, transformational leadership, strategic planning, and innovation and co-creation exhibited and implemented in an effective public institution?	Literature review, subject matter expert interviews, sample instructive cases, randomly selected case studies
How can we use the applied conceptual framework to emphasize the SDG mindset and apply innovative strategies and leadership characteristics among local public institutions? What are the barriers and constraints to applying the applied conceptual framework?	Literature review, subject matter expert interviews, sample instructive cases, randomly selected case studies

strategic planning, and innovation, examining scholarly literature to determine the relatedness of these elements to the general effectiveness of a public institution.

Semi-Structured Expert Interviews

The research team conducted semi-structured interviews with four subject matter experts to complement our literature review. These experts included academics and practitioners specializing in governance, leadership, and strategic planning. These interviews aimed to gain insight into the required elements for institutional effectiveness both from an academic and a practical view. These subject matter experts' profiles and interview questions can be found in Appendices A and B, respectively.

Instructive Case Studies

Based on the UN PSIB/DESA's recommendation, we studied two cases from UN PSAI: SAKALA Mission (2017) and Decide Madrid (2018). Because the UN identified these cases as poignant examples of effectiveness, we chose to use them as instructive cases for understanding institutional effectiveness from the perspective of the UN PSIB/DESA. In addition, these cases allowed us to understand better the determinants for effectiveness envisioned by our client. Based on our analysis, we developed comprehensive evaluation criteria to guide our selection of six meaningful cases from our randomly selected sample from the Knowledge Base. These 17 criteria are divided into 7 classifications, each highlighting critical case selection areas. Table 3.2 lists the evaluation criteria sorted by classification.

Phase 2: Random Selection

We constructed our sample of six award-winning case studies from the Knowledge Base using a two-tiered random cluster sampling method. During the first tier, we selected a random sample of 27 cases from the Knowledge Base of UN PSAI. During the second tier, we meaningfully selected six cases to serve as case studies using a list of developed evaluation criteria. As the Knowledge Base contains several hundred cases from many years, we narrowed our initial sample by only including case studies submitted in 2017. This process restricted our initial sample to 391 cases. We clustered the cases from this group into United Nations Region Groups (see Table 3.3). Within each group, we created four sub-clusters that reflected four levels of development, according to the Human Development Index (HDI). These subclusters were adopted as "Very High HDI," "High HDI," "Medium HDI," and "Low HDI." We selected six cases from each UN Region Group cluster, two from each development level. We selected these cases using a random number generator found in Microsoft

TABLE 3.2 Evaluation Criteria

Classification	*Criteria*
Accountability	Transparency: information on public entity activities and performance Legal mechanisms that establish rules and principles
Assessment	Ongoing external and internal monitoring and evaluation Initial diagnostics to help determine the solution(s) Assessment of public's opinion and satisfaction with services
Co-creation	Employee inclusion in innovative solution(s) Public and stakeholder participation
Convergence with the 2030 Agenda	Initial issue(s) and solution(s) linked with SDGs
Distinct Cases	Initial problem and solution(s) unique from other selected cases Technologically distinct from other cases Community/municipality and its context distinct from other selected cases (i.e., HDI, UN Region, etc.)
Equity	Bottom-up approach Focus on diminishing existing inequities Focus on vulnerable groups Focus on increasing inclusiveness (i.e., public participation)
Sustainability	The solution is durable in time The solution is resilient concerning the environment and political and cultural context

TABLE 3.3 Statistics of Cases by UN Region and HDI Level

UN Region	*Very High HDI*	*High HDI*	*Medium HDI*	*Low HDI*
Africa	0	4	25	6
Asia-Pacific	77	49	107	1
Eastern Europe	2	3	0	0
Latin America and the Caribbean	23	65	1	0
Western Europe and Other	25	2	0	0
UN Observers	0	0	1	0
TOTAL	**127**	**123**	**134**	**7**

Excel. We chose these cases randomly to conduct a fair and accurate assessment of the information, as we could not analyze all the available data in the Knowledge Base.

Furthermore, as every case in the database is award-winning, we assumed each case involves a public institution that qualifies as effective. Thus, analyzing any case in the database would convey the required elements for effectiveness. However, to increase the likelihood that we were selecting a meaningful case study that would provide insight into our analysis, we read each of the six chosen cases. We chose the most significant of those six for our in-depth analysis.

From each UN Region Group cluster, we selected two cases from each level of HDI at most. For groups with only one case in an HDI level, we selected only that one; for groups with no HDI level, we selected zero cases at that level within that UN Region Group. Thus, after coding every case under the clusters of both UN Region Group and HDI, we obtained three random numbers for each level of HDI in each UN Region Group (see Table 3.4).

The formulation for Random #1 and Random #2 is:

$$= \text{RANDBETWEEN}\,(1, 4)$$

Here, (1, 4) refers to "from 1 to 4," which means there are four cases with High HDI in the Africa Group.

The formulation for Random #3 is:

$$= \text{IF}\left(\text{B3} = \text{VLOOKUP}\left(\text{B3}, \text{B3}:\text{C3}, 2\right), \text{RANDBETWEEN}\left(1,4\right), \text{B3}\right)$$

TABLE 3.4 Results of Random Selection

Africa Group	**Random #1**	**Random #2**	**Random #3**	**<>?**
Very High HDI	0	0	0	Y
High HDI	4	3	4	Y
Medium HDI	16	16	5	Y
Low HDI	6	6	4	Y
Asia-Pacific Group	**Random #1**	**Random #2**	**Random #3**	**<>?**
Very High HDI	36	58	36	Y
High HDI	8	26	8	Y
Medium HDI	93	100	93	Y
Low HDI	1	1	1	Y
Eastern Europe Group	**Random #1**	**Random #2**	**Random #3**	**<>?**
Very High HDI	1	2	1	Y
High HDI	2	1	2	Y
Medium HDI	0	0	0	Y
Low HDI	0	0	0	Y
Latin America and the Caribbean	**Random #1**	**Random #2**	**Random #3**	**<>?**
Very High HDI	7	19	7	Y
High HDI	12	65	12	Y
Medium HDI	1	1	1	Y
Low HDI	0	0	0	Y
Western Europe and Other	**Random #1**	**Random #2**	**Random #3**	**<>?**
Very High HDI	7	16	7	Y
High HDI	1	1	2	Y
Medium HDI	0	0	0	Y
Low HDI	0	0	0	Y
UN Observers [only 1 case]				

To generate two random numbers from Random #1–3 while avoiding repetitive numbers, we employed "Y" to indicate that the random numbers in the row were qualified, meaning it is possible to obtain two different numbers from the three. We first inputted "Y" in those cells corresponding to HDI levels with only zero or one case in a particular region highlighted in gray in Table 3.4. Then, we adopted "<>?" to monitor whether there were AT LEAST two values among the three random numbers in each row that were different. The formulation for "<>?" is:

$$= \text{IF}\left(\text{OR}\left(\text{B3} <> \text{C3}, \text{B3} <> \text{D3}\right), "\text{Y}", ""\right)$$

We then observed the "<>?" column and checked whether we obtained a "Y" in every cell (except for header lines). If not, we refreshed the page to conduct the random selection again until a "Y" appeared in each cell in the "<>?" column. If "Y" appeared across all column cells, we checked the three random numbers in each row. We chose Random #1 and Random #2 if they were different; otherwise, we chose Random #1 and Random #3. After completing our numerical selection, we referred to the Knowledge Base to determine the cases corresponding to the random numbers.

After we gained 27 randomly selected cases, our team conducted a cursory analysis of each case using the evaluation criteria created during Phase 1 of our research. Finally, we collectively chose six meaningful cases (e.g., one from each UN Region) to analyze these evaluation criteria in greater depth.

Phase 3: Case Analysis

Using the six meaningfully selected cases from our tiered random selection, along with the two instructive cases recommended by UN PSIB/DESA (SAKALA and Decide Madrid), our team conducted a comprehensive case analysis of eight case studies from the Knowledge Base of UN PSAI. These cases gave insight into our initially selected framework elements and allowed us to develop a more comprehensive understanding of the required elements of an effective public institution. In addition to the knowledge gained from scholarly literature and expert interviews, we used the observations gathered from our case analysis to assemble our applied conceptual framework. The following section contains a factual description of each selected case.

Case Studies: Overview

Figure 3.1 shows the eight case studies chosen based on our tiered random selection. Consistent with our evaluation criteria, each case is distinct, regionally diverse, and congruent with the SDGs. Further information about each initiative can be found in Table 3.5 and the following sections.

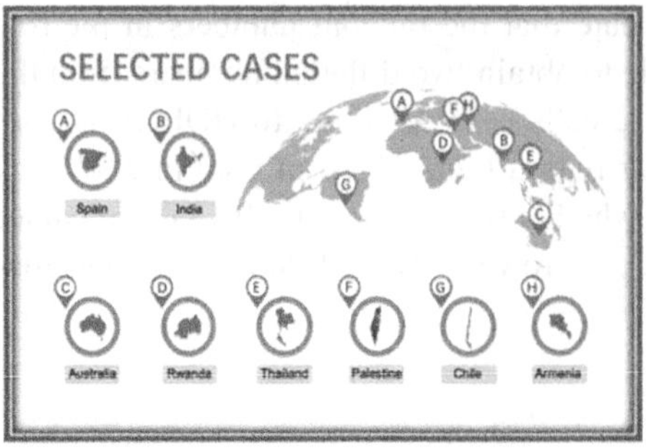

FIGURE 3.1 World Map with Highlighted Selected Cases

TABLE 3.5 Eight Selected Cases for Case Analysis

Initiative	*Country*	*UN Region*	*HDI Level*
Elimination of Mother-to-Child Transmission of HIV	Armenia	Eastern Europe	High
Cape York Region Package [infrastructure]	Australia	Western Europe and Other	Very High
Port Works Management	Chile	Latin America and the Caribbean	Very High
SAKALA Mission [e-governance]	India	Asia-Pacific	Medium
Establishment of the Palestine Public Finance Institute	Palestine	UN Observers	Medium
Automated Passenger Clearance System [border crossing]	Rwanda	Africa	Low
Citizen Participation Project	Spain	Western Europe and Other	Very High
Sa Kaeo Shelter for Children and Families	Thailand	Asia-Pacific	High

Armenia: Elimination of Mother-to-Child Transmission of HIV

Armenia suffered from a lack of preventive mother-to-child transmission of HIV (preventive mother-to-child transmission of HIV (PMTCT)) services (Figure 3.2). Without treatment, up to 45% of the children of HIV-positive mothers were also found to be HIV positive. While the likelihood of HIV mother-to-child transmission can be primarily reduced with PMTCT interventions, Armenia did not provide access to PMTCT and other relevant services before 2002. This problem had many causes, including lack of a regulatory framework, lack of trained personnel, lack of tests and antiretroviral (ARV) drugs, and lack of financing.

To solve this problem, Armenia has undertaken large-scale measures over the past 15 years by establishing the National Center for AIDS Prevention (NCAP). In 2002, the government approved the first National AIDS Programme (NAP), 2002–2006, in which it set PMTCT as one of its primary goals. Through the NAP, the government also initiated the national HIV testing and counseling system. In addition, it approved the National PMTCT strategy to set up a multi-sectoral Country Coordination Mechanism (CCM) on HIV/AIDS Prevention. After developing the nationwide project proposal, the Armenian government also accumulated further financial resources and approvals for funding. In addition, the Ministry of Health facilitated the establishment of supply chain management and monitoring and evaluation systems for ARV drugs and distributed tests, consumables, and ARV drugs to the NCAP, antenatal clinics, and HIV-testing laboratories nationwide. Further, the country introduced the Obstetric Care State Certificate Program for pregnant women in 2008 and the Child Health State Certificate to children under age seven in 2011 so that healthcare services related to pregnancy and childcare would be free.

The program results were impressive. By 2004, the number of HIV tests taken among pregnant women rapidly increased. Up to 2011, testing and counseling sites were available in all antenatal clinics, and over 95% of pregnant women had taken an HIV test. This test allowed them to know their HIV status and take measures at the early stage of the illness. Since 2007, no cases of mother-to-child HIV transmission have been registered among those who received PMTCT. Through systematization and coordination of the national AIDS response, Armenia's National Center of AIDS Prevention ensured access to PMTCT nationwide, promoted its healthcare system, and worked toward advancing the SDGs for health.

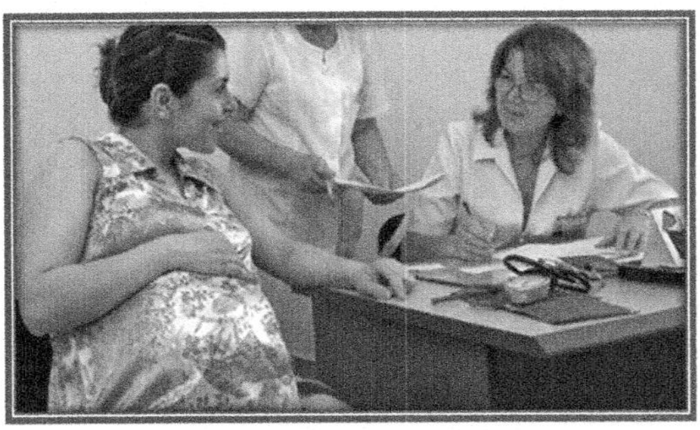

FIGURE 3.2 Elimination of Mother-to-Child Transmission of HIV

Source: United Nations Armenia

Australia: Cape York Region Project

Australia's Cape York Peninsula is a remote region populated by 18,000 people, 60% of whom are indigenous. This region is accessible only through the Peninsula Development Road (PDR), a 570-km road, 72% of which is unpaved as of 2013. This lack of infrastructure has had significant adverse effects on indigenous communities. During rainy seasons, flooding severely damages the unpaved sections of the PDR, limiting access to Cape York for as long as six months. The PDR costs at least $38 million annually for maintenance and disaster relief in this state. In addition to high costs, the lack of access to the Cape York region has contributed to a lack of economic opportunity and social inequality for the Cape York indigenous communities.

To increase access to Cape York and improve the quality of life for its indigenous communities, the Queensland Department of Transport and Main Roads (TMR) co-sponsored an infrastructure initiative with the Australian National Government. As a result, the Cape York Region Project (CYRP) allocated $260.5 million for three projects designed to improve Cape York's infrastructure by engaging local indigenous communities (Figure 3.3). The first project allocated $200 million to pave priority sections of the PDR, increasing paved roads from 28% to 60% by 2019. The second project gave $10 million for roadwork on the Endeavor Valley Road, which leads to a particular indigenous community. The third project allocated $50.5 million to infrastructural development in eight indigenous communities.

In all CYRP projects, TMR prioritized the involvement of indigenous community partners to lead and participate in construction. TMR specifically

FIGURE 3.3 Cape York Region Package [infrastructure]

Source: Queensland Government TMR

designed programs to incentivize the inclusion of indigenous businesses as contractors and subcontractors for construction. Additionally, TMR developed several training programs in partnership with indigenous leadership groups to increase employment opportunities for indigenous community members, whose unemployment rate is approximately 80%. TMR has built roads with input from several indigenous stakeholders while complying with indigenous cultural heritage legislation and creating an infrastructure based on the needs that the communities themselves identified. The work completed with CYRP funding led to several positive outcomes for the Cape York community, including improved travel conditions along the two major roads leading to indigenous communities, reduced annual maintenance costs for the roads, and increased economic opportunity for participating indigenous communities. Through this initiative, TMR was able to meet its primary goal of connecting communities to change lives.

Chile: Port Works Management

With the enactment of the Ports Act of 1997, the Ministry of Public Works broadened its focus on port management to include services provided to citizens in public recreational areas associated with edge coastal, maritime, fluvial, and lacustrine activities (e.g., artisanal fishing). The port serves 45% of the Chilean population (4 million people). This initiative aimed to guarantee effective services that ensured accessibility and connectivity. To identify the inequities of the existing infrastructure, the Ministry created a service diagnostic tool. Combatting inequity required making the Ministry beneficiaries visible and formalizing their participation using this diagnostic tool. To incorporate inclusiveness, the Service for the Strategic Products of Connectivity, Artisanal Fishing, and Coastal Border incorporated themes related to gender, ethnicity, and age in the development of pre-investment and investment studies, capturing the diversity of the Ministry's constituency. This diagnostic tool enabled an inclusive analysis of the port's economy, environment, and culture to ensure its activities reached all its citizens. When diagnosing the port's infrastructure, the Ministry considered its constituents' varying needs and roles in its plan to improve services (Figure 3.4).

The inequities detected with the diagnostic tool include high costs for lighting, the need for public spaces, inadequate access and services for vulnerable groups (i.e., elderly and physically disabled), poor access and sanitary conditions for women in male-dominated activities (e.g., gutting, network repair, incarnation, seaweed drying, etc.), and poor access to transportation affecting men's labor, women's health, food, and children's education.

FIGURE 3.4 Port Works Management
Source: Ministry of Public Works

Once inequities and needs were determined, interdisciplinary teams implemented a management and modification plan for the port in partnership with experts and stakeholders (i.e., National Service of Disability, Ministry of Women and Gender Equity, Service of the Elder, and National Tourism Service). The outputs of this initiative included access to all people, including those with special needs (including gender, age, different sensorial capacities, etc.), to the bathing and sunbathing sectors on the Coastal and Lacustrine Border; to leisure sports areas; reduction in operating cost; and reduction in the port's carbon footprint through alternative energy sources (i.e., solar, wind, water, and thermal). In addition, this initiative's improved service delivery is illustrated in the increase in citizen requests to the Port Works Directorate and a decrease in claims, consisting of complaints and disagreements, between 2015 and 2016.

India: SAKALA Mission

Even after many years of independence, the citizens of India feel that the government has not effectively responded to their needs. Citizens often encountered unpleasant experiences while seeking common services from any government agency. Undue delays, poor enforcement, careless attitude of public officials toward citizens, and mushrooming corruption were a few prominent problems faced by ordinary citizens.

In response to this dissatisfaction, SAKALA Mission introduced citizen-friendly governance with a time-bound service guarantee (Figure 3.5). This groundbreaking program of the Karnataka state government aimed to standardize and simplify its service delivery system and make the government more

FIGURE 3.5 SAKALA Mission [e-governance]
Source: The Hindu (Newspaper)

accountable to its citizens. As a result, the state government passed a bill, the Karnataka SAKALA Services Act, in 2011, empowering citizens to avail services on time and claim compensation for any delays or defaults caused by the government. The mission used information technology as a tool to revolutionize the delivery system of government services to citizens. When applying for any service, a citizen receives a unique Guarantee of Service to Citizen (GSC) or a SAKALA number to track the process of their application online, enabling them to claim compensation in case of delays or defaults. The impact of the SAKALA initiative was so effective that 96% of services were delivered ahead of time, and 100% transparency in workflow and accountability for officials was achieved. Additionally, the program reduced the human interface, reducing the number of follow-up visits to the application processes saving valuable time and resources for citizens and government officials.

Palestine: Establishment of the Palestine Public Finance Institute

In response to growing public distrust and tax compliance issues, the Palestinian Ministry of Finance developed a program to augment the Palestinian public administration's weak capacity for public fiscal management. This program, called the Palestine Public Finance Institute (PPFI), focuses on capacity-building and employee development for all staff involved in public fiscal management through various trainings and events (Figure 3.6). PPFI was born out of a partnership between the Palestinian Ministry of Finance and Expertise France, whose goal is to create a program that builds effective public fiscal management systems based on transparency, accountability, and efficiency.

This program includes in-house training to cultivate hard and soft skills, develop up-to-date management tools, and standardize practices to improve customer service. While initially focused on employees within the Ministry of Finance, PFI's efforts have expanded to include all public finance management staff.

Motivated by its core values, PPFI prioritizes creating a culture that instills a collective sense of belonging among its members. PPFI believes this sense of belonging will increase employee investment and create a more productive organization, improving constituent experiences and greater public trust. As part of its objective to build the capacities of all public fiscal management officers, PPFI has developed a coaching and mentoring system that hosts workshops and develops mentorship plans for all newly appointed, newly promoted, and freshly transferred employees. On a broader level, PPFI's primary goal is to cultivate employees at all levels through in-house training modules. These training courses are intended to serve all public fiscal management officers in the Palestinian public administration. Additionally, PPFI creates space for innovation and exchanging ideas by hosting events that bring together several communities, including the media, business sector, academia, and the international community.

Since its launch, PPFI has provided thousands of training days, involving almost every public fiscal management officer in at least one training course. As of 2017, PPFI also had over 40 Ministry of Finance employees engaged in its train-the-trainer program, implementing public fiscal management training within the Ministry. PPFI also operates a documentation center available to members of the public seeking reliable financial information. PPFI's programming continues to grow, allowing more employees of the Palestinian administration to participate in its capacity-building efforts.

FIGURE 3.6 Establishment of the Palestine Public Finance Institute

Source: Palestine Public Finance Institute

Rwanda: Automated Passenger Clearance System

The Directorate General of Immigration and Emigration (DGIE) of Rwanda confronted crowded passenger clearance at Poids-Lourds, Rwanda's land border with the Democratic Republic of Congo (DRC). Poids-Lourds received an average of 45,000 travelers crossing the border daily, most from the two cities neighboring the border. Although the bilateral agreement between the two countries had simplified the documents required for entry and exit, long waiting lines caused congestion daily due to the inefficient clearance process. Citizens had to wait for a manual verification process to receive a stamped single-entry border pass, valid for 24 hours. Then, upon crossing the border, citizens were required to present the pass coupon and identification to officials on the other side. This process brought inconvenience to disabled constituents and school children who needed to cross the border daily. The process also prevented the government from knowing the exact statistics of cross-border movement and created fatigue among the clearance staff, especially in bad weather conditions.

This issue was remarkably solved by introducing the Automated Passenger Clearance System (APCS) at Poids-Lourds in 2013 (Figure 3.7). This innovative information technology-based solution allowed each traveler to undergo a self-clearance process with fingerprints in no more than 16 seconds. After registering their identification information and fingerprints, members of the border community received a card, which they would use to open the first gate at the border. After entering the first gate, they used their fingerprints to open the second gate, while the next traveler could start to pass the first gate simultaneously. Furthermore, APCS was designed with two special lanes dedicated to disabled travelers. These two wheelchair kiosks issue a border pass right after travelers successfully verify their fingerprints.

FIGURE 3.7 Automated Passenger Clearance System [border crossing]

Source: Quest Africa

This 24-hour system followed the core principle of immigration work: balancing security and facilitation. It contributed to the free movement of people, optimized space usage at the border, and improved productivity. With the help of APCS, the border clearance time was reduced to under one minute, which improved the lives of the border community, enabling travelers to cross the border more frequently and increasing cross-border trade. As a result of increased trade, the governments of Rwanda and DRC made other policies to exempt 168 commodities from import duties, and mechanisms for the transportation of goods were also developed.

Spain: Decide Madrid

Before 2015, planning for Madrid accounted for the opinions of experts and other associates while failing to include significant public stakeholders. As of 2015, strategic planning for the city was recentralized toward encouraging honest and direct citizen participation to develop transparency and inclusiveness (Figure 3.8). The government website Decide Madrid aimed to create a computer-based tool to be used as a platform for listening and communicating citizen ideas and needs as they relate to public services. This platform implements and encourages many types of citizen participation, including citizen proposals, consultations, and participative budgets. As an innovative form of citizen participation, this virtual platform allows the population's strategic planning demands for the city to be imparted individually or collectively, and the direct involvement of citizens becomes institutionalized and strengthened by binding procedures.

This innovative system's use of technology expanded the quality and quantity of the participating citizens. The fast and straightforward virtual platform is accessible to many of the population; any citizen can formulate a proposal or demand regardless of age, gender, or other characteristics. To ensure the inclusion of all citizens within this platform, the city government created the Department of Inclusion, Neutrality, and Privacy, in which members meet with social organizations and other entities that defend the rights of disadvantaged communities and detect existing barriers in the applicability, access, and use of the tool. For example, the platform incorporates facilitators to help communities negatively affected by the digital divide participate in the Decide Madrid program. Thus, even the most vulnerable groups are included in the participatory process, fulfilling the desired quality of inclusiveness for all participants.

This quality can be seen in the participatory budgeting process, where citizen participation has funded 26% of projects supporting social inclusion services (e.g., services for the disabled, elderly, children, women, etc.). The 362,702 registered users can illustrate the effectiveness in terms of the number

FIGURE 3.8 Citizen Participation Project

Source: Decide Madrid

of participants in the platform's initial launch. Additionally, 5,000 debates, 21,000 proposals, and more than 4 million votes have been recorded, resulting in the creation of 517 new government services proposed by Madrilenians to improve their quality of life.

Thailand: Sa Kaeo Shelter for Children and Families

Sa Kaeo is in the eastern part of Thailand near the border of Cambodia. Transit points along the borders between Thailand and neighboring countries have increased migration into Thailand. Due to illegal migration from Cambodia, Sa Kaeo is facing human trafficking and other social issues. Many trafficking victims from various countries willingly migrate to Thailand, seeking employment through illegal and informal recruitment networks.

FIGURE 3.9 Sa Kaeo Shelter for Children and Families

Source: Sa Kaeo Shelter Facebook page

Brokers and employers reportedly continue to exploit the situation of victims. Generally, victims of human trafficking suffer because they are assisted under false pretenses and do not know how to request help from the government. The project, "One Home for Development on Assisting Victims of Trafficking," of Sa Kaeo Shelter for Children and Families, has been launched to assist victims of human trafficking, including children and women (Figure 3.9). The program works with multiple stakeholders like private sector entities, nongovernmental organizations, and Japanese organizations. It uses four critical criteria to combat human trafficking: capacity-building, intelligence exchange, campaigning, and remedy and rehabilitation. This initiative protects victims of human trafficking by safeguarding the rights of trafficked persons and providing dignity to all people regardless of gender, race, age, religion, or other features. Sa Kaeo reduces social problems such as organized crime, drug abuse, crimes against vulnerable populations in the community, and health problems.

4

EFFECTIVE INSTITUTIONS—APPLIED CONCEPTUAL FRAMEWORK

Overview of Framework Elements

Based on the research methods mentioned above, we identified four critical elements required for a public institution to work effectively. These elements are Values and Ethics, Transformational Leadership, Strategic Planning, and Innovation and Co-Creation.

Like the Sustainable Development Goals (SDGs), these four elements are interconnected, interrelated, and interdependent. Each element carries equal weight in achieving institutional effectiveness, and each element relies on the other elements to function at its full potential. While our applied conceptual framework manifests in a linear model, these elements share a nonlinear relationship. Each element must be equally and continually applied throughout the institution's life cycle to achieve the desired outcome of effective public administration. Figure 4.1 demonstrates the interdependent nature of these four elements as they work together to build an effective institution.

The following sections present our findings on each element of institutional effectiveness and examples of the ingredients in practice, as seen through our chosen case studies.

Values and Ethics

Ethical behavior is critical for allowing democracy to thrive. Ethics are standards of conduct and behavior that distinguish between right and wrong. To act ethically is to be consistent with what is right and moral. Ethical or moral behavior is dependent on strong democratic values. When a code of ethics is

DOI: 10.4324/9781003497097-4

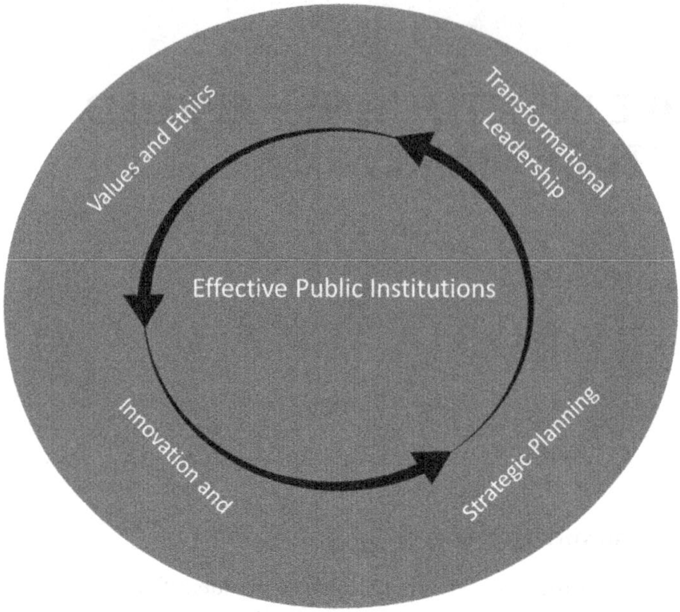

FIGURE 4.1 Interdependent, Interrelated, Interconnected Elements of Institutional Effectiveness

established through values, leaders (and public sector employees) have the guidelines to carry out their tasks responsibly and with integrity.

Values and Ethics in Addressing Corruption

The public sector emphasizes maintaining high ethical standards and values in public administration to combat corruption. Fraudulent and dishonest conduct by those in power erodes efforts toward sustainable development and the strengthening of democratic institutions. The selfish behavior of powerful individuals who abuse their public positions—often for monetary gain—does so at the community's expense (especially the most vulnerable community members). This lack of integrity drives activities that negatively affect equity and fairness. Corruption undermines development and stability, and it diminishes public trust and confidence. Consequences of corruption are realized in the ineffectiveness of the institution, where there is a lack of quality service and resources, poor management, and bad governance.

To ensure effective public service delivery, mitigating corruption extends to mitigating its less well-known form, "quiet corruption." This form of corruption leads to long-term consequences and disproportionate effects. Quiet corruption is malpractice where wrongdoers are motivated by reasons other than monetary gain; it occurs on the frontlines of public service, creating failures in delivering government-based services or goods to the public. This quiet corruption includes teachers, doctors, and other government representatives who fail to provide services or deviate from expected conduct, such as excessive absenteeism, lowering effort and productivity, and bending the rules. These direct actions negatively affect beneficiaries and harm vulnerable groups relying on government service delivery systems. Thus, ensuring public institutions' effectiveness and good governance relies heavily on mitigating corruption in all its forms.

Ray Rood, Founder and Senior Consultant at the Genysys Group, recognizes the challenges that the public sector faces due to its diffused nature, where public servants and the constituents of public institutions are not coordinated in their values and agendas. Rood states, "If you don't have a value system that holds people together, then you bring individual agendas and personalities." A public institution must operate according to its values; without it, individual agendas rooted in diverse politics and misguided values will result in corruption.

Studies combating quiet corruption have stressed on the need for qualitative changes to service delivery as they pertain to the public servants working at the institution's forefront. These qualitative changes refer to values and leadership outputs that motivate public servants toward more efficient service delivery. In many cases, adverse effects on organizational culture, which have ethical implications on employees, result from organizations and employees perceiving leadership philosophies as putting ethics on the "back burner." While establishing a code of ethics and values is necessary, ensuring they are well practiced and applied by leaders is essential in combating grand forms of corruption and encouraging employees to behave ethically to limit quiet corruption.

The literature suggests that trust, "the positive perception about the actions of an individual or an organization," is a core element of the "fair and effective functioning of government institutions ... or the delivery of basic public services." Ray Rood notes that an effective public institution must have basic morality grounded in values. Values create a structure for the institution to carry out its mission to achieve its purpose. They are critical to accomplishing the tasks and goals at hand. Without values to lead an organization to make ethical decisions in response to the needs of citizens, the organization may not achieve efficiency. This structure is because values shape behavior. When ethical behavior is enacted in delivering services, its application helps combat corruption in many forms. When corruption is limited, the institution's performance is strengthened. With improved performance (or the efficient delivery of services), citizen expectations and experiences with service delivery are positively perceived. In essence, trust is generated as citizens rely on the institution to meet their needs, and it grows with their confidence in knowing that the institutions will deliver. As synthesized by Ray Rood, "the output of values is [the public's] trust."

Trust in an institution is correlated with shared values between the public and the institution, strengthening service delivery effectiveness. This correlation is further highlighted when considering citizens' role in an institution's effectiveness. My former colleague, Janet Denhardt, a Professor of Public Administration at the USC Sol Price School of Public Policy, describes effective public institutions as having strong and supportive relationships with citizens and stakeholders—"their organizational culture is based on trust." Trust is also necessary to create a dialogue between public institutions and stakeholders, without which the goals of the institution—which are focused on supporting the public—will not be realized. As Ray Rood emphasized, without morally grounded values, the mission and purpose of the institution will fail. The core of establishing trust is the necessary positive perception of stakeholders. When consistency between promises made and actions taken are achieved, the institution will facilitate partnership and participation from civil stakeholders crucial to strategically delivering services effectively and efficiently.

As such, values must be focused on appropriately practicing and establishing democratic norms to limit corruption and create trust. Integrity, transparency, and accountability are value-based prerequisites to public trust, as they generate fair and reliable public services and predictable decision-making that produces good governance. The most compelling values in the literature (including the 2030 Agenda documents) and expert interviews include Accountability, Commitment to Excellence, Empathy, Equity, Monitoring and Evaluation, Predictability, Resilience, Responsiveness, and Transparency. The significance of these elements as they correspond to the "Values and Ethics" in this framework is outlined.

Accountability

Accountability in the public sector refers to responsibility, the extent to which government and its institutions are held answerable for their actions, regardless of their level of authority, position, or power. Accountability is vital to demonstrating democratic governance, as it is necessary to control the abuse and unethical actions of those in positions of power.

Commitment to Excellence

Commitment to excellence refers to employees and public servants who clearly understand the importance of their position and the difference they are making in the lives of those they serve. Civil servants with this understanding are committed to the institution's mission and goals and enhance their skills and competencies for efficient service delivery.

Empathy

Empathy refers to the ability to "recognize, understand, and respond to the needs and feelings of another." In public administration, this "other" refers mainly to those being served. Public servants, leaders, and employees must know who they serve, including their constituents' feelings, experiences, and various social influences. Empathy is necessary to improve and mediate interactions between public servants and constituents. It enhances relationships by promoting unity, cooperation, and an appreciation for the circumstances and needs of constituents that allow the public servants to correspond appropriately and make "compensatory adjustments ... for known distinctions."

Equity

Equity considers the heterogeneity of a population and its beneficiaries to achieve a democratic, fair, and equal society. All members (even the most vulnerable) should feel included and that their well-being is a priority. Equity consists of various elements, including fairness, justice, inclusiveness, diversity, participation, and accessibility. Other qualities embody accounting for heterogeneity and incorporating the unique individual in an institution's strategic planning to attain a fair and equal society.

Monitoring and Evaluation

Monitoring and evaluation aims to identify, track, measure continuously, and document outputs and impacts to determine the program's effectiveness. These mechanisms help establish institutional programs and provide opportunities to make the needed modifications to ensure that an institution's actions are executed predictably and with excellence. Monitoring and evaluation are essential for making an institution's contributions and operations transparent and accountable.

Predictability

Predictability refers to the extent to which stakeholders, especially beneficiaries, are confident in the public institution's service. An institution's predictability is generally grounded in laws and regulations that provide political stability in the processes and outcomes relating to governance. As a result, predictability generates reliability in the public institution's systems and structures. Beneficiaries can anticipate occurrences pertaining to public services when there are stable and unambiguous rules. This stability will enable constituents to rely on the institution, knowing that the institution will consistently deliver its services.

Resilience

The resilience of a public institution refers to the capacity that it possesses to recover from crises. This resilience encompasses the institution's preparedness and anticipation of adversity and harm. Resilience requires the institution to adapt and remain stable despite difficulties; the institution must also understand capacities that extend beyond short-term expectations. One of my favorite quotes from Nelson Mandela is, "The greatest glory in living lies not in never falling, but in rising every time we fall."

Responsiveness

Responsiveness is about meeting the public's needs within a reasonable time frame. The prompt provision of quality public service helps promote access and equity.

Transparency

Transparency is disseminating readily available and easily understood information for scrutiny and supervision. Transparency increases openness, and accountability protects public interests and reduces maladministration. Transparency is "openness so that people know what's happening."

Values and Ethics as Seen in the Case Studies

Chile: Port Works Management

A strong value for equity has driven a majority of Chile's port-related work. To evaluate the infrastructure and services provided, Chile's Port Works Management identified significant inequities within public port recreational areas. Valuing equity led to ambitions, such as making beneficiaries visible in their different social identities, considering age, gender, and presence of disability, among other defining characteristics. This valuation allowed for further identification of solutions that make the port accessible to all. Notably, identifying gender-based inequities led to a strong focus on modernizing the infrastructure to address the specific needs of women and girls without distinction of social class. For example, artisanal fishing has enhanced the infrastructure to allow hygienic services and workspaces for women in a male-dominated sector.

Additionally, a value for equity has produced technical instruments that allow for citizen participation despite differences in beneficiaries. In the design and implementation stages, the institution conducted pre-investment studies that included economic, social, participatory, and gender assessments, prioritizing relationships with various stakeholders (including the Ministry of Women and Gender Equity, Service of the Elderly, and various Indigenous groups). Equity-based evaluation of the port has led to such things as designing accessible beaches for those in wheelchairs.

The institution's strong focus on monitoring and evaluating the project's effects and the beneficiaries' satisfaction also led to several positive outcomes. Environmental baselines and energy efficiency evaluations have been established to avoid unwanted environmental impacts. While these metrics evaluate the effects of the services on environmental efficiency, they also incorporate elements that value resiliency. The port's evaluation examines the durability, good construction, and fragility of the project and services in an environmentally sensitive infrastructure. Transparency is also well-valued, as it is generated through citizen participation and the Ministry of Public Works Integral Information and Citizen Assistance System (SIAC). Through the SIAC, constituents can mandate requests for access to public information. The predictability of information access is anticipated due to Law No. 20,285.

Additionally, information is further predictable by regulated response time. Currently, access requests to public information have a maximum response time of 20 business days, and consultation, claims, and suggestions have a maximum response time of 10 business days. Field visits are even appropriately used to allow for a more effective response to citizens. In 2015, there were 22,921 applications through SIAC, where only 1.4% of applications corresponded to the port works. Of this relevant 1.4%, only 5% were complaints or disagreements, suggesting that most applications are service requests from citizens rather than complaints.

Palestine: Establishment of the Palestine Public Finance Institute

As defined in its strategic framework, the Palestine Public Finance Institute (PPFI) defines six critical core values: excellence, credibility, integrity, dedication, transparency, and accountability. Through its commitment to excellence, PFI aims to uphold high professional standards that are ethical, responsible, and consistent with international norms of public fiscal management. PFI's credibility value reflects its commitment to customer service, as seen through policies and practices aimed at harmonizing inconsistent procedures (i.e., inconsistent tax policies) so that constituents have a predictable and satisfactory experience when working with public finance officials. The initiative seeks to establish practices that are congruent with its policies. In valuing integrity, PFI aims to address underlying corruption issues by promoting honest and fair dealing with all constituents. PFI's emphasis on dedication demonstrates its value of resilience and responsiveness through its goal of equipping public finance officials with knowledge in high-quality, comprehensive training. While not part of its mandate, PFI is also dedicated to achieving gender balance in its programming, strategically seeking to create opportunities for women trainers and trainees. As of 2017, 13 of its 22 training coordinators were women. Lastly, PFI's addition of transparency and accountability highlights its understanding of the importance of monitoring and evaluation. This value is operationalized through 14 indicators that provide quantitative measures of progress based on PFI's mission and strategic goals. These indicators include the number of in-house trainers, training days, training modules, and trainees. Using these indicators, PFI aims to uphold an evaluation structure that contains quarterly, biannual, and annual reporting on these indicators.

Thailand: Sa Kaeo Shelter for Children and Families

The values and ethics found in Thailand's Sa Kaeo Shelter for Children and Families are essential to its humanitarian vision and goals. These values include transparency, resilience, commitment to excellence, and empathy. As a basis for humanitarian aid, empathy is the principal value in the Sa Kaeo initiative. The program must show empathy toward victims of human trafficking who have suffered physical and mental trauma. The Sa Kaeo Shelter for Children and Families envisions children and youth embodying good citizenship, happiness, and creativity. Espousing empathy as one value has led to understanding victims' lives and circumstances. This value recognizes the resulting struggles and difficulties of designing multi-faceted aid for victims, including medical care, legal assistance, psychosocial care, recreational opportunities, education, and livelihood training. Sa Kaeo described the staff's compassion toward the victims as essential for producing the victims' informed consent, as the staff guarantees anonymity and confidentiality for the victims. Without this empathy, staff members would be limited in their ability to understand and show compassion for victims, hampering their reintegration into society due to a lack of trust. Furthermore, a staff that is incapable of appreciating the position of a human trafficking victim may struggle to recognize trafficking indicators and could fail to identify victims.

Sa Kaeo also values equity in its many forms. The initiative understands that victims of human trafficking are inherently diverse—men, women, and children all from bordering countries—and they believe in the need to help all of them equally. A commitment to excellence is another such value. The fragility of helping and identifying victims requires staff members and volunteers to perform their work diligently and with care. Assisting the police, hospital clinics, shelters, and networks is delicate work and requires well-trained, dedicated volunteers and staff to carry out quality operations. Enhancing employee skills, capabilities, and knowledge is one focus of Sa Kaeo Shelter's commitment to excellence.

Transformational Leadership

Transformational leadership is defined as a leadership approach that causes reform and change in individuals and social systems. It generally has a moral purpose larger than self, increasing the commitment and effort made by organizational members to achieve the organization's goals and improving the capacities of members to increase productivity. This form of leadership focuses on reform and social change to improve the status quo. It helps achieve the organizational transformation to higher levels of efficiency and effectiveness with its three dimensions: setting direction, developing individuals, and redesigning the organization.

Transformational leaders pay special attention to improving organizational qualities, dimensions, and effectiveness. They interact with others to allow leaders and followers to help each other bring their motivation and morality to higher levels. They provide an inspiring organizational mission and vision, and they love to motivate followers to design new ways to change the status quo and surrounding environment. As a result, the followers of this type of leader feel

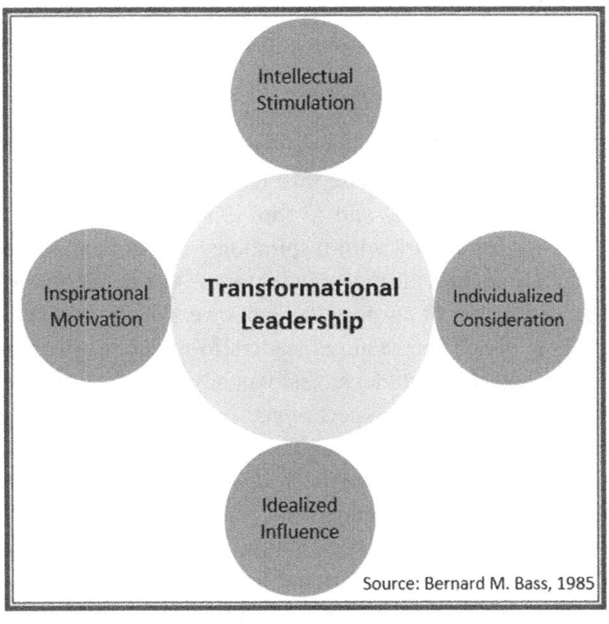

FIGURE 4.2 Transformational Leadership

that trust, admiration, loyalty, and respect motivating them to work harder than initially expected. According to the theory of Bernard M. Bass (1985), transformational leadership comprises four key elements: individualized consideration, intellectual stimulation, inspirational motivation, and idealized influence (See Figure 4.2).

Individualized Consideration: Mentor or Coach with Empathy and Support

A transformational leader acts as a mentor or coach for each follower. This leader listens and pays enough attention to each follower's concerns and needs. Transformational leaders give empathy and support, maintain open communication in the organization, and willingly assist followers when facing challenges. In supporting their followers, these leaders fully respect and celebrate the contribution made by everyone, sparking each follower's will and aspiration for self-development and spurring inner motivation for accomplishing tasks.

Intellectual Stimulation: Encourage Creativity and Innovation

Transformational leadership plays an essential role when supporting trial-and-error practices. Although public institutional leaders lack precedence for defining how operatives or professionals deal with their tasks, they can provide room and tools for designing and testing any practices that may be confirmed as effective and beneficial to the institution. In addition, these leaders stimulate innovation and inter-organizational learning.

Inspirational Motivation: Motivates Associates

Transformational leaders always define an appealing and inspiring vision for followers at the beginning and regularly revise this vision according to the circumstances faced by the institution (Bass and Avolio, 1994). Transformational leaders set ambitious standards for work with inspirational motivation, deliver optimism about future goals, and provide meaning for tasks. As a result, followers are embraced with a keen sense of purpose that empowers them to advance the institution's work. This dimension requires leaders to maintain trust and respect with their followers, especially under stressful or adverse circumstances requiring followers to work beyond their expectations.

Inspirational motivation requires leaders to develop and communicate a strategic vision. Vision refers to long-term goals or ideas that benefit the entire system and its members. A charismatic leader may develop a pseudo-vision without a clear vision and easily persuade naive followers to believe its value, though the vision is destructive. Transformational leaders must have a clear and deep perspective about the status quo before creating an organizational vision, which is an intellectual task. These leaders must be knowledgeable, intelligent, and professional in the field and maintain an awareness of the changing task environment. However, according to our colleague Janet Denhardt, transformational leadership is not just about leaders themselves having a grand vision after brainstorming to transform an institution. It is also about working through and with followers and having followers and leaders raise each other to higher levels of attainment. As such, a leader must employ proper communication skills to deliver the vision and keep that vision understandable, precise, robust, and engaging. Several scholars identify the significance of communication associated with inspirational motivation. Transformational leaders can communicate effectively with their colleagues with specific competencies, such as language, rhetoric, metaphors, images, symbols, or nonverbal cues. They inspire followers to remain optimistic about the organization's future and themselves, motivating followers to take delight in investing more effort in their work.

Idealized Influence: Role Model

Leaders with a great vision must have enough followers for implementation and also the powerful eloquence to communicate that vision, indicating the importance of personal charisma. Charisma originates from the Greek word "charismata," meaning "the gift of grace" or "gifts presented by the gods." It is generally applied when describing personalities whom language cannot depict. Charismatic people can be easily identified by how they attract others. They always use their power for good (like Mahatma Gandhi or Nelson Mandela) or evil (like Adolf Hitler or Talat Pasha) to influence others. In an institution, successful transformational leaders stand as role models for high moral and ethical behavior. They are respected, trusted, and admired. They maintain high self-efficacy and self-discipline as the consistent base for how their followers view and treat them. Furthermore, rather than personal gain, transformational leaders pay great attention to promoting the autonomy and accomplishment of their followers and make efforts to develop them into new leaders.

An excellent example of a successful transformational leader is Theodore Roosevelt, the 26th President of the United States, who contributed to national environmental protection. When Theodore Roosevelt took office in 1901, the United States was significantly overusing natural resources, notably the large-scale overharvesting of renewables such as wood, water, birds, and other animals. Despite the prominent value given to free-market economics around the country, Theodore Roosevelt prioritized educating citizens about environmental protection at public forums. He used visits to national parks and natural preserves as education platforms. He pleaded with local citizens to regard the environment as a limited treasure with economic, aesthetic, moral, and spiritual value.

Consequently, Roosevelt achieved his goals with the help of his energy, appeal, and charisma. He could attract enthusiastic followers to support his political views wherever he was. Many scholars believe that Roosevelt's charisma outshines most other U.S. presidents based on his accomplishments. As a result of his environmental campaigning, Roosevelt successfully initiated the emerging American conservation movement, which protected hundreds of millions of acres of natural resources. He also effectively set up a bridge between concern for nature and good citizenship and changed American attitudes toward controlled use and systematic protection of natural resources. Thus, Roosevelt demonstrates the idealized influence of a transformational leader and the ability of transformational leadership to benefit the institution. Notably, this form of leadership should not be confused with pseudo-transformational leadership, in which charisma can be wielded as a dangerous tool for personal gain rather than the benefit of constituents.

Transformational Leadership as Seen in the Case Studies

Armenia: Elimination of Mother-to-Child Transmission of HIV

Before the National Center for AIDS Prevention's initiative, Armenian women and children faced significant harm due to HIV. In the absence of services aimed at the Prevention of Mother-To-Child Transmission (PMTCT) of HIV, Armenia suffered a rate of 45% HIV mother-to-child transmission, and patients with HIV encountered challenges of discrimination and misunderstanding from the public. However, how the Armenian government combatted this issue displayed sufficient individualized consideration. As a result, the PMTCT initiative benefited HIV-positive mothers and children by issuing programs to provide HIV testing and counseling services and coordinate the national AIDS response. In addition, the initiative was proposed to reduce the stigma and discrimination toward people living with HIV and meet the demand for universal access to PMTCT countrywide.

The Armenian Ministry of Health developed inspiring and appealing visions and established a working group with various stakeholders to build the National PMTCT Strategy. The group consisted of specialists, the Ministry of Health, the Institute of Reproductive Health, UN Agencies, multilateral organizations, and patients living with HIV. As a result, a wide range of opinions was accepted after a deep discussion among public institutions and beneficiaries, which guaranteed the effectiveness of program implementation.

The National Center's initiative also faced challenges during the process of eliminating mother-to-child transmission of HIV. In addition to providing relevant healthcare services, the government also gave out medical and dietary supplies, such as milk formula, to the HIV-positive women who had given birth. However, many women did not apply for the milk formula because they were afraid of disclosing their HIV status. The government solved this problem by releasing a new mechanism for distributing milk formula. The women living with HIV could access the milk formula through a network of local pharmacies. With respect and support from the government, Armenian women aspired toward self-development and actively participated in establishing the nationwide HIV testing and counseling system.

India: SAKALA Mission

The Karnataka state government received regular complaints about the state's poor governance, as public services could not be delivered on time. By showing outstanding personal charisma and focusing on public benefits, the Chief Minister of Karnataka appointed a nodal minister to supervise and guide a solution to this problem. The nodal minister delegated responsibilities to the department's secretary to spearhead the initiative. The Secretary took steps to engage citizens, civil society, and employees of the organization in intensive deliberation, supporting and encouraging their contributions to create a systematic solution. The vision created by the Secretary was appealing and inspiring to the people inside and outside the organization. She was a role model who worked tirelessly to achieve better governance, monitoring, and evaluation of the impact of the SAKALA mission in an ongoing manner to improve its performance. Proactive steps were taken to get citizens who applied for public service under the SAKALA mission. Through this mission, the SAKALA leadership created trust, admiration, and respect for themselves and the government system.

Rwanda: Automated Passenger Clearance System

The Directorate General of Immigration and Emigration (DGIE) of Rwanda displayed outstanding transformational leadership through the implementation of the Automated Passenger Clearance System (APCS) at the Rwandan border with the Democratic Republic of Congo (DRC). After initiating this innovative technology-based infrastructure project, the government created an internal program team with technical engineers to discuss construction feasibility and spark creativity. The team was eventually expanded to a committee that involved multiple stakeholders, including the Rwanda Development Board (RDB), National Identification Agency (NIDA), Ministry of Local Government

(MINALOC), Rwanda National Police, Rubavu district authorities, Private Sector Federation, and representatives of cross-border traders. Considering the lack of experience operating this type of system in Rwanda, the committee participated in deep discussions, accepted views from various stakeholders, and even sent a group of technicians on a study tour in Hong Kong. This exploratory team learned much from the Hong Kong Immigration Department, which employed advanced techniques of APCS. After the study tour, the Rwanda government summarized the information gathered and invited an independent consultant from Hong Kong to help generate design ideas for the system in Rwanda based on its local context. Finally, the DGIE successfully transferred the Hong Kong model to Rwanda and established a unique information technology system to solve crowded passenger clearance.

Strategic Planning

As an application of effective transformational leadership, strategic planning drives public institutions toward their goals by supplying a method for determining a clear vision and translating it into action. While strategic planning has traditionally been incorporated in private sector organizations, its methodology may be applied to public institutions to provide these institutions with clarity of action about serving their stakeholders best. Our UN Team 2019 consulted two of the best strategic planning scholars and practitioners, my colleague Rick Cully and Professor Ray Rood.

A successful strategic plan provides an opportunity for organizational diagnosis and learning by establishing seven elements: comprehensive environmental assessment, vision, values, mission, goals, strategy, and tactics. These components interact with each other in an ongoing, parallel process throughout the institution's life. Strategic planning is inherently nonlinear and requires participants to continually revisit parts of the plan through regular evaluation and vision casting. Establishing planning periods during which the strategic planning process occurs regularly allows participants to proactively approach this endeavor, creating avenues for assessment and adaptation to the institution's current reality. While each strategic plan component requires its evaluation and analysis, the components together provide public institutions with direction and equip them with an action plan to serve their constituents.

Components of a Strategic Plan

In application, each component of a strategic plan challenges an institution's stakeholders to answer a critical question about the institution's place in its community and ability to carry out its services to meet constituent needs. Figure 4.3 provides an overview of the components and the accompanying question that each component presents to participants in the strategic planning process.

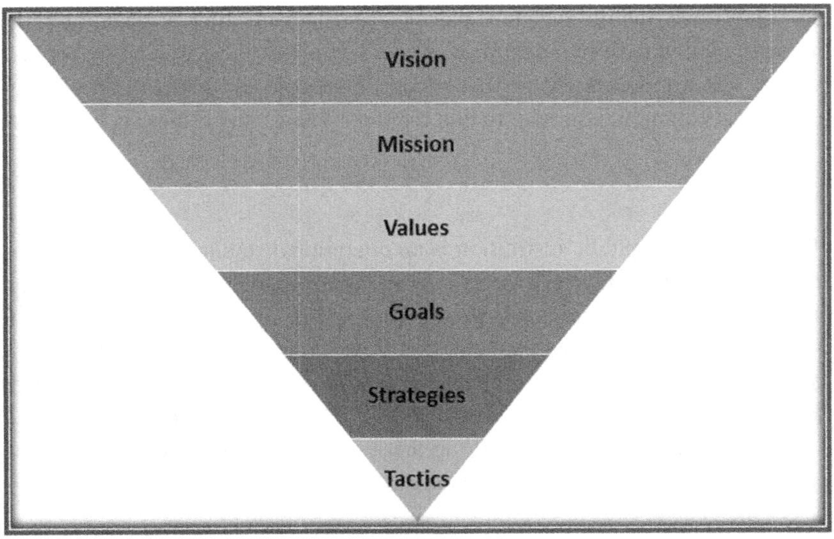

FIGURE 4.3 Strategic Planning Components

Comprehensive Environmental Assessment

Developing an effective strategic plan for a public institution begins with an appraisal of the social, political, environmental, and technological factors that comprise the institution's environment. The institutional leadership must also consider the relevant statutes and regulations that determine the institution's function within the public sector. Finally, based on this assessment, the institution can begin crafting a framework to assess its precise mission in serving its stakeholders.

Vision

A public institution's vision comprises its long-term, intended direction for the future. The vision answers why the organization exists. According to Professor Culley, the institution's vision is primarily aspirational, serving as "True North," guiding the institution as a compass guides a traveler. All members and stakeholders must share an institution's vision, as it reflects where the institution is headed, considering its current reality.

Values

Organizational values present a framework for a public institution's ethics and management. As the pillars of an institution's work, values set standards for how an institution carries out its mission to achieve its purpose. As these values are established, institutions must place these values in a hierarchical order; this hierarchy will determine institutional priorities in instances of conflict between values. For a more extensive discussion of the role of values in an effective public institution, please refer to this chapter's Values and Ethics section above.

Mission

The mission of a public institution is an operational statement clarifying what the institution will do to achieve its vision. The mission also identifies the constituency the institution intends to serve through its operations. As public institutions exist for the public's benefit, their mission is based on the requirements of the public; the mission may change over time or with changing public needs. Finally, this mission must be clearly understood by those responsible for leading the institution and those working there so that the institution can carry out its intended work effectively and efficiently.

Goals

Goals determine a public institution's operational policies. They clarify the institution's focus on achieving its stated mission. Goals should be strategic and span multiple years; some may last indefinitely. An institution should limit its strategic goals to between three and seven (optimally, five). As with the broader components of the strategic plan, every department in the institution must identify with the goals to play a role in accomplishing them.

Strategies

If goals determine *what* an institution aims to accomplish, strategies determine *how* an institution will achieve its goals. Thus, strategies are categorical and provide a practical basis for operationalizing organizational goals. To achieve these goals, a public institution's strategies establish its rationale for decision-making in practice.

Tactics

Strategies are effectively implemented through a specific and detailed action plan that delineates a series of tactics. These tactics can be thought of as time-sensitive objectives that are updated during every planning period. According to Professor Rood, to be effective, these objectives must be SMART: Specific, Measurable, Achievable, Results-oriented, and Time-bound. As opposed to broad aspirations, SMART objectives create opportunities for tangible achievement.

Strategic Planning Best Practices

Community Engagement

After gaining an understanding of its general purpose, an effective institution must engage its stakeholders in assessing the institution's strategic plan. The institution must identify and differentiate its organizational stakeholders from its beneficiaries in conducting its stakeholder analysis. Organizational stakeholders are members with a vested interest in the institution's mission and implementation. Beneficiaries are external stakeholders that the institution is designed to serve. Including stakeholders in the strategic planning process allows for the inclusion of various knowledge bases and experience levels, ensuring greater depth and breadth in terms of who is responsible for the implementation of organizational objectives and who is eventually served. An inclusive stakeholder analysis ultimately leads to developing a holistic framework for strategic planning.

Mindful Implementation

After creating a successful strategic plan, an effective public institution must implement this plan by establishing actionable objectives and mechanisms to ensure its achievement. Successful strategic planning is further contingent on an institution's effective and sufficient leadership. Institutional leadership should establish reward systems to incentivize institution members to work efficiently. Additionally, institution leaders should take steps to fill gaps between creating and implementing a strategic plan. These gap-filling measures may include aligning the allocation of resources with strategic priorities.

Monitoring, Evaluation, and Celebration

An effective public institution must regularly evaluate its progress throughout the implementation process and adjust its implementation strategy to match its strategic vision. A review of the strategic plan and its implementation motivates organizational learning and promotes clarity of action. This systemic monitoring and evaluation process must occur quarterly or semiannually to appraise the institution's progress toward goals. The quarterly review allows for the creation of regular planning periods; the beginning of each new period provides for assessing progress and establishing new goals, strategies, and tactics depending on the institution's current progress.

Finally, institutional evaluation must be accompanied by celebration. Institutions must take time to celebrate what has been accomplished and do so in partnership with their constituents.

Planning as Seen in the Case Studies

Armenia: Elimination of Mother-to-Child Transmission of HIV

In response to the prevalence of mother-to-child transmission of HIV in Armenia, the National Center for AIDS Prevention undertook efforts to increase preventive and curative care to reduce HIV in this population. This initiative responded to a local context that indicated that approximately 45,000 pregnant mothers were diagnosed with HIV. In addition, up to 45% of children born to these HIV-positive mothers were also HIV-positive. To combat this fatal health concern, Armenia's vision was to eliminate the transmission of HIV from mothers to their children. This vision was grounded in values of service accessibility, quality of life, accountability, and equity, especially for women in rural and remote areas. The National Center operationalized its vision by creating government-facilitated systems and structures for preventive and curative HIV care—including testing—ensuring access to all who need it across the country. To execute this mission, the National Center identified several goals (what the National Center calls "objectives") that center on creating avenues for receiving care. Three of the salient goals include (1) access to HIV treatment and counseling services for all pregnant women, (2) access to ARV drugs for all HIV-positive pregnant women and newborn children, and (3) capacity-building for medical and non-medical personnel working on this issue. In designing strategies to accomplish these goals, the National Center considered various political and legislative factors to execute its action plan effectively. Finally, the National Center created a comprehensive, time-based list of tactics that outlined actions from 2002 to 2016. It comprised a step-by-step action plan allowing the National Center to accomplish its mission of creating a healthcare structure to eliminate mother-to-child transmission of HIV.

Palestine: Establishment of the Palestine Public Finance Institute

In designing its policies and programming, the Palestinian Public Finance Institute (PPFI) comprehensively understood its social and political environment. PFI's leadership was acutely aware of the Palestinian administration's weak capacity to deliver quality goods and services, resulting in public distrust and low tax compliance. These administrative shortcomings led the PPFI to develop programming to counteract these negative consequences and increase its public fiscal management officers' transparency, accountability, and efficiency. Additionally, in considering its capacity-building efforts, PPFI prioritizes professionalism to reinforce its social and political legitimacy as an administrative authority considering the Palestinian administration's political tensions. According to its strategic framework, the vision of PPFI is "to become the center of excellence for public financial management education and to learn in the Palestinian public finance system." PPFI operationalizes this vision through its mission to offer educational and development opportunities to build employee skills, competencies, and practices in public fiscal management. In its three-year framework, PPFI lays out goals and tactics to accomplish each strategic objective, including a list of intended results for each objective. To incorporate monitoring and evaluation into these objectives, each objective is accompanied by a list of indicators that measure progress. Overall, PPFI emphasizes the need for SMART strategic planning that, when incrementally executed, will lead to the institution's long-term success.

Spain: Decide Madrid

In Decide Madrid, the institution identified in its contextual assessment that the city's strategic plans were developed in partnership with the interested associations and experts to exclude constituents affected by the city government. To address this issue, the institution envisioned an avenue for direct

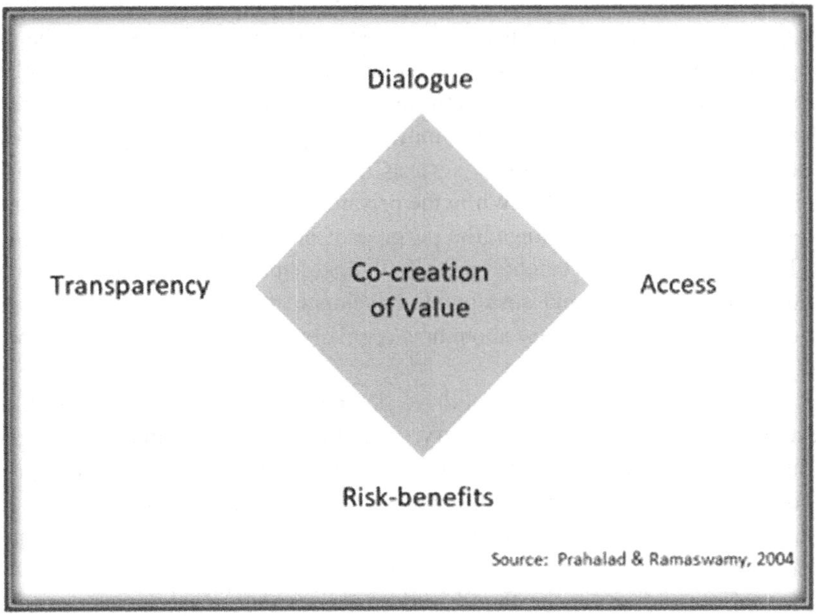

FIGURE 4.4 Factors of Co-Creation

communication between citizens and the government to implement programs that meet community needs through participatory processes. This vision was operationalized through the creation of the government website Decide Madrid. The mission of Decide Madrid was to mobilize citizen engagement through participatory processes, including citizen proposals, consultations, and participatory budgets. The institution prioritized creating a transparent, participatory, and inclusive municipal government to provide a structure for the institution's participatory interactions with its citizens. To achieve this higher level of morality, the municipal government explicitly prioritized equity, sustainability, human rights, participation, and peace as its core values. These core values were applied to three key objectives laid out in the Decide Madrid initiative: citizen proposals, consultations, and participatory budgets. Each area of emphasis created opportunities for citizen engagement and participation for the municipal government in Madrid to realize its vision of a more inclusive, equitable, citizen-focused city.

Innovation and Co-Creation

Forms of Innovation

Innovation involves creating a new product or a new way of looking at an old problem—it constitutes a radical discontinuity with the past. In public institutions, innovation focuses on finding creative and better means to achieve public ends. Public sector institutions strive to balance their priorities, including effective resource allocation and meeting pressing societal challenges. In a changing world, new ways and approaches are required to address society's complex problems. The notion of public sector innovation—new ideas that create value for society—is not new. However, innovation in public institutions must tackle inherent barriers and dilemmas, such as the traditional risk-averse approach and bureaucratic work style. While the private sector needs innovation to support its competitive advantage, the purpose of innovation in the public sector is less clear. However, current trends, including demographic changes, poverty reduction challenges, and sustainable development, have supported governments in thinking differently about how regulations and policies are developed and services are provided.

Leaders must understand what drives the need for innovation, such as allocation of resources, service delivery, or policy design and implementation. Further, leaders should clearly understand the circumstances needed to promote innovation in public institutions. Innovation brings governments numerous benefits, such as optimal resource allocation, increased accountability and transparency in public service, and enhanced equity and inclusiveness. Several types of innovation can be found in the public sector; these include service innovation, process innovation, regulatory innovation, and policy innovation.

Service innovation by a local public institution involves using various technological implementations or developing modernized service delivery mechanisms. Process innovation refers to rethinking the institution's complete set of end-to-end processes. The primary objectives of process innovation are to increase productivity, reduce complexity, and drive down costs. For example, an institution may engage in process innovation when redesigning an application form for an education system by removing unnecessarily complex questions and introducing simpler ones written in plain language. This change reduces the time and complexity required to complete the form while providing the necessary information.

Regulatory innovation stems from the need to balance the interests of multiple stakeholders. It must maintain a balance of social, environmental, and economic values. Regulations must be synchronized with changes in the economic and social environments to stimulate harmony in society. Regulatory processes also affect other innovations, as the regulation and innovation interface are mutual and dynamic. An understanding of this interface is crucial for regulatory innovation. Policy innovation involves identifying constituent needs and shortening the time required to develop, test, implement, and diffuse a policy. This form of innovation may focus on mission-oriented policies, invention-oriented policies, or system-oriented policies. Policy innovation promotes efficient and accurate policy formulation for the benefit of stakeholders.

Innovation by Co-Creation

Public sector organizations and leaders should identify the processes and structures that can foster innovation. Public leaders must find ways to build capacities that can support and accelerate the innovation process. A new paradigm of leading innovation in public institutions is co-creation. The term co-creation was first used by the management thinkers Prahalad and Ramaswamy. It is a process where novel solutions are designed with people and not for them. This process changes how public managers or leaders think about their role in policy development. It goes beyond committee meetings, formal stakeholder hearings, and customer research. Co-creation is about participatory design, co-design, design attitude, and design rethinking, which have been emphasized as essential to innovation in recent years.

Co-creation is about the joint creation of value by public institutions and their target populations. It allows citizens to co-construct service experiences to suit their context. It encourages different creative processes, a different involvement of people, and a different mode of knowledge, bringing them to the forefront of public sector innovation and decision-making. Co-creation engages stakeholders inside and outside the organization throughout the process, recognizing that everyone is essential in the innovative process. Engaging non-state actors, including social innovators, private sector entities, local communities, individuals, and citizens, is critical to jointly developing creative public sector environments to benefit all.

The critical components in creating innovation by co-creation are dialogue, access, risk-benefits, and transparency. These factors of co-creation are significant to breaking the status quo or monotony of public institutions and their processes to bringing about the necessary change for innovation. In addition, connecting end-users and other stakeholders to the entire creative process is a powerful way to drive public sector innovation. Figure 4.4 visualizes the four factors of co-creation in what is known as the DART Model.

Dialogue entails interactivity and engagement with citizens. It is more than just listening to stakeholders. It implies shared learning and communication among equal partners. However, it is difficult to envisage dialogue between unequal partners or problem-solvers. Thus, it is vital that capacity-building occurs among communities and organizations to stimulate discussion for partner-based innovation.

Access refers to ensuring that information is accessible to citizens. Institutions should aim to provide on-demand services to their constituents. Without this access, information asymmetry creates a knowledge gap that hampers successful dialogue.

Risk-benefit refers to the probability of harm to citizens. With access to information, transparency, and dialogue, citizens can debate the trade-offs of an institution's potential policy decisions. All stakeholders of co-creation can share responsibility through the risk-benefit component.

Transparency allows public institutions to build trust with all stakeholders. Institutional transparency, in turn, creates effective dialogue, access, and risk-benefit analysis.

In a public institution, innovation by co-creation opens the institution's value chain to the stakeholders it serves. It shifts the focus from the work process to the human engagement process.

Innovation and Co-creation, as Seen in the Case Studies

Australia: Cape York Region Package

The Cape York Region Package (CYRP) implemented innovative and co-creative strategies by engaging Indigenous community actors during every stage of project development. Although the CYRP's overarching objective was to improve the quality of roads and infrastructure in the Cape York Peninsula region, the Queensland Department of Transportation and Main Roads (TMR) designed every initiative in this project in partnership with local communities to promote economic opportunity and social equality for the Indigenous communities involved in the program. TMR outlined three Key Result Areas (KRAs) with attached monetized incentives to ensure the inclusion of these Indigenous communities in the construction process. These KRAs focused on maximizing Indigenous individuals' employment, education, and training opportunities and promoted Indigenous businesses as project contractors and sub-contractors. Additionally, TMR partnered with various Indigenous councils and institutions in the project's strategy and implementation phases. Notably, through the Peninsula Development Road Priority Agreement (PPA), TMR partnered with the Land Council Aboriginal Corporation and Indigenous Traditional Owners (TOs) to ensure that roadwork is fully compliant with all cultural heritage legislation. In addition, PPA enables the TOs to serve as cultural heritage monitors and surveyors throughout construction. TMR negotiated with Indigenous communities to establish the Indigenous Economic Participation Plan (IEPP) through the Indigenous Land Use Agreement. IEPP provides workshops for Indigenous businesses involved in construction and scholarship opportunities for high school and college students pursuing careers in construction-related fields. By applying companies in IEPP, TMR aims to train these businesses to manage the maintenance of the Peninsula Development Road.

Within the community works infrastructure efforts undertaken in this program, TMR partners with eight Indigenous communities to implement construction projects chosen by the communities themselves based on community needs. Local Indigenous governing authorities oversee these projects and focus on giving local businesses and individuals employment opportunities. Finally, in response to concerns about nonindigenous companies usurping employment and training opportunities from Indigenous businesses, TMR partnered with the Department of Aboriginal and Torres Strait Partnerships to certify that legitimate Indigenous businesses are engaged in all CYRP projects. Through its many partnerships, CYRP emphasizes innovation and co-creation to achieve lasting success for the Indigenous constituents it aims to serve.

India: SAKALA Mission

SAKALA's mission introduced service and process innovation efficiently and effectively. It reduced the complexity of the process, saved time for both citizens and employees of the institution, increased the system's performance, and decreased the costs associated with the process. Through service innovation, SAKALA empowers citizens to avail themselves of services in a time-bound manner and claim compensation for any delays or defaults. This initiative revolutionizes the public delivery of services by standardizing and simplifying the government system. The government was reinvented as a single, citizen-friendly unit, converging heterogeneous departments onto a single platform for the application and delivery of services. Information technology was used to create an innovative model of public service delivery. This model centers on a single-window system for the application, which tracks citizen service requests, processing, and delivery. This system simultaneously monitors delays, defaults, rejections, complaint redressals, and generates monthly reports to evaluate progress. Within the development of this initiative, co-creation processes were engaged to stimulate innovation. Citizens, civil society, and government employees participated in the dialogue before drafting the initiative. Access was given to non-state actors to analyze the situation and provide innovative design solutions. SAKALA's mission was created with people and not for them. Risk benefits were discussed among stakeholders to assess the status quo and determine the penal-based provisions that should accompany the initiative. These provisions incentivize government compliance and compensate citizens for service delays and defaults. Through innovation by co-creation, SAKALA has become a citizen-focused and reliable public delivery system.

Spain: Decide Madrid

Decide Madrid demonstrates innovation by co-creation in practice, specifically through process and policy innovation. The initiative allows the citizens of Madrid to participate in the city's decision-making processes. Any citizen, regardless of gender, appropriate age, or circumstance, can give their opinions and formulate proposals. People participate in presenting their ideas and needs and proposing public services necessary to meet those needs. To participate in the Decide Madrid digital platform, citizens must register and be over 16 years old. This platform represents a significant advancement since Decide Madrid promotes cooperative governance to establish shared priorities beyond enabling direct communication between citizens and government. Citizens dialogue in the form of debate with the government and among themselves while voting for any initiative. Madrid gives access to information about any government program, creating an inclusive process that allows citizens to make informed voting decisions based on measured risks and benefits. The initiative's transparency and web-based access build trust between the government and the citizens. Through this participatory platform, citizens pass initiatives binding on the municipal government.

Additionally, citizens participate in the management of the budget. They present, support, debate, and vote on proposals for investments, expenditures for goods and services, and grants or subsidies that impact their immediate environment. This collaborative legislation process creates value jointly and creates an innovative environmental experience. It is one of the most complete and innovative citizen participation tools for open, transparent, and democratic government.

Applied Conceptual Framework

Figure 4.5 captures the application of the four essential elements outlined above. Though the visual flows in a linear order, the framework is not linear in operation. For one, the elements are codependent and interconnected. We cannot have meaningful co-creation without morally rooted strategic planning and established democratic values. Second, given that the elements are multilateral and constantly working in relationship, their real-world operation has a fluctuating nature. However, even considering their fluid relationships, the conceptual framework can still be applied using this quasi-linear approach.

Beginning with a contextual assessment, a public institution can understand its environment to effectively develop a plan to meet the needs of its constituents. At the macro-level strategic planning, the institution can create a vision, values, and mission based on the contextual information discovered during its initial environmental assessment. By employing a code of values and ethics, an organization's transformational leaders can engage in practices of co-creation

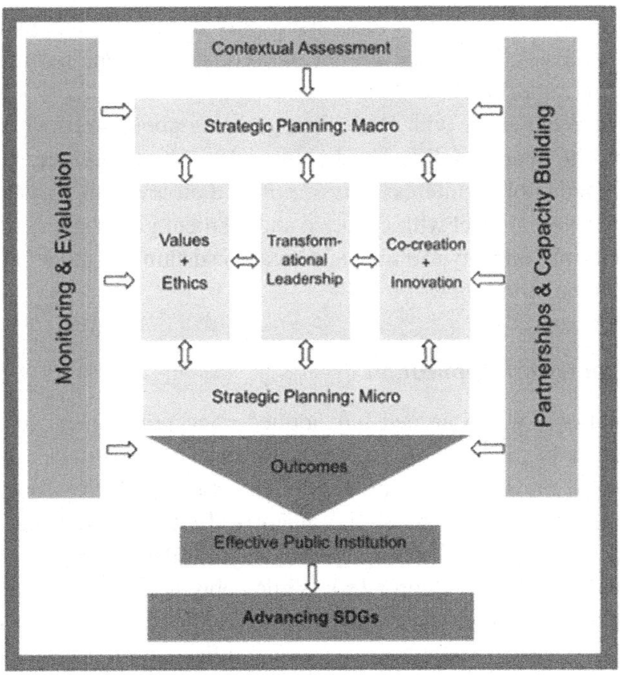

FIGURE 4.5 Applied Conceptual Framework

and innovation to partner with constituents and stakeholders to develop action plans. At the micro-level of strategic planning, an institution can outline goals, strategies, and tactics to execute its mission effectively. Provided that the institution includes regular monitoring and evaluation within its efforts, the institution will achieve its purpose by applying this framework effectively.

Before delving into the best practices for applying this framework and the intended outcomes of application in the following sections, it is essential to note the extensive doctoral research by our former student, Dr Michael D. Falkow (2020), who leveraged this conceptual framework's four main components and created a robust and detailed framework for effective and resilient local governance. Dr Falkow's in-depth framework, detailed in an upcoming book, comprises 16 subcomponents. He began with values and ethics, transformational leadership, strategic planning, and innovation and co-creation as his primary building blocks, and he ultimately subdivided them into four subcomponents. Then, through a comprehensive and in-depth qualitative interviewing process, Dr Falkow captured the lived experiences of municipal leaders (both policymakers [elected council members] and public administrators [city managers]) to determine the structure, definition, and importance of the framework and its elements. Dr Falkow contends that using a bottom-up strategy (rather than a top-down one) where good local governance might "trickle upward" and provide a foundation for good governance at the state and national levels is desirable and necessary. Examining current events and trends at the state, national, and even international levels, finding governance-based fractures and fissures in dire need of repair is not difficult.

We hope to leverage our work with Dr Falkow to bring about worthwhile change. The overarching goal of political and public administrative processes must be to maximize the public's interest. It is essential at all levels of government. If we begin at the local level with effective and resilient governance, we can improve municipalities one city at a time and create a sustainable model for higher levels of government to follow.

Best Practices for Framework Application

In the preceding sections, we examined our applied conceptual framework elements and how those elements are reflected in the various case studies. In this section, we turn to the application process of the framework to various public institutions. The application process is categorized into four best practices: (1) Contextual Assessment, (2) Capacity-Building, (3) Partnerships, and (4) Monitoring and Evaluation (see Figure 4.6). While applying the framework tool to various local public institutions, there is a high likelihood of facing contextual differences and barriers. Therefore, leaders of public institutions should identify those differences and obstacles to create a supportive and conducive environment to foster institutional effectiveness.

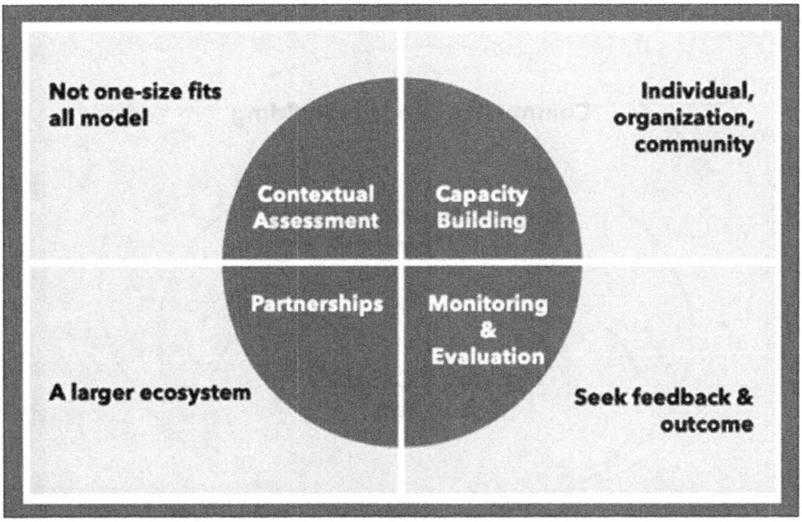

FIGURE 4.6 Overview of Application Best Practices

Contextual Assessment

The applied conceptual framework is created to support and stimulate the process of transferring good practices from one region to another to enhance the effectiveness of local public institutions. Through this transfer process, however, it is essential to note that applying this framework tool does not entail copying or emulating the same framework in different settings. This framework is not a one-size-fits-all model for developing effective institutions. Before applying this framework tool, users must understand that an institution's local circumstances are characterized by considerable diversity in terms of political and institutional arrangements, cultural conditions, social and economic settings, local capacities, and so on. Our research found that effective public institutions must prioritize values and ethics, transformational leadership, strategic planning, and innovation and co-creation. The success of instilling these effective elements depends on how well an institution recognizes and adapts to its local context. Analysis of this local context is an invariable pretext for applying this framework. Thus, the first step to the application must be a contextual assessment that considers the public institution's environment.

Local public institutional actors must study the local political and economic resources and their bureaucratic size and efficiency. Borrowing the framework model does not mean it can bypass the complexities of local public institutions. Leaders who want to apply this model should expect natural resistance to change, mainly when it is a new method seeking to transform organizations

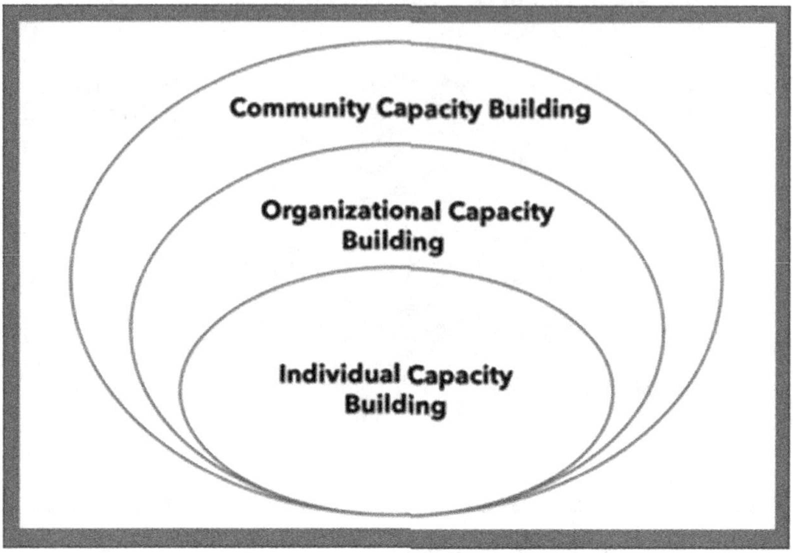

FIGURE 4.7 Levels of Capacity-Building

fundamentally. Further, some places have weak institutional structures or lack the necessary leadership skills to transfer the model. All these and other difficulties must be identified to localize the framework's application. Analyzing the local context will help determine what opportunities and challenges local public institutions will face when applying the framework.

Capacity-Building

A critical finding of our research is that capacity-building plays an essential role in applying the framework. Institutions must be prepared for the implementation of the elements of the framework to enhance their performance. Capacity-building is a broader concept; in addition to showing concern for human resources and the organization, it covers the overall environment within which public organizations operate and interact. While different institutions use distinctive types and strategies, capacity-building serves as the comprehensive bridge between applying the framework and the effectiveness of the institutions. It strengthens participants' abilities to acquire the skills required for transformational leadership, learn the co-creation process that brings about innovation, assimilate strategic planning skills, and comprehend the values and ethics required for effective public institutions.

Capacity-building may include education and training, soft skills development, institutional and legal reforms, and scientific, technological, and financial assistance. Overall, environmental capacity-building contains community capacity-building, an ongoing process emphasizing social justice, and a bottom-up approach.

Capacity-building often starts with assessing individuals, organizations, and the environment or community (see Figure 4.7). There are several tools available for this process. Depending on the needs and local context, capacity-building can combine human resource, organizational, or community-based efforts to bolster and equip the organization to apply the framework. A comprehensive, multi-level understanding of the local context must design capacity-building solutions that best fit specific circumstances. The capacity-building process will be more effective when partnering with non-state actors such as private and non-governmental organizations. These partnerships can provide valuable inputs that strengthen and reinforce institutional capacity.

Partnerships

Public organizations exist in a broader ecosystem that involves a network or web of other entities. Public institutions need active partnerships to act as responsible ecosystem members (i.e., community or society) and better respond to constituent concerns. Previous sections in this chapter discussed the new paradigm that innovative solutions to societal challenges could be found through co-creation. This process entails dialogue, access, transparency, and risk benefits. Through the scholarly literature and case studies, our research found that the framework elements will be received well in institutions when there are mutually supportive partnerships. Partnerships are strong when ideas, information, strategies, implementation, and evaluation are shared. In addition, partnerships need to be open and transparent so that all stakeholders are mutually accountable.

Partnership stakeholders might be diverse in their fields of action; however, they share the goal of improving governance to address society's problems and meet its needs collectively. Local communities want to be a part of the decision-making process for policy formulation; they aim to play a central role in creating solutions for process or service transformations. Partners together can decide the values and ethics they require in the public institutions they deal with regularly. Community members want to be part of strategic planning and the leadership process. Stakeholders of partnership can create best practices and networks that can influence innovation in public institutions. These partnerships can encourage and enable the participation of underprivileged people, leading to a more comprehensive and sustainable community impact.

The path toward partnerships is threefold:

Build Engagement Platform

Public institutions should provide stakeholders with physical or virtual platforms where they can engage with each other. For example, Spain's Decide Madrid initiative created a virtual platform for engagement of citizens with their municipal government. In Thailand's Sa Kaeo Shelter for Children and Families, a physical platform created opportunities for different stakeholders to assist victims of human trafficking.

Foster Stakeholder Interactions

Partnerships in public institutions should motivate participants to use the new engagement platform (or platforms) to enable new kinds of relationships. In turn, this will foster interactions between the institution and its various stakeholders, including citizens and private entities.

Enable New Experiences

Creating opportunities for stakeholder interaction and engagement leads to valuable experiences for all stakeholders involved; these experiences can intrinsically improve the quality of their lives.

The partnership extends the transformation of a public institution beyond the institution's internal capacity, leading to more robust and more effective work for the public good.

Monitoring and Evaluation

Program evaluation is a valuable tool for public leaders and institutions to seek feedback on a program's operations and assess constituent experiences. It answers fundamental questions about a program's effectiveness and addresses the common concerns of public leaders. This factor is critical to applying the framework, as it provides information about the utility of the framework in bringing about institutional effectiveness. Our research recommends two types of evaluation: (1) process evaluation and (2) outcome evaluation.

Process evaluation discovers whether the conceptual framework was applied as planned, whether the application factors (i.e., contextual assessment, capacity-building, and partnership) were considered while doing so, and the significant challenges and successful strategies within the framework application.

Outcome evaluation assesses whether and to what extent the expected effectiveness is achieved in the public institution, whether changes in effectiveness can be attributed to the framework or its elements, and what barriers hamper success in the process.

While its merits are clear, the program evaluation process raises concerns about institutional priorities. Program evaluation may be seen as diverting resources from an institution's core activities, as complicated and subjective, and as imposing additional burdens on employees. Despite these concerns, program evaluations are essential in determining whether elements of the framework have been effectively applied. The evaluation shows an institution's effects on stakeholders, enabling the institution to improve its partnerships with non-state actors. This factor also suggests modifying an institution's strategies to implement the framework to allow it to address the local context in implementing effective programs. Both process and outcome evaluation provide information about the barriers to institutional effectiveness. These barriers may include the rigidity of the government system, political unwillingness, the role of unions, and so on. Identifying and taking the required steps to address these barriers is crucial.

Limitations

Although we designed our research methodology to accurately analyze a representative sample of case studies from the Knowledge Base of UN Public Service Award Initiatives, several limitations must be considered when reviewing our findings. These limitations are related to internal and external validity and information availability.

Validity

Our selected case studies were chosen from a database containing only award-winning initiatives executed by public institutions concerning internal validity. As a result, our dataset contained no counterfactual situations or examples that would allow for analysis and evaluation of the causal effects of an initiative's success. Our case analysis-based approach to the research focused only on observing changes in the status quo within each case through a posttest-only evaluation. A more complex research design allowing for non-equivalent group comparison of pretest and posttest environments, or a single-group Interrupted Time-Series Analysis (ITSA), would have led to more robust findings.

The transferability of research results and recommended framework presents a question of external validity. Due to our limited time and resources, we narrowed the scope of our research to only eight case studies, two of which were chosen by our client. As we could only analyze a small sample of cases from the Knowledge Base, it is difficult to say whether our applied conceptual framework is effectively adaptable to every local public institution. An analysis of a larger sample of cases may reveal the need for a more nuanced framework design. However, to combat this limitation within the scope of our study, we have emphasized the need for continued contextual assessment. Continued partnerships with constituents and community stakeholders are required to conform the planning and execution of public programs to the community's needs while considering relevant contextual factors (i.e., political considerations, social norms, etc.).

Information Availability

As we conducted a transnational research study, we faced language comprehension and information-gathering limitations. The Knowledge Base of UN Public Service Award Initiatives contains case files written in several languages. When we conducted our random selection, several cases appeared in other languages, including Spanish and French. To overcome this barrier, we used the Google Translate function embedded in our web browsers to translate these files electronically. This translation method aligned with our limited time and resources and allowed us to read the files in English; however, we recognize that there may have been minor inaccuracies in the translation. A more comprehensive translation method may have improved our analysis of the cases.

Within each case file, we faced the limitation of varying levels of data availability. As several of the initiatives in the Knowledge Base came from under-resourced communities, the abilities of these institutions to gather data about their local contexts or the quantitative impacts of their programs may vary significantly. To understand the elements required for an effective public institution, we needed case files containing essential data regarding the carried-out initiatives. Thus, during the second tier of our random selection, we focused on the cases with more robust information when choosing meaningful case studies.

When analyzing our eight case studies, we were limited in communicating with the institutional leadership in each of the eight initiatives. Our initial research design included a semi-structured interview with a critical actor within each case study to gather more information about strategic planning and operations in each public institution and observe characteristics such as leadership and ethics. However, despite numerous efforts by our team and the client, we could not contact the institutions except the Thailand Sa Kaeo Shelter. Thus, these semi-structured interviews were not included in our analysis.

Recommendations for Further Research

Considering our research's limited scope and timeframe, we have identified several areas that require further exploration to understand the complexity of institutional effectiveness. First, a large-scale quantitative analysis of all cases in the Knowledge Base of UN Public Service Award Initiatives would provide insight into the causal factors of institutional effectiveness. This study would require a research design that enables coding all case files and identifying critical variables to be measured. Second, an empirical analysis of the four identified best practices would strengthen our conclusions about framework application to quantitatively demonstrate the benefits presented by these best practices. Third, within this analysis, a deep dive into the factors required to assess the context to adapt the framework to various institutions effectively would enable the ideas present in our research to be more narrowly tailored to the needs and circumstances surrounding each institution's work. Finally, as co-creation is a more recent form of innovation, more research should be conducted to determine best practices for engaging co-creation methods in the public sector.

Conclusion

Our research design allowed us to identify the elements of our conceptual framework through scholarly research and comprehensive case analyses. We did this analysis by assessing the application of framework elements in each case study. We identified best practices that allow this framework to aid the work of public institutions in various contexts. Based on this synthesized research, we have concluded that the framework's application will lead to the creation of effective public institutions. This outcome will exhibit the following characteristics:

Good Governance

By adhering to their stated values and ethics, public institutions will achieve good governance through increased transparency, accountability, and responsiveness. In addition, the culture set forth by these values will motivate institutional actors to behave ethically, combating instances of quiet corruption. This framework safeguards the institution's ability to serve its stakeholders effectively.

Efficiency

Public institutions will be able to ensure predictable, timely, and consistent delivery of services to their constituents. Contextual assessment and comprehensive monitoring and evaluation promote efficient government practices and allow institutions to streamline their systems in structures to reduce costs while meeting constituent needs effectively.

Public Participation

Effective institutions incentivize citizen involvement and view citizens as equal partners in solving community issues. Public engagement opens opportunities for community-based innovation, leading to more holistic and equitable solutions to specific community needs.

Trust

As the research indicates, the outcome of an institution putting values into practice is trust from the public. Trustworthy institutions demonstrate their reliability through transparent, efficient, and citizen-friendly systems. Improved public trust promotes the dignity of all citizens. It enables public institutions to meet constituent needs more effectively due to the equal investment of government and citizens in improving society. Trust is essential for strengthening the efficiency and effectiveness of public institutions, especially in their ability to generate participation and involvement in programs that require public investment. Trust creates space for honesty, open conversation, and innovation, leading to the effective delivery of public services.

Resilience

Application of the conceptual framework will build the capacities of local institutions, equipping them with resilience. Resilient institutions can effectively serve the public despite changing circumstances. In their continued assessments of the local context, resilient institutions identify and address community issues that constrain the delivery of their services. Ultimately, resilience enables institutions to withstand crises and adapt to the changing needs of their constituents.

Overall, applying this framework will improve the capacities of participating public institutions to advance the Sustainable Development Goals.

5

NEWGOTIATION—AN ETHICAL AND METHODIC PROCESS

Team UN 2021 researched, developed, and presented a negotiation framework based on our Newgotiation model in our book *Newgotiation for Public Administration Professionals* through case study analysis of exemplary projects across the globe. This chapter highlights the core of the Newgotiation process as we set up the adaptation of the Newgotiation framework for later chapters to evaluate the chosen SDGs. The goal is to distil critical elements further to generate several recommendations for UN DESA.

The word "Negotiation" finds its roots in Latin "neg," meaning to deny, and "otium," meaning leisure. The English called this as "being busy," "occupied," or "doing business." Unsurprisingly, "business" in Latin is "negocio." Time and evolution, managing feelings and emotions, matching desires and necessities, along with the game of power or the search for common ground, shape the modern art and science of negotiation. Various scholars and practitioners have studied and defined negotiation in legal, psychological, and business or economic terms in recent times.

Fisher, Ury, and Patton define negotiations as "back-and-forth communication designed to reach an agreement" or a "communication process with joint decision-making objectives." Similarly, Rubin and Brown define negotiations as "two or more parties attempt[ing] to settle what each should give and take." Carnevale and Lawler claim that negotiation is a "form of symbolic communication that involves two or more people attempting to reach agreement on issues where there are perceived differences of interest."

DOI: 10.4324/9781003497097-5

Rubinstein defines negotiation as:

> a situation in which two individuals have before them several possible contractual agreements. Both have interests in reaching an agreement, but their interests are not entirely identical. So, what will be the agreed contract, assuming that both parties behave rationally?

The *Black's Law Dictionary* defines negotiation as "the deliberation, discussion, or conference upon the terms of a proposed agreement; the act of settling or arranging the terms and conditions of a bargain, sale, or other business transaction."

The *Business Dictionary* generally refers to negotiation, a "bargaining (give and take) process between two or more parties (each with its aims, needs, and viewpoints) seeking to discover a common ground and reach an agreement to settle a matter of mutual concern or resolve a conflict."

Finally, Herb Cohen, an accomplished practitioner, said about negotiation, "Life is a constant series of actions where we attempt to influence others. We seem forever absorbed in trying to get people to agree with us." This process is where vocal expression plays a role in our training as negotiators:

> Above all, negotiation is a pervasive process in which people ultimately attempt to reach a joint decision on matters of common concern in situations where there is initial disagreement. Thus, a negotiation always requires both shared interests and issues of conflict. Obviously, without commonality, there is no reason to achieve resolution. So, without discord, there is nothing to negotiate about.

With the backdrop of these diverse definitions highlighting and focusing on conflict, we define our Newgotiation for Public Administration Professionals paradigm as "an ethical and elegant process of rational and collaborative decision-making aimed at mutual benefits." Our definition promotes relationships and trust, which we discuss in later chapters. Relationships and trust are two critical pieces of currency that every public administration professional must possess to remain productive. As we discuss throughout the book, our Newgotiation paradigm is about a collective learning and decision-making process to score a win–win.

Negotiation, as a primitive concept, rises from the conflict or tension we sense from seduction, rivalry, honor, jealousy, the sense of competition to win, and envy to "destroy" our opponents. Challenging another man to a duel was considered a pinnacle of honor and a practice reserved for gentlemen. Dueling began in ancient Europe as a form of "justice" in which two disputants battled it out; whoever lost was assumed to be wrong. The first American duel took place in 1621 at Plymouth Rock. While the rule of law has improved on the types of conflicts and the levels of violence associated with them, we continue to experience the biological and cognitive impulses and reactions related to dueling. After all, we are still human.

The primitive and intuitive nature of negotiation comes from the limbic brain. This is the part of the brain that our prehistoric ancestors developed before the neocortex. The neocortex is the analytic brain developed with vocal expression or language. The limbic brain is a part of the brain that does not speak. Instead, it feels like it is all about the five senses. Hence, it is the value we place on aesthetics, which in Greek means sensation. This feeling is why we dress well or smell good to impress our partners, relatives, friends, customers, or constituents. In prehistoric times, smell became a factor of attraction and, therefore, the basis for persuasion or conflict. In more modern times, humans invented perfume, drinking and dining, and other enhancements to precisely cause a chemical reaction in our limbic brain to please. Some cultures still value "drinking and dining" as part of the negotiation process.

There are four anatomical steps to anchor our Newgotiation technique. They are preparation, value creation, value distribution, and implementation. Our study of thousands of negotiations also demonstrates that ten simple (but most relevant) elements directly correlate to these four steps. These elements include context, interests, options, power, communication, relationship, concession, conformity, criteria, and time. Therefore, to create a common language and a workable collective blueprint of Newgotiation, we discuss our four steps below and apply each of the ten elements to the four steps in every negotiation. Also, to ensure success through implementation in each negotiation, we propose ten benchmark criteria for implementing and evaluating our Newgotiation paradigm for future use. We call this entire process the 4-10-10 Technique of Newgotiation. This logic model is for every negotiation, especially for public administration professionals. While the model is not a "magic bullet" that solves all conflicts, we recommend its methodic use to improve productivity, probability, and value in all negotiations. Our Team UN 2021 did just that. We discuss their research and findings in later chapters.

We see the profile of all Newgotiators as movable with education and training. Newgotiation is all about transformation. While controversy may be necessary to negotiate, facilitating a frank discussion accelerates the meeting of the minds and the collective good decision-making process. Jack Welch calls this "friendly frankness."

Before we get to the substantive content or the anatomy of our Newgotiation technique, some preliminary basics on the process are critical to the outcome's success. First, accurately knowing the profiles of each participant in this Newgotiation is crucial to our approach and preparation.

We teach that preparation is critical. First, identifying the context and the frame of the negotiation is vital. Typical questions might start with who, what, when, and how. For example, is an elected official or a political appointee participating? Is there staff representation in the group? Are lawyers present?

Are consultants facilitating? Are all stakeholders with authority or legitimacy present? As to frame, are we competing on positions or discussing interests for collaboration? After these preliminary steps, a skilled Newgotiator lays down the strategy before approaching the negotiation.

Good negotiation is all about the frame. The key here is to avoid conflict between different actors. The priority is to strategize the process using a collaborative structure (win–win) rather than a competitive frame (win–lose). Also, one must consider what to do and who to call if the frame is competitive. Sometimes, simply knowing when to walk away from a competitive frame and wait for a better collaborative frame is critical. Here, thinking about the appropriate social capital and human capital is beneficial to the process. This is when breaking bread or building a relationship may be vital to the future of the negotiation.

Building a relationship among the participants explores the multiple approaches to transforming beliefs, perceptions, emotions, and visions. It is all a pedagogical process of joint decision-making through various life skills, such as empathetic listening, communication, ethics, passion, reconciling interests through collaboration, enthusiastic vision building, or perhaps dreaming. Rushing to negotiate may have severe, long-lasting, and disastrous consequences compared to taking time to build a relationship based on mutual respect and trust. We discuss these life skills throughout the book and the framework we apply in Newgotiation.

We all are familiar with the adage "preparation is everything" or the sports cliché that a football team on game day is as good as its last practice. Negotiations are won or lost before any substantive meetings between negotiators. Therefore, preparation and the quality of that preparation are essential. Good preparation considers a well-designed process, meticulous stakeholder analysis, and good decision-making.

A stakeholder analysis is a framework for analyzing stakeholders. This analysis helps us understand stakeholders' behavior, intentions, interrelationships, and interests in the negotiation. The analysis also helps us assess the influence and resources that stakeholders bring to bear on decision-making or implementation processes.

A good amount of negotiations or projects fail because we miss or misidentify a stakeholder. For example, ignoring the coastal community residents may be a fatal mistake in offshore drilling negotiations. Likewise, ignoring the equestrians in an equestrian community while attempting to build a golf course may lead to the project's demise. Good preparation through listening and collecting relevant data also postpones anchoring the critical event in the negotiation.

Most negotiators fail because of a lack of preparation and for anchoring the critical moment, primarily the project's price or contract, too soon. Once the price is exposed, a commercial transaction's Zone of Possible Agreement (ZOPA) becomes one price against the other or no deal. This anchoring of the price is the third step in our four-step process. Ignoring steps 1 and 2 can be fatal to any negotiation. Everything else to achieve the win–win becomes secondary or much more challenging to discuss and, more importantly, much more difficult to achieve.

Value creation defines the "why" for the Newgotiation by identifying interests, options, and possible alternatives. This is the moment to be creative, innovative, and descriptive. The more creative the negotiator, the more opportunities are created; the more options are made, the more possibilities there are for a deal. During value creation, empathetic listening matters. The more we explore "what ifs," the more we propose solutions to problems. The value creation step addresses or suspends criticism and invents options and alternatives to solve problems.

For example, options to improve productivity, product quality, organizational climate, or culture are crucial to success in an organizational context. This culture is the step to building trust by brainstorming, asking, and listening. Value creation is all about getting to "yes." H. Raiffa, in his book entitled *The Art and Science of Negotiation*, emphasizes the importance of building trust, shared purpose, and belief. Most negotiators do not even agree about the hypothesis without this step, let alone agree on the solution to the equation. The key is to expand the focus on creating coherence between the limbic brain and the neocortex. The value creation step (our second step) is the only way to achieve the desired outcome by getting to "yes" with incredible velocity and value.

A small number of negotiations are distributive or single-issue negotiations. Negotiation over a tractor, for example, may involve a single price issue. These negotiations are not our focus here. Rather, negotiations that involve multiple problems are where we will direct our attention, as they are more common in the public sector. These types of negotiations are known as integrative or value-creating negotiations because they allow the negotiating parties to integrate various sources of value through creative exchanges.

We offer as a case study our negotiation of building a fire station for a California city. While we proposed a public–private partnership through a methodology called lease/leaseback, our creativity and value creation did not stop there. The method helped the city finance a brand-new fire station with private funds through bonds. It also shifted construction and delivery risk to the private sector. But more importantly for the city, it allowed the municipality to take possession of a "turn-key," all-inclusive fire station operation, including fire trucks and engines, as part of the deal. This creativity brought about an efficient and effective public–private negotiation based on interests and values to serve those interests. The city focused on good governance and public administration, while the private sector delivered a state-of-the-art fire station using its building and procurement strengths. A holistic discussion about various interests maximizes negotiation potential. This rationale is why we claim that our Newgotiation process improves the public value of a deal by creating and enhancing the probability of a better deal.

In the fire station negotiations, we asked ourselves how to make the most integrative negotiations, creating as much value as possible to distribute among the private and public sectors. The negotiation literature about guidelines to create value tracks our practical experience in this case study.

Generally, when negotiators encounter differences with negotiating parties, as we did in this case study, they tend to view this as a roadblock. However, differences are often "opportunities to create value in negotiation," writes Harvard Business School professor Max H. Bazerman and the University of California, Berkeley professor Don A. Moore in their book *Judgment in Managerial Decision Making.*

Negotiators often get stuck because they remain focused on one aspect of the deal or transaction. We broke through that impasse by asking many questions to identify all interests in our fire station case. For example, we would not have been able to structure the deal if we did not know that the city had specific tax revenues for 15 years. This knowledge helped us structure the lease term, making ownership of the fire station by the city a reality at the end of those 15 years. In addition, if we had not asked what an ideal deal for a fire station looked like for the city, we would not have known about the necessity to procure fire apparatuses (e.g., trucks and engines) as part of the deal.

Negotiators think that methodic organization is critical to resolving one issue at a time. That may be true in some instances. However, in integrative negotiations, especially in the public sector, discussing multiple issues is better. Then, only settle when everything is discussed and agreed upon between the parties. Negotiating one point at a time prevents capitalizing on differences with trades across problems.

Integrative negotiations do not require sacrifices in the name of cooperation. On the contrary, they allow negotiators to get more of their wants by identifying what each party values most. For example, our fire station project made sense once we recognized and categorized all stakeholder interests, such as the deal's timing, equipment, etc. We were prepared to distribute values once these interests were identified and aligned with elegant options and solutions.

Our third step in our four-step technique is value distribution. This stage is when we describe or justify the critical moment for the negotiation or the price. Again, having explored all interests and generated all viable options without commitment, this is the time to expose and justify our decision or price with objective standards based on evidence obtained during our preparation.

The moment of value distribution is when we transform the options of each interest into reciprocal concessions and divide the equities. The opportunity created by this step before getting to ZOPA cannot be understated. This step is also commonly known as the compromise.

Once the value distribution is over, the fourth and last step is all about the follow-through or implementation of the agreement as negotiated. This step is also about compliance with the law and a sustainable future. Given the complexity and importance of the first three steps in our technique discussed above, the fourth step yields results as good as the quality of the first three. Finally, as much as preparation is critical to any good negotiation, implementation is everything. Even the best negotiations have no value if the negotiated agreement cannot be implemented.

6

NEWGOTIATION OF SDGs—THE 4-10-10 TECHNIQUE

In our 4-10-10 technique (see Figure 6.1), we create a logic model or a common language for Newgotiators. We take our four steps through ten elements identified through our research and practice of all negotiation types. The ten elements play a substantial role in the outcome of the negotiation. Like a stakeholder analysis, discussing each relevant element in detail during all four steps is crucial to the technique's success. In our matrix at the beginning of this chapter, we identify each suitable piece vis-à-vis each step of our approach. Not surprisingly, the crucial preparation step bears relevance to most of our elements.

Context

The first element, "context," impacts the environment in which the negotiation takes place. For example, in the demographic context, one age group's bargaining power may be stronger than the other. In an aging municipality, advocacy for a senior community center may be more successful than a playground with a swing set at the park. Conversely, the park will win the day in a municipality full of young families.

At the personal or organizational level, the negotiator's history, educational background, friends, customers, partners, socioeconomic status, culture, values, and religious beliefs all provide context to impact the relationships from the first contact to the end of the negotiations. Remember, negotiation is a human endeavor.

The context analysis in negotiation occurs during our first and perhaps the most critical step, preparation. This step is used to gather information and data

DOI: 10.4324/9781003497097-6

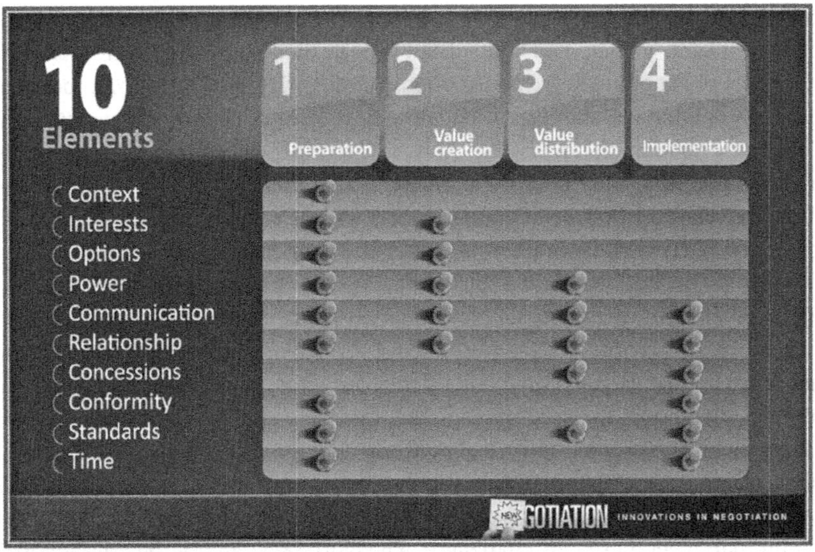

FIGURE 6.1 Newgotiation 4 Steps and 10 Elements

Source: Newgotiation for Public Administration Professionals

to create value. This step is also used to tell a story or describe the "why" of the negotiation.

Defining the context also determines the form or channel of negotiation, which we identify below as direct talks, negotiations through an agent, a facilitator, a mediator, auctions, multi-stakeholder dialogue, and parallel informal negotiations.

Direct talks are appropriate between friends or organizations with existing relationships. The social capital already in place between two friends is all that may be necessary to begin direct negotiations. Newgotiations through an agent like a real estate agent, lawyer, or trade union representative facilitate more distant relationships or perhaps relationships needing professional or technical expertise such as law. In other words, a functional relationship between actors bound by a social structure may be used to produce an economic or non-economic outcome.

In the context of an environmental dispute, two competing organizations may request a neutral facilitator to advance negotiations. Facilitators like the United Nations, World Bank, or NGOs such as Doctors Without Borders or the Red Cross are helpful in negotiations, public policy creation, and administration. Their established social and human capital helps them design and implement the needed administrative remedies in negotiations between countries or international organizations.

Newgotiations through a neutral mediator are to resolve legal disputes. An entire field of alternative dispute resolution is becoming a precious tool for bench officers, judges, and trained lawyers to mediate disputes. In a context where there is not much left to negotiate but the price, such as a commodity or public procurement, auctions provide the best form or channel for negotiation. Electronic auction platforms like eBay, E*TRADE, or Bloomberg help supply and demand efficiently and productively. While our Newgotiation model may improve relations between suppliers and customers when buying and selling products, auctions remain the most efficient channel for concluding a transaction; we do not address these types of negotiations in this book.

Another form or channel of Newgotiation is the multi-stakeholder dialogue in a more 21st-century collaborative context. We argue that the three sectors are more predisposed to collaborate than ever before due to various contextual settings involving the new media, the Internet, and globalization. Nicolas Berggruen, in his book entitled, *Intelligent Governance for the 21st Century*, suggests that in a genuinely multipolar world, no single power dominates the bargain. He further argues that a new "intelligent governance" system is required to meet these new challenges. The North Korean missile crisis of 2017 illustrates the difficulties of this context and the importance of multilateral relationships and discussions with various stakeholders.

Multistakeholder dialogue provides the platform for exchanging ideas to harmonize beliefs, interests, and convictions to reach a collaborative state and result. This harmonization is more useful in framing. Finally, parallel informal negotiations may be helpful in more delicate or potentially hopeless public negotiations. An excellent example of the direct but parallel approach through informal channels is when a representative of General Secretary Khrushchev approached President Kennedy during the Cuban Missile Crisis in October of 1962. History tells us this crisis may not have been averted without this intervention. As we know, the situation ended with Russia agreeing to remove the missiles from Cuba. In return, the United States decided to remove Jupiter missiles from Turkey and Italy and pledged not to invade Cuba.

Interest

Our second element, "interest," is about defining the "why" or the purpose of our negotiation. Why are we here? In our Newgotiation paradigm, the general answer is always to maximize the value of our cooperation and create a sustainable, long-term relationship. In other words, defining the win–win approach begins right here.

From a technical sense, interest is defined in our preparation and value-creation steps. Interest is our mission, vision, goals, and the target we want to achieve through this process. If interest were only about price, it would be a single-dimensional definition of purpose leading to a swift win–lose frame or, at best, a compromise between the contemplated price A and price B.

We want more in multilateral and integral negotiations. Most leaders in the 21st century cannot afford less. Our constituencies demand more effective, efficient, cost-efficient, successful, and sustainable collaborations. Our Newgotiation paradigm addresses these needs. Notice that for this element, we said "interest" and not "position." Interest defines the problem and motivates people to find solutions to the problem. Interest is "something that concerns, involves, draws the attention of, or arouses a person's curiosity."

Every interest has several potential solutions that could satisfy it. Shared and compatible interests lie behind opposed positions. Each side has multiple interests, but they also have basic human needs consistent with their personal characteristics we discussed earlier. A good Newgotiator acknowledges the other side's interest and attacks the problem without blaming them. Separating the people from the problem allows the parties to address the issues without damaging their relationship. It also helps them to get a clearer view of the substantive problem that may need a satisfactory solution for both parties.

Emotions are a second source of problems. Negotiation can be a frustrating process. People often react with fear or anger when they feel that their interests are threatened. Our Newgotiators are excellent and empathetic listeners who give the speaker their full attention, occasionally, respectfully, and accurately summarize their points to confirm their understanding. Generally, the principled Newgotiator uses questions and strategic silences to draw the other party out to discover more. Discussions lead toward a desired solution rather than focus on past events. Sometimes, the solutions are simple but not readily apparent. Only a good listener can detect the nuances of various interests to satisfy.

In our world of Newgotiation, parties keep a clear focus on their interests but remain open to different proposals and solutions. Interests are critical to discuss options, but premature judgment hinders imagination, creativity, innovation, and the quest to think creatively to develop novel and worthwhile solutions.

Newgotiation balances interests, as it is predisposed to seek the "why" or "why this project?" We often discuss with our real estate development Master's students that gracing us with their presence as developers in our municipalities is not enough to serve all interests, including our constituents. Yet, bureaucratizing our cities is not in their or our interest either. We need a collaborative approach instead of an adversarial process at this moment. This time is when we should generate imaginative, creative, and innovative solutions to deal with collective interests. These interests may include creating or maintaining parks, open space, and storm drains, limiting or relieving traffic, addressing climate change concerns, and, of course, evaluating the monetary profit or marketing interest of the developer. Profits are not measured by just dollars and cents or sectors but by benefits to all project participants, including the municipality.

Transitioning from the preparation step to value creation is an exciting brainstorming process. The discussion about interest in defining mission, vision, and goals transforms into discussing the joint mission, joint vision, and joint goals. The development of a definition of common purpose, the search for mutual gains, and the invention of ways of making decisions easy are conducive to value creation and, ultimately, value distribution in our system of Newgotiation. Good stakeholder analysis and overall preparation facilitate this process.

Despite these optimistic prospects, it would be naïve to think and approach any negotiation without a "plan B." Remember, it is all about the frame. William Ury, Roger Fisher, and Bruce Patton call this Best Alternative to a Negotiated Agreement or BATNA. BATNA gives us the power to walk away if we cannot reach mutual gains at any negotiation stage. The better the BATNA, the stronger our ability to negotiate. In our Newgotiation paradigm, we advocate using BATNA as a tool to collaborate and strengthen the deal at hand rather than a means to support walking away.

In our classrooms and executive education courses, we teach students how to postpone the moment of anchoring the price (only at the value distribution step) by discussing interests and creating options to improve the probability of closing a better deal.

Options

The third element in our 4-10-10 system is "options." Like context and interest, options are created in Newgotiation steps one (preparation) and step two (value creation). Options are about imagination, creativity, and innovation. Finding elegant options for the interests we create in the previous step of our Newgotiation process makes Newgotiation pleasant. There is no tension or friction here; there is only an opportunity to solve problems through creativity.

This element is about building a rapport and personalizing, customizing, and matching interests with options for solutions. A word of caution here is appropriate. Collaboration in our Newgotiation context does not mean capitulation. A good Newgotiator assures that there are sufficient options for both sides to distribute and, more importantly, never reveals the order of importance of each option. Walking away from the wrong frame is critical. This moment is also where BATNA comes in to help shape these options.

Finally, people are sometimes confused about options and alternatives. Alternatives are means to say no (e.g., a BATNA outside the deal). Conversely, options are invented to match the interest inside the deal as a package. As such, options and various alternatives to those options add value and improve our ability to cut a better deal. The more options available, the easier the distribution and the more room for concessions in ideal deal-making. Uneven option creation yields disproportionate concessions. The purpose of our Newgotiation paradigm is the equitable and balanced distribution of options. The win–win opportunity demands nothing less.

Power

Our fourth element, "power," is potentially more destructive than constructive or productive. However, for public leaders especially, power is very much part of every negotiation and relationship in some form or another. As such, we spend several important and cautionary pages identifying the minefield power can create. We also organized our discussion about power into three distinct categories: (1) self-centered motivations, (2) tactics that misfire because they damage relationships, and (3) qualities that lubricate negotiations because they improve relationships.

Self-centered Motivations

The power of money helps us determine authority and ability to transact a deal, but it also helps to corrupt. The power of money, like the power of sex, is an incredible source of influence. Moreover, either power is quite addictive. The chemical imbalance these powers provide for the human brain removes the capacity to fear or adhere to civil society rules, norms, or laws.

Unfortunately, the power of money and sex are the two most dangerous causes of disgrace for public leaders. We have known presidents, governors, ministers, legislators, mayors, and council members who lose the trust of their constituents and sometimes their office because of the addictive and destructive nature of these kinds of power. This is one more reason our Newgotiation technique focuses on the purpose of the negotiation rather than the price. Identifying the "why" through the creation of interests and inventions of options reduces the risk of corruption or self-interest.

Purpose, mainly public purpose, grounds us and reminds us of our responsibility as public servants. Negotiating on behalf of the public to create value for the community is a collective interest. The power of money or sex is rooted in self-interest. Our Newgotiation technique is designed to pursue collaboration and cooperation to improve the deal for everyone instead of someone. Good governance measures such as transparency and accountability help expose self-interest, which is often kept a secret.

The power of ego is not a distant third to the first two examples we identify here. An egomaniac is sure of his true being—the only truth. They have difficulty learning. More importantly, they think that listening is a waste of time. Given that we identify listening, in fact, empathetic listening, as an essential tool to invent solutions in our system of Newgotiation, an egomaniac is a liability in value creation. Manipulating or seducing the egomaniac with skill may be the only way to transform the negative into a positive.

Envy and jealousy are engines of power and weakness in negotiation; both create conflict. More importantly, both envy and jealousy lead to loose–loose outcomes. How often have we encountered siblings fighting over a family heirloom, which gets sold in an estate sale because neither agrees to let the other have it? Being envious of the other party's benefits from the options created in the negotiation is indeed dangerous. This consequence results in a competitive rather than a more productive collaborative frame.

Earlier, we discussed the importance of having equal options at the value distribution stage to ensure that the negotiation leads to a win–win. We now emphasize the importance of the quality and quantity of the possibilities created. While jealousy may be used as a motivator, which may be a good thing, quality and balanced options avoid the harmful and destructive human emotions of jealousy or envy.

In the negotiations with a real estate developer for entitlements, a mayor is never negatively concerned with the potential benefits of the developer but only with the benefits to their constituents because of the proposed development. They look for quality and balance in the duties and responsibilities of each side. They look for fairness and justice for the community but are never envious of the benefits to the developer. The goal is to make the developer and the community winners in the negotiated outcome. Both deserve success, and the mayor's job is to facilitate that success.

Tactics that Misfire because They Damage Relationships

The power of the threat can be productive if used properly. Confidence, posture, and the skill to dissuade are great resources to avoid a conflict or fight. In its proper context, the old Roman adage "si vis pacem, para bellum" or "if you want peace, prepare for war" demonstrates the power of the general threat to be prepared for the accomplishment of the good. On the other hand, specific threats frustrate the collaborative approach and reduce the chances that prolonged discussions will create interest and invention of options needed to solve problems.

Like the tactic of domination in negotiation, the power of the bluff can work, but it is short-lived. Bluffing may be a skill for a poker game, but complex negotiations for our organizations or communities are not a game. Pretending through silence or misrepresentation ruins social capital and reputation, not to mention that it is dishonest. It takes years to build trust and reputation, and one bluff to destroy them. And for those negotiators who think they escaped, there is always a next time; once discovered, suspicion plagues that relationship forever. Therefore, we always advocate ethics before anything else in our Newgotiation. No deal is worth compromising our reputation for integrity. Another way of saying this is that bluff and misrepresentation cannot possibly achieve the opportunity to win–win, especially in the long term.

Among the powers that are not helpful to our paradigm of Newgotiation is what old negotiators call "salami tactics." This is a tool to manipulate more than collaborate. It prolongs the negotiation as a drawn-out, step-by-step process, forcing small concessions in "thinly cut slices." In our classes, we create a set of learning tools by gathering intelligence and information in our preparation step to avoid being the victim of such archaic power tactics. Also, using a facilitator with social capital helps change the narrative from manipulation to collaboration. Unfortunately, salami tactics do not add value; they serve only to detract, destroying trust.

Another dreadful power trick in the old repertoire of negotiation is the unwelcomed and unsolicited "last bid." Asking yet another concession before signing off on long and sometimes painful negotiations is a power tactic. It is dishonest, undermines collaboration, and ruins any trust that may have been built during the negotiation process. This tactic is short-sided and will surely ruin a reputation. One way to respond is to revisit the interests to reset the negotiation. This may also be a suitable place to use BATNA to either recast the agreed deal or potentially walk away.

Perhaps old negotiators' most classic power tactic is called "good cop/bad cop." Put in practice by the cooperative and competitive side of negotiation into one. This 2-in-1 strategy does not help relationship or reputation building either. It is inconsistent with our ethical and elegant standards to strive for the collaborative win–win. The "bad cop" is intentionally looking to intimidate through deception.

We see the "good cop/bad cop" tactic as the opposite of our Newgotiation paradigm, where both parties win through sharing. Honesty in labeling and diplomatically exposing the tactic with a request to start over is beneficial to defuse such an ugly scenario. Assurances that all interests are discussed openly and fairly are persuasive. Good preparation and the power of anticipation are good tools to avoid the tactic altogether. Our purposeful, methodic, and thoughtful preparation leads us to negotiate with one person with authority or legitimacy, building trust and avoiding the bad cop altogether. If this tactic persists, bringing your bad cop may remind you that a relationship reset may be helpful to all.

Qualities that Lubricate Negotiations because They Improve Relationships

The power of media and, more importantly, new media is quite remarkable and undeniably potent. Image or reputation and the intangible value it provides to various actors in Newgotiations is substantially enhanced or otherwise affected by media. Therefore, we must pay attention to this power and use it to promote the value of the win–win.

As companies fight for revenue, growth, market share, and loyalty in an increasingly competitive environment, measuring and managing corporate reputation has become the critical driver of business value. Yet, although most companies agree that reputation management is essential, relatively few organizations have figured out how to harness its value. Almost 80% of companies polled agree that we now live in a "Reputation Economy," a marketplace where who you are matters more than what you produce; however, only 20% say their company is ready to compete.

The battle for corporate social responsibility is being waged across the globe. According to the Reputation Institute Report 2020, LEGO tops this chart, followed by The Walt Disney Company. LEGO and Walt Disney perform according to consumer expectations while being intentional about their corporate purpose and the social impact of their businesses. We find this intangible value of the image helpful to our new paradigm of increasingly distributed or shared governance, promoting the opportunity to win–win. Reputation creates trust, and trust makes deals.

Next in our review is the valuable power of social capital. The World Bank defines social capital as "institutions, relationships, and norms that shape the quality and quantity of a society's social interactions." In an article we assign in our classes about "Social Capital in the Creation of Human Capital," James S. Coleman writes, "Social capital is productive, making possible the achievement of certain ends that in its absence would not be possible." We believe this productivity is paramount in our Newgotiation. Social scientists conclude that social capital improves economic, political, administrative, and overall human behaviors because, indeed, it is comprised of concepts such as "trust," "community," and "networks."

While these concepts are difficult to quantify, the challenge is increased when one seeks to measure social capital's quantity and quality on various scales. Therefore, the World Bank encourages social scientists to identify methods and tools to qualify and quantify social capital so that policymakers can make decisions about subjects like poverty, economic development, and democracy, all of which are part of the SDGs.

Results in the qualification and quantification of social capital are fascinating. Measures of trust in government or interpersonal trust, strong voting trends, membership in civic organizations, and volunteerism all contribute to the prosperity of a city, state, or nation. John F. Helliwell and Robert D. Putnam, in the *Eastern Economic Journal* (1995), examine social capital by comparing Northern and Southern Italy. Their research and conclusions support social scientists and are pretty compelling in terms of the power of social capital. In Northern Italy, where indicators like civic involvement, voter turnout, newspaper readership, membership in football clubs, and confidence in public institutions are high, we see significant improvement in governance. These indicators are compared to struggling Southern Italy, which is much poorer and disengaged from government and institutions.

In simple terms, there is no substitute for trust, community, or networks when seeking to improve the probability of closing a better deal, improve value through collaboration, improve productivity by sharing, and prevent conflict. There is no better way to Newgotiate than "putting an arm around someone" we know in our community or network who we trust to describe the "why." But again, Newgotiation is a human endeavor.

Starting with similar interests is more than half the battle in negotiations. In this context, the World Bank's research finds "increasing evidence that social cohesion is critical for societies to prosper economically and for development to be sustainable. Social capital is not just the sum of the institutions underpinning a society—it is the glue that holds them together."

Moreover, our leadership with trust assures happier Newgotiations and happier communities. Stéphane Garelli is a professor at the International Institute for Management Development (IMD) and the University of Lausanne. He leads the team that publishes the IMD World Competitiveness Yearbook—the most comprehensive and reputed study on the competitiveness of nations. Not surprisingly, countries with high interpersonal trust rank among the world's top ten most prosperous countries. Happiness is very high among the Nordic countries. Sweden ranks at about the same level as Norway and Finland but after Denmark. The United States, among the countries with more than 150 million people, ranks number ten.

Our Newgotiation paradigm thrives on trust, social capital, integrity, elegance, and ethics. As a result, our Newgotiators have a higher success rate at striking a better deal. Similarly, we do not advocate naiveté either. When facing negative power tactics, good Newgotiators anticipate what may be missing. Max H. Bazerman and Michael D. Watkins, in their book entitled, *Predictable Surprises: The Disasters You Should Have Seen Coming, and How to Prevent Them*, show us in the business context how to reduce risk by understanding and lowering the psychological, organizational, and political barriers preventing us from foreseeing some of the manipulations we discuss here. They then describe the powerful tools—including incentives and formal coalitions—that business or public leaders can use to uncover and deflect threats invisible to insiders.

Perhaps more simply put is the old Russian proverb American President Ronald Reagan adopted, "trust but verify." This phrase has since passed into the American lexicon to warn against predictable surprises. Negotiators need to foster this good sense of suspicion by asking through trusted channels, relations, and networks about the integrity of the information provided during preparation. In our technique, accurate information is vital in identifying interests, making decisions, developing options, and designing elegant distribution solutions during our value distribution step.

The *Harvard Business Review* reports on this new principle of shared value, which involves "creating economic value in a way that also creates value for society by addressing its needs and challenges." This power is perhaps the power of empathy and care, not quite seen or practiced before. As a result, companies are reconnecting their success with social progress.

Shared value is not necessarily social responsibility or philanthropy but a new standard to achieve economic success. A growing number of companies known for their business savvy and accomplishments, such as GE, Google, IBM, Intel, Johnson & Johnson, Nestlé, Unilever, Costco, and Wal-Mart, have already embarked on significant efforts to create shared value by restructuring the intersection between society and corporate performance and success.

In our classes for intersectoral leadership, we are teaching and imploring the government leaders of tomorrow to wisely regulate in ways that enable shared value rather than deter it. This overall theme of empathy or empathetic listening to address needs and challenges through our Newgotiation technique should not surprise our readers by now. Newgotiation is all about compassionate listening to align interests, create options, and invent solutions. One of our favorite quotes from the Greek philosopher Epictetus is, "We have two ears and one mouth so that we can listen twice as much as we speak." Epictetus' advice remains one of the best we give our students.

Our colleague, Robert Denhardt, in his book, entitled, *Just Plain Good Management*, starts lesson one with:

> [L]isten, listen, listen. The first and most important idea in good management is simple: listen, listen. Failure to listen attentively, genuinely, thoughtfully, and completely is the cause of an incredible number of organizational breakdowns. On the other hand, listening carefully builds trust, engagement, and, in turn, productivity. Practice not just hearing but listening to others. Encourage people to listen to each other. And, who knows, people might even listen to you.

We agree. Perhaps more impactful than lesson one, Professor Denhardt concludes, "Remember the first management lesson: listen, listen, listen. Assuming you've got that down, now twist it. Listen empathetically." He continues, "Walk a mile in their shoes, even if their shoes don't quite fit and are the wrong color. Sympathize, empathize—but then take the next step." These are lessons that fit what we teach in Newgotiation. Failure to empathetically listen in the preparation and value-creation steps of the technique we describe in this book leads to missed opportunities to create value. Lack of value decreases the probability of closing a better deal.

We also think of intuition as a magical phenomenon—what many call "gut instincts" are formed from our past experiences and knowledge developed over time. One can build intuitive capabilities by being wise, attentive, detail-oriented, curious, and repetitive.

Many studies show that the average learning retention rate from a lecture is about 5%; by contrast, the retention rate by doing increases the rate to 75%. Those trained in the FBI and general law enforcement academies master these skills by developing an intuition about someone lying, embarrassed, or hiding something.

In more recent psychology, intuition can embody the skill to develop fast and practical solutions to problems, the importance of which we discussed in creating options in our paradigm. Gary Kline, a pioneer in the field of natural decision-making, found that under time pressures and fluid conditions, experts use their "base of experience to identify similar situations and intuitively [choose] feasible solutions." Developing these skills is at the core of our Newgotiation paradigm. Finding feasible and elegant solutions is what we teach for value creation and, ultimately, value distribution. In our experience, intuitive negotiators are better at finding and negotiating a higher-quality deal. Steve Jobs said, "Have the courage to follow your heart and intuition. They somehow know what you truly want to become."

Finally, the power of humor is, of course, a great strategy to captivate and to be enchanting. We teach our students and trainees to be entertaining and not dull during their presentations. We insist on crisp and yet informative presentations delivered with charm to draw others into our stories. Some people might call this charisma. We describe it as the ability to enlighten the brain to make people feel positive and enthused. Studies show that when participants in a negotiation smile and dream, the results are highly positive.

In our classes, we practice storytelling interspersed with clean and understandable humor. We encourage our students to be passionate about their stories. Passion shows that we care. When we care, we tend to listen more attentively. We learn about interests and potential problems attached to those interests when we listen closely. Only when we know the issues can we invent solutions. The more elegant and collaborative the solutions we design and develop, the greater the chances of striking a better deal. Our paradigm of Newgotiation is all about the value-added and the "better deal."

Communication

Storytelling nicely correlates to our fifth element to pilot Newgotiations: effective communication. Spoken, unspoken, and written communication remain critical to our Newgotiation paradigm. Since we focus on the "why" by telling a story, writing and effective communication skills are paramount for a successful negotiator. First impressions count greatly; sometimes, a wrong first impression is irreversible. The elements of communication and relationship, which we will discuss next, are two of our ten elements that have applications in each of our four steps for Newgotiation (i.e., preparation, value creation, value distribution, and implementation or follow through).

Nothing is more important than preparation for an excellent communicator to present effectively and efficiently. Before beginning the negotiation, our investigation or preparation must ascertain the identity and characteristics of our negotiating partner(s) context, including the impact of culture, values, acquaintances, networks, and habits. For instance, based on our experience in teaching or coaching in various countries or cultures, we find apparent differences and tendencies in communication. In Nigeria, top-down negotiations are the norm. In China, a trusted facilitator is preferred. In France, social status, job title, and educational credentials make a substantial difference in the negotiation process. Also, political context or image cannot be ignored in communication. Negotiation with a "labor party Mayor" for a Labor Day celebration in Brazil will most likely not succeed if the negotiator shows up in a designer suit, attaché, and expensive watch. Since 80% of communication is nonverbal, we must consider our appearance, mannerisms, and gestures during negotiations.

Elegance, passion, care, and consideration go a long way. The perception and reality of civility make a good impression and help start our negotiation's branding and collaborative process. Making others feel important is a skill that rewards the participant in our Newgotiation paradigm. The number one reason an employee leaves a job is not the money or the work but the relationship with superiors and colleagues. Nurturing that relationship from day one is extremely important in the negotiation process.

The use of technology to communicate is now quite acceptable in all circles. Platforms like Zoom, Teams, and WebEx became the norm during the pandemic. However, visual and audio presentations to present documents, slides, or any other media type must look and feel professional. This digital footprint is typically our first impression after our physical appearance.

The first minutes of a digital presentation and conversation are critical to the outcome. Ricardo Bellino's book, *You Have Three Minutes*! offers his successful wisdom on the impact of the first impression, the power of intuition, and the importance of image and nonverbal behaviors. These things we embrace in our Newgotiation paradigm.

Consistency and commitment communicate trust, and trust builds reputation. To succeed in negotiations, we need both. We previously discussed trust in the context of building social capital and the importance of social capital in improving our ability to transact a deal. In our world of Newgotiation, there is nothing like the success of a closed deal influencing the next deal. Indeed, implementation is everything!

Researchers and practitioners are always intrigued to know how to deal with critical communicative moments during a negotiation. This research and the literature on communication during negotiations provide a guide to best practices. A non-comprehensive but instructive list for our Newgotiations is shown in Figure 6.2:

Proper communication is paramount in telling the story, describing interests, finding and applying solutions, and even determining the hypothesis of the problem or the subject matter of the negotiation. However, what could be critically and fatally flawed is a miscommunication on the premise. In other words, how can we solve a problem if we disagree with its definition?

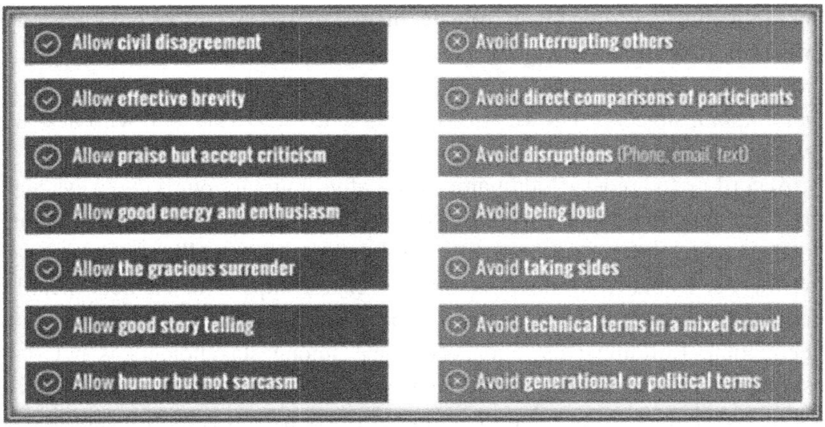

FIGURE 6.2 Proper Communications

Source: Newgotiation for Public Administration Professionals

Describing "what" is essential for two reasons. One is to operate from the exact definition to define interests. The other is to customize options. For example, buying oranges for a juice manufacturer differs from buying oranges for a bakery. One needs the pulp, and the other needs the skin. A collaborative approach to purchasing the same oranges may yield substantial benefits and, therefore, a better deal for the farmer, juicer, and baker.

The value creation step is to connect interests, preferences, and options to harness a better deal. Etymology and epistemology are both essential to effective communication. Understanding the origins of the interests of the parties and the origins of the surrounding knowledgebases will help Newgotiators use framing knowledge management to reduce the gap between information and perception, which can be a source of disagreement.

Our culture of Newgotiation focuses more on the cognitive tools we describe in this book and on resolving any differences elegantly. The empathetic listener and the elegant Newgotiator would say, "Here is how I see this; if I am wrong, please help me see it differently." This statement is authentic, honest, and truthful. This effort is about joint fact-finding and not about persuasion or advocacy. The exercise is about reducing the gap between perception and reality so that both parties have accurate data to craft options and solve problems. No one benefits from a deal constructed on a false premise or bad decisions.

Relationship

The sixth element in our Newgotiation technique is relationship, which involves emotions, identities, values, culture, and beliefs. In his book entitled, *The Feeling of What Happens*, Antonio Damasio says that we can often observe emotions but not feelings, as they are a "private, mental experience of an emotion." It is important to read body language and identify behaviors and emotions. Daniel Goleman, in his book, *Destructive Emotions: A Scientific Dialogue with the Dalai Lama*, suggests that we must learn how to effectively deal with destructive emotions by taking time to pause, meditate, and reset our hormones.

According to Frédéric Saldmann, it takes five hours for our body to evacuate the hormones produced during a stressful or angry conversation. We must create a shared perspective—a sentiment that the other is like us, as it paves the way for empathy, kindness, and good relationships. This element includes people at the negotiation table and people who can affect the outcome of the negotiation. Building trust and acceptance among stakeholders is not only essential but also necessary for public negotiations. To amass a comprehensive list of stakeholders to develop the required relations and data for negotiations, we offer the following strategies:

1. Involve internal stakeholders as early and as frequently as possible. They are professionals with remarkable resources. The more involved they feel, the more they are invested in the idea and likely to agree with the direction of the future negotiation. The earlier they are involved, the earlier you can address their needs and concerns instead of discovering them late into the process. These people are responsible for carrying out the policy decisions you make.
2. Set proper metrics and expectations before work begins to prepare for the negotiation. Clear directions, metrics, and reasonable expectations engender trust, which improves the chances of success.
3. Identify key staff to build a team, but do not ignore the rest. Recognizing everyone's agendas, goals, and expectations is critical while including staff at all levels. Addressing staff-related needs helps gain momentum from the bottom up and ensures that we tackle potential concerns from all directions during our preparation step.
4. Tell stories and describe scenarios when presenting policy or projects. Stories bring meaning and value beyond how policies or projects appear on the surface. Stories help us establish a connection with our staff on both analytical and emotional levels, which can be highly effective in the preparation, value creation, and value distribution steps of Newgotiation.
5. Express tradeoffs that occur if policy or project compromises are made. Whenever someone questions the approach or suggests an alternative way of doing things, be ready to explain elegantly the tradeoffs that will occur if those changes are made. For example, while something may be less expensive and easier to build, an increase in usability issues may positively affect the overall conversation. Feedback is not always a damaging compromise.

Stakeholder feedback can often result in beneficial gains to the user experience and product success—embrace options.

6. Relate ideas and policy or projects to the needs of stakeholders. When presenting policy or projects, consider the perspectives of the stakeholders or constituents at large. These participants are people whom the decisions of the policymakers will impact. These people also have an emotional or relational interest in the policy outcomes.
7. Support policy or projects with data whenever possible to reduce subjectivity. Data should influence policy or projects (not necessarily "driven"). While not everything can be affected by data, being able to refer to both qualitative and quantitative research that helped influence the approach can help reduce subjective opinions during policy or project discussions.
8. Speak their language. This approach will help you connect with your stakeholder audience and help stakeholders focus on what is important. Ultimately, this concept is essential for building competency, effective relationships, and trust.
9. Do not be overly defensive or let pride get in the way. Stakeholders offer a critical perspective; their insights are vital to the project's success. If the feedback comes off as critical without being constructive, it is because challenges must be articulated about what does not feel right with a policy or project. Listen actively to all feedback and focus on genuine issues instead of always jumping to defend an established position. Those of us in public office know the embarrassment we feel when facts or figures destroy a position we advocate during a public hearing. Back to Professor Denhardt's lesson, "Listen, listen, listen."
10. Communicate well. It may be best to present diagrams and storyboards to help visualize ideas and to tell the grander story; seeing the macroscopic view can help eliminate misunderstandings.
11. Offer methods of testing various approaches when consensus cannot be reached. There are times when stakeholder feedback may seem perfectly valid, but there is no straightforward way of determining whether one idea or approach is better. Informal mediation may be a viable solution—the more options there are, the more chances there are to settle or mediate desired outcomes.
12. Foresee and address technical concerns. Consult with technical experts as often as needed, as technical mistakes are easy to make but difficult to correct once the negotiation is underway. These are people who have the knowledge or information required for you to make good policy decisions. Help them help you.
13. Engage people whose diverse ways of thinking or working bring novel ideas to policymaking. "Think different," said Steve Jobs, "if you don't cannibalize yourself, someone else will." Most importantly, remember essential resources like the youth.

Concessions

The most common approach in conventional negotiations is positional bargaining. This is also known as old-fashioned "haggling," often done in an open bazaar for a product. First, the shop owner stakes out a high price, expecting the customer to offer a meager price. Then, after a series of concessions, our seventh element of Newgotiation, either ZOPA is reduced to an agreed-upon price or the customer moves on to the next shop owner, who might represent the BATNA.

The two good arguments that can be made for this negotiation style are that it goes back to the beginning of time and is relatively simple; little preparation is necessary. It is quick, inconsequential, universally recognized, and frequently used. There are also tactical and strategic advantages for one side or the other depending on which anchors the better or more favorable position.

In other words, positional bargaining has the makings of or is predisposed to win/lose. It is competitive, like arm wrestling, and focuses on conflict rather than collaboration. As previously stated, this is shortsighted and unsustainable in multilateral negotiations, especially in the public sector. Perhaps the most significant of its shortcomings is the lack of opportunity to discuss interests, explore additional or better options, or consider the "why" of the negotiation.

Moreover, all the value-maximizing opportunities and benefits of collaboration, creativity, and commitment to data and standards are completely diluted. Positional bargaining also promotes all the unpleasant habits we discussed earlier in our power element, including salami tactics, good cop/bad cop at best, and bluff and misrepresentation at worst. Finally, positional bargaining produces arbitrary results by "splitting the difference" or what might be labeled lose–lose. This outcome is complicated for a public leader to explain why they bargained to lose to the constituency.

Our Newgotiation paradigm contemplates mutual concessions based on a plurality of options created due to examined interests. Making concessions is often seen as a weakness to obtain a desired result, whereas they can be opportunities to create value and get a better deal. For instance, conceding that you get six and the other person gets seven is better than getting zero and the other person gets 1. Newgotiation aims to find a common good, which Jean Tirole calls "Le Bien Commun." Thus, our concessions only occur at the value distribution step, which consists of transforming the package of options created without commitment during the value creation step into a series of mutual concessions that both parties are prepared to adopt.

The value distribution step is critical for Newgotiators to reveal all viable options and anchor their expected price. Value distribution is also the moment to justify the price and the best available options through standards, conformity to law, and data. By this step, our Newgotiators are expected to have established a working relationship, a level of trust, reputation, objectivity, fairness, and credibility. Only then can a fair distribution of an effectively lengthy list of balanced options be accomplished. Finally, Newgotiators use concessions to establish a distributive win–win frame.

Conformity to the Rule of Law

The ultimate facilitator or constraint for negotiations is the eighth element of Newgotiations, which is conformity to the rule of law. The use of the law in negotiations is much more strategic. Deep knowledge and understanding of laws may facilitate negotiations by allowing negotiators to shape legal interests for better options and solutions within the bounds of the law. The rule of law limits the contemplated negotiation process and the expected outcome.

For example, even assuming the necessity of pension reform for the financial health of a municipal organization, the law may prohibit those reforms, or the collective bargaining agreement in place may bar the reduction of previously bargained and vested benefits. Thus, legal compliance, including the authority to contract, directly impacts the credibility and leadership of the public leader. It is better to know at the onset if the subject matter of the negotiation is legally achievable or even subject to negotiation in the first place. Therefore, consulting a lawyer is necessary for a public leader during the preparation phase and, ultimately, the implementation or follow-through phase of the talks.

We offer a caveat here about what we generally mean when we use the word "legally." We suggest literal compliance with the law but also compliance with local customs, conventions, and behavioral expectations. Especially in the public domain, the role of politics is substantial, and perceptions in politics are reality. Therefore, adhering to these customs and expectations must be part of the preparation and implementation steps.

Our ethics and leadership classes typically teach that the law is the minimum requirement. So, just because it is legal does not mean it is ethical or customary. So, for example, granting a contract to a friend's company in which the public leader has no financial interest may be legal but not necessarily acceptable for the constituents of the public leader in the United States. And, of course, geographic context, like your own home and neighborhood, adds another dimension to normal or legally acceptable behavior or interaction.

For example, unlike the United States, sexual innuendos may be culturally and legally acceptable in Europe. Therefore, the broader legal requirements contemplated and mapped by trained facilitators like lawyers significantly impact preparation and, ultimately, the outcome of each negotiation.

The impact during preparation may also be about assessing the laws regarding risks, investments, and interventions for different rules. If the negotiation is about whether to invest in a country like Brazil, labor laws, social security, and tax laws may significantly impact the decision. In addition, the rules and customs about self-interest, conflicts, courts, and the time it takes to resolve disputes may also be significant during preparation.

The lack of laws or the need for different rules will always influence negotiation strategy—industries with strong lobbies shape laws to their advantage to negotiate better deals. Sizable corporations, as well as trade unions, are known to use this tool quite effectively. Therefore, we withhold judgment as to whether this tool enhances our Newgotiation paradigm. Suffice it to say we are comfortable using it if the proposed law aims for the win–win.

Finally, legal compliance often preserves integrity. Respect for the law demonstrates discipline. Integrity and discipline build reputation and brand. Reputation builds trust and facilitates sustainability. We note, however, that not everything legal is necessarily ethical. And not everything ethical is necessarily legal.

Standards

Our ninth element of the Newgotiation technique is what we generally call "standards." We rely on experts to influence our policy decisions. Consulted experts can influence negotiations when and if they are asked. Therefore, some standards are necessary to appreciate the value of the expertise provided. During preparation, standards are reviewed in the value distribution step, primarily to anchor the price, and finally, reviewed again during implementation. Solid and reliable standards help our negotiation process by improving interests, alternatives, options, and legal compliance. Next, we describe various known examples of standards influencing public policy and administration and, therefore, the negotiation.

The market standard is typically the voice of the market or people through polls, statistics, and averages. For example, it would be irresponsible to negotiate hiring a new city manager without knowing the market standard for a city manager with, say, ten years of experience. This standard can relate to competence as well as monetary value.

Market research organizations or publications like "Consumer Reports" have developed a fundamental science about this standard to influence product buyers. In the financial sector, indices for every part of the stock market affect investors' participation in the overall economy. Investors, in general, are familiar with these indices through index funds and exchange-traded funds, which track the performance of a particular index. The Dow Jones Industrial Average, New York Stock Exchange, Standard and Poor's 500, Wilshire 5000, Russell 2000, Nasdaq 100, and the 10-Year Treasury Bond are all examples of widely acceptable and reputable indices. These guides and indices are standard bearers in negotiations dealing with the markets they represent.

As in the "Consumer Reports" example, objectivity is paramount to credibility and sustainability in the expertise provided. Objective market standards offer solid tools for our Newgotiation process and our Newgotiators. These standards frame the "what" and the "how" in our approach. They are proof of the truth, fairness, and neutrality in our discussions to close a deal.

Accounting and management standards are also pivotal in some negotiations. Of course, accounting is not a perfect science in that various outcomes can be obtained depending on who and what is doing the accounting. Nevertheless, governments have typically observed as a standard what we call generally accepted accounting principles. In the United States, the phrase "generally accepted accounting principles" (or "GAAP") consists of the basic accounting principles and guidelines with detailed rules and standards issued by the federal agency in charge of regulating the industry. GAAP are exceedingly helpful because they attempt to standardize and regulate accounting definitions, assumptions, and methods, bringing consistency from year to year in preparing a public company's financial statements. GAAP is also helpful in this context to establish a standard of trust.

Management standards in the 21st century are all about collecting and distributing data through behavioral principles that benefit and define an organization. Technology is a powerful tool to manage, control, influence, and facilitate negotiations. An organization like Alphabet (Google) constantly searches for data to customize its products and services and presumably deliver a better deal.

In our Newgotiation paradigm, where collaboration and collaborative governance are critical, the management standard provides excellent analytical and practical opportunities to our Newgotiators. We highly recommend using this standard to add value to any deal that benefits from good data. Governments are incredible resources that go untapped in preparation for most negotiations. Tap your data and analytics to improve preparation and enhance value for a better deal.

Simply put, governments are in the data business. For example, they know how much electricity and water we use in each dwelling unit. They have a record of our land ownership and land use approvals. They know what types of licenses we hold. This data yields terrific opportunities to collaborate and deliver a better deal when used correctly.

Finally, harmonizing standards like accounting and management are part of the negotiations, for example, in multinational discussions. Some international mergers and acquisitions face these types of challenges. As articulated by Fisher and Ury in "Getting to Yes," the key to resolving these conflicts is to focus on objectivity and adaptation of a fair, equitable, purposeful, and lawful standard. These are challenges that highly qualified experts typically overcome based on their technical knowledge and practice.

Like compliance with the law, standards may also become limiting factors framing the substance of the negotiation. For example, manufacturing and logistics businesses are highly regulated. Therefore, not knowing the emissions standards promulgated in regulation by an air quality management district for a chemical factory or refinery may substantially alter negotiations about locating a plant in a particular municipality. In short, collecting and distributing data, creating patterns, identifying procedures, and establishing standards all help generate a Newgotiation strategy and convey trust. They also help design elegant and informed options to negotiate better deals.

Time

Our last but certainly not least element of our Newgotiation paradigm is time. According to many studies, time is known to be one of the primary sources of conflict. Also, this tenth element is perhaps the most undervalued commodity in the negotiation process. While positional bargaining is slow and inefficient, time is misused to make the slightest concessions to frustrate, dominate, and force the marginal win–lose or lose–lose frame. Jean de La Fontaine, one of the most widely read French poets of the 17th century, wrote, "Patience and time do more than strength or passion."”

In Newgotiations, time is essential to describe the vision or the "why." Time is vital to discuss interests to create elegant options without commitment. Creativity during this process needs time. Our collaborative approach explicitly delays all formal commitments or concessions toward the end of our Newgotiation process.

Time is needed to develop the relationship or build social capital between participants to explore mutually beneficial options and create and distribute value. Robert Mnookin and others point out that while the creation and distribution of value may create a type of tension (how much value to keep and how much to distribute), also known as the "negotiator's dilemma," studies show that through a collaborative process, Newgotiators work through a "gradual and reciprocal disclosure of interests while brainstorming options without commitment."

Our Newgotiation process deserves and requires time during each step. Therefore, we emphasize the importance of preparation throughout our writing. Timely preparation yields a productive value-creation step by discussing interests and brainstorming options without commitment.

No deal is successful without implementation, which is our last step. Time in this step is a double-edged sword. On the one hand, it is necessary to implement the deal promptly to close and consummate it. On the other hand, there is the need to implement the agreement forged by the negotiators properly. Therefore, the only wisdom we can offer is that implementation dates and times must be set and adhered to as much as possible. Regular and consistent human contact builds relationships and trust.

Scheduled meetings with deliverables promote accountability and collaboration. On the other hand, we feel it is ill-advised to set deadlines that rush any Newgotiation process at the expense of our four timely and necessary steps.

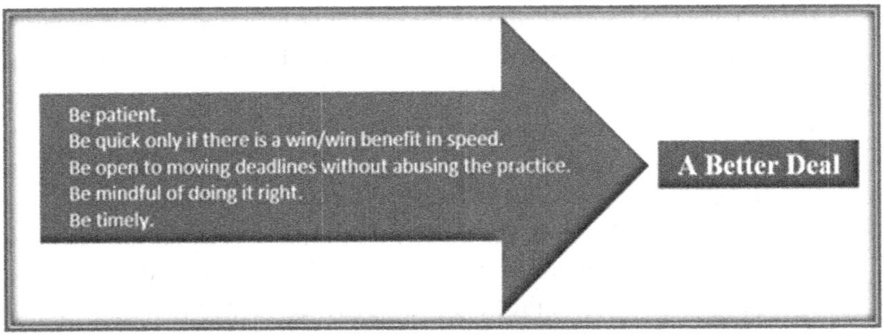

FIGURE 6.3 Treating Time as an Essential Element

While there is a risk of lower productivity, we know that the probability of making a deal is higher when there is no deadline. We also see the deal's value tends to rise with no deadline, as the collaborative process facilitates a better deal.

Finally, time must be evaluated in the context of culture. Some cultures appreciate and expect more time to build relationships before transacting business. Others feel they have no time to waste on relationships other than the business relationship necessary to transact a deal. To be clear, we advocate a balanced and thoughtful approach to the element of time. Figure 6.3 lists several suggestions about the treatment of time as an essential element in the Newgotiation process:

Evaluation of the Completed Newgotiation—the Last Ten of the 4-10-10

Our Newgotiation paradigm has no value if we cannot implement what we negotiated or learn from the process. These indicators evaluate an entire agreement and, perhaps more importantly, its implementation. This step has intrinsic "intra" and "extra" organizational value for a sustainable relationship. Especially for our public administration professionals, trust and relationships are too valuable to waste. Most of our public administration professionals do not negotiate only for one deal but a series of deals, often with the same stakeholders. So, we created ten steps to evaluate a negotiation process and to complete our 4-10-10 technique for Newgotiation.

1. Satisfaction and Optimization: Concluding or closing a deal is already a success, given that only 30% of all negotiations finish with an agreement. Our Newgotiation paradigm exponentially improves this percentage, but we are always looking for more. Therefore, we ask ourselves, are we happy or satisfied to close this deal? Is this a total win–win? Is each step productive now or in the future? Are there any regrets? What could we have done

to optimize each step? Was there a need for more preparation? Would the process have been enhanced with more data or more or different experts? Did we miss any stakeholders or fail to evaluate their stakeholdership properly? Is it perhaps an undervalued BATNA? Is the move toward value distribution too fast? Was more time necessary for implementation? A full assessment of our process can optimize results for this and future relationships in public sector Newgotiations.

2. Rationality of Decision: Is the outcome of this negotiation rational? Did options correlate to interests? Did we solve the problems we heard from participants? Are there unintended consequences that may require adjustments during implementation? How can we mitigate unintended consequences or unknowns in the future?
3. Emotion: How do we feel at the end of this negotiation? Are destructive emotions still due to the long and arduous value distribution process? Did one side concede much more than the other, creating a deal and emotional imbalance? Are we still collegial and respected post-closing? What is our reputation likely to be after this negotiation? How would we feel in their position? And more importantly, will we return for another deal? SDG negotiators do not have the luxury of picking up and leaving for another market or community. They must forge a relationship that lasts. Negotiators must establish credibility and build a brand reputation to be trusted now and in the future.
4. Ethics/Fairness: How did we deal with self-interest? Did anyone lie or mislead? What about fairness? Were our solutions indiscriminate? Did we deal with each other fairly and with respect? Did we use stereotypes? Did we build sufficient trust and integrity to create a good reputation for another deal?
5. Justice/Legal Compliance: Was the deal just? Was there any risk in not adhering to the rule of law? Did everyone have authority or legitimacy? Is our contract legally enforceable? What about legal liability? Are there any risks of post-agreement lawsuits? Are the lawyers satisfied? What is our legal plan going forward? A word of caution here is that not everything legal is just, and not everything just is necessarily legal. Raising pharmaceutical prices may be legal, but is it just for a financially vulnerable community that may need the drug? Peaceful protests during the Civil Rights Movement may have violated the law, but no one will claim that such protesting was not just.
6. Productivity: Were we productive, given the time allocation? What is the average speed of a similar deal? Were we too fast or too slow? What could we have done to improve our productivity? For example, companies like Pfizer have enhanced productivity by 25% by improving collaboration between departments and sound ergonomic practices. Others used technology to enhance their processes, like the cities of Palo Alto or New Orleans,

with their land use planning, decisions, or implementations. This boost in productivity is an area of continued opportunity within the public sector, especially with the effective use of data and analytics.

7. Social Responsibility/Environmental Sustainability: How will this negotiation impact the community or the organization in five or ten years? What will be the impact on public policy or public administration? Are the outcomes sustainable? Are we good stewards of the environment? Are we acting responsibly for future generations? Are we creating sources of prosperity and development based on demographic changes? Millennials are good facilitators and consumers of all these responsibilities. Did we incorporate the youth in our decisions? A well-balanced approach here, incorporating economic action, community action, and environmental action, is what we seek in this step. The World Commission on Environment and Development at the United Nations defined this as "development that meets the needs of the present without compromising the ability of future generations to meet their own needs." Sustainable development has emerged, in fact, as the guiding principle for long-term global growth.
8. Control and Execution: Once the negotiation is complete, the legal document or contract is signed. The next question is whether there will be operational readiness to start the implementation. Do we have assurances that what we said or agreed upon will be done? Are there any consequences for delays? Should there have been more consequences? For example, is there a penalty for overdue payment or late delivery of products or services? Or is there a bonus for early delivery? Is there a confidentiality clause to protect intellectual property? What about penalties for unauthorized disclosures? Are we sure that the project is fully funded? Is there a stakeholder missing that can stop the project? Are there contingencies built into the contract?
9. Adaptability for Post-settlement: For example, in case of a change in a currency rate, is there a clause to mitigate the risk of this conflict? Are all the expectations included in the contract? If one of the parties dies or files for bankruptcy, how do we deal with such an eventuality? Are there letters of credit or performance bonds? Does the contract contain a mechanism for naming a mediator in a conflict? Is there an arbitration clause in case the mediator does not solve the dispute? Which country or state will have jurisdiction to hear the matter in the case of litigation? Is there insurance covering the implementation or lack thereof? Is there a mechanism of supervision to ensure success in the long term? The management of expectations is one of the best means to prevent conflicts. Learning from and practicing these suitable measures will make us accomplished Newgotiators.
10. Technical Standards: Did the experts correctly interpret the technical standards? Here, we are discussing technical standards, such as Generally Accepted Accounting Principles (GAAP), American Society of Mechanical Engineers (ASME), and European Commission minimum standards for

public consultations, to name a few. Did we evaluate them correctly? Did we consider possible changes in laws or regulations about the technical standards? Technical data assures the customization of options. Did we meet the expectations of the parties with our technical requirements? Is there a supply of technically required parts? Do the technical standards facilitate future purchasing in the contract? Do we have a competitive advantage here? Is risk managed? Most companies make money by buying well and mitigating risk. For example, Exxon-Mobil, the largest oil, perhaps energy, and third-largest company globally, creates value by cautiously reducing costs and properly evaluating the risks it manages. The art of negotiation is about respecting technical standards, mitigating risks, and using experts to realize better value every time.

7

NEWGOTIATION APPLIED—RESEARCH AND CASES

This chapter shares Team UN 2021's proposed conceptual framework for policy negotiations at the local government level. This framework aims to enhance SDG achievement through effective and collaborative policy negotiations.

We outline project objectives, research methods, and case analyses to develop the applied conceptual framework. Two research questions guided this inquiry that assessed the collaborative negotiation paradigm to promote the 2030 Agenda and create a tool kit for UN DESA. The first research phase included conducting a literature review. The team then interviewed subject matter experts and conducted a targeted survey of UN experts to create a conceptual framework. This new conceptual framework combines policy negotiation theory and insights from the team's in-depth analysis and qualitative evaluation of case studies across different continents. The case studies are the Seoul Smart City Platform in the Republic of Korea (ROK), Decentralized Cooperation to Democratize Cities in Brazil and Mozambique, Careers by Design in the United States, Shanghai's One Net Office in China, and Endearing Homes for our Silver Generation in Singapore. The framework consists of the four steps of Newgotiation described in previous chapters applied to evaluate the chosen SDGs-oriented case studies. Chapter 8 concludes with a discussion of the framework's application, limitations, recommendations for further research, and conclusions.

Methodology

The team employed several qualitative methods to answer our research questions. These methods include combining a review of collaborative negotiation literature, a survey, a case study analysis, and semi-structured interviews.

DOI: 10.4324/9781003497097-7

Phase 1: Qualitative Method—Literature Review

By engaging with UN DESA and conducting a review of collaborative negotiation literature, Team UN 2021 ultimately decided to use the Newgotiation framework developed in our book *Newgotiation for Public Administration Professionals*, the basic framework of which is republished in this book in Chapters 5 and 6.

For this project's purpose, the team chose our Newgotiation framework as the best among the negotiation frameworks processed because it uses a versatile model applicable to any negotiation activity. In addition, the framework promotes collaboration, which we learned is critical to the success and adaptation of SDGs.

The Newgotiation framework comprises four steps: (1) Preparation, (2) Value Creation, (3) Value Distribution, and (4) Implementation. To bolster our understanding of each step, we investigated the literature on how each step contributes to the overall collaborative negotiation process. Finally, we used the insight gained from this process to execute the other qualitative methods of our research.

Phase 2: Qualitative Framework—Survey

We distributed a survey with 26 multiple-answer and five optional-answer, open-ended questions (33) among the UN staff seeking to understand how they perceive local government effectiveness in advancing the SDGs and the role of negotiations in the process. We received 38 responses to the multiple-answer questions and varied reactions to the five optional-answer, open-ended questions (Appendix B). Respondents were from several countries in Northern Africa, the Middle East, Northern Asia, and South-East Asia.

The survey results are limited, given the geographical concentration, the small number of respondents, and the lack of randomness integrated into our survey delivery. Nevertheless, the results did indicate that collaborative negotiation could improve a local government's ability to advance the 2030 Agenda.

Phase 3: Qualitative Method 3: Case Study Analysis

Unlike our previous projects with UN DESA, Team UN 2021 could not design a random selection of our case studies using the United Nations Public Service Innovation Hub Database ("UNPSA Initiatives and the SDGs," n.d.). This limitation was because our team had to assess whether a project sufficiently met the criteria found in the Case Identification table (see Table 7.1). This restriction substantially narrowed our ability to identify appropriate cases. Additionally, the nature of investigating the negotiation process required our team to depend on information not provided by the United Nations Public Service Awards

TABLE 7.1 Case Study Analysis and Identification

Case Identification	
Classification	*Criteria*
Collaborative	The negotiation exhibits stakeholders who are interested in the well-being of their counterparts.
Complete Information	There is sufficient information available that permits analysis.
	At least one person on our team understands the language of the case study materials.
Convergence with the 2030 Agenda	Initial issue(s) and solution(s) linked with SDGs.
Distinct Cases	Initial problem and solution(s) unique from other selected cases.
Negotiation	The case must involve some negotiation.
Local/Regional Level	The stakeholders work at a local or regional level.
Sustainability	The solution is durable in time.
	The solution is resilient concerning the environment and political and cultural context.

TABLE 7.2 UNPSA Cases Reviewed

Location	*Program*
Singapore	Endearing Homes for Our Silver Generation
City of Los Angeles, California, United States	Careers by Design LA (CDLA)
Guarulhos & Porto Alegre, Brazil Nampula & Inhambane, Mozambique	Decentralized Cooperation to Democratize Cities
Shanghai, China	Shanghai's One Net Office
Seoul Republic of Korea	Seoul Smart City Platform for Mayor

(UNPSA) database, as negotiation process information typically is not included in the program documentation.

We identified three of our case studies from the UNPSA database (Singapore, Seoul, and Shanghai) and found the city of Los Angeles case study through interviews and networking. Finally, we found the Guarulhos & Porto Alegre, Brazil, and Nampula & Inhambane case through the United Cities and Local Governments (UCLG) learning forum (see Table 7.2).

Qualitative Method 4: Interviews

The case studies of Singapore, Los Angeles, and Seoul used semi-structured interviews with project leaders from their respective cases. Before engaging in an interview, our team developed a list of 18 questions that guided our interviews

(Appendix D). This methodology provided detailed information about perceptions among project leaders concerning how the negotiation process played out in each of these cases.

Strengths and Weaknesses

Since the SDGs are a global initiative, using cases from various places will give a more comprehensive understanding of the problem. Furthermore, through the survey and project leader interviews, we learned that those people familiar with the SDGs could provide helpful information on the subject. Also, surveys and interviews can compensate for the deficiency of studying static cases by bringing dynamic interaction to our analysis.

However, this research method's limitations include access to the required information. Three of our case studies did not include interviews directly with project leaders. Another weakness is that our case studies are limited in geographical scope. The disadvantages of surveys may be participant knowledge level and bias. Lastly, while we used a criteria filter to select cases, our preferences regarding what is sufficiently collaborative likely influenced the cases we considered.

Characteristics of Negotiations in the Literature

Public policy negotiations between local governments and public stakeholders are generally multi-stakeholder negotiations. Stakeholder competition for finite resources from the government characterizes these public policy negotiations. Public policy negotiations also allow local governments to communicate policy positions to achieve their policy goals effectively.

Theoretically, a conducive environment for effective negotiations provides an objective and neutral discussion arena. This neutral arena involves all stakeholders in the policy (or as many as possible). It isolates the negotiation process and roundtable from other policymaking or stakeholder-specific strategies that the government or public stakeholders undertake to achieve their specific goals regarding the issue.

The hallmark of a successful negotiation is reaching a desirable and workable consensus. Effective collective action under the agreement and outcome of the negotiation has been effectively communicated and subsequently undertaken. Conversely, ineffective communication during the negotiation process causes insufficient collective action in most unsuccessful negotiations.

An important consideration when studying multi-stakeholder negotiations is understanding that some situations yield relatively more negotiating power among the various stakeholders than others. More powerful stakeholders are likely to have strong financial backing, be societally solid with commanding political influence, or, in some cases, possess deeper ties to the local government involved in these public policy negotiations. However, this power structure implies that there will often be disadvantaged groups at the losing end of the final negotiated agreement.

Therefore, a primary challenge to effective public policy negotiations between local governments and public stakeholders is to increase the decision-making power of disadvantaged stakeholders. Engaging and giving disadvantaged groups increased capacity through education in a negotiation process is cardinal because underprivileged groups are the stakeholders who are more likely to reject the final negotiated terms and, hence, not follow through and cooperate with the agreed-upon collective action. This lack of a level-playing field hinders effective negotiations and outcomes.

Research on negotiation theories has shown that communicative rationality and liberal pluralism schools of thought define multi-stakeholder negotiations. We also discuss alternative approaches that propose giving disadvantaged and less powerful stakeholders a more influential voice in radical pluralist thought. Finally, we also address feminist post-structuralist theories.

Establishing Common Spaces for Negotiation

Creating a typical, fair, and neutral negotiation space is known as the communicative rationality approach in negotiation literature. This approach aims to increase the effectiveness and credibility of the negotiation process. In so doing, proponents of the theory suggest that this neutral space creates conducive environments for formal negotiation processes that promote social justice. This environment is achieved by adhering to proper legislation, government policies, and constitutions.

Hence, the communication process takes a back seat in negotiations because due processes ensure that participants achieve a fair and unbiased negotiated outcome. However, power imbalances between the stakeholders involved in negotiations make completing this seemingly fair and non-contentious negotiation process challenging to achieve realistically. Proponents of this theory have also recognized the presence of different policy networks and stakeholders with antagonistic goals of negotiation and radically different viewpoints, both of which may render communication difficult or even impossible.

Establishing a Workable Consensus from Individual Interests

On the other hand, the perspective toward negotiations posits that individual stakeholders come to the negotiation roundtable to realize their respective self-interests and specific organizational/personal goals, known as the liberal pluralist view. Then, in negotiations with local governments, these stakeholders organize collectively to form the "public interest" through synthesizing and bargaining their perspectives, creating a consensus.

A vital characteristic of liberal pluralism is that public stakeholders negotiate the notion of "public interest." Liberal pluralism considers and justifies all stakeholder viewpoints that are ethical and reasonable. Hence, a good, fair, and effective negotiation outcome is where all rational and ethical opinions and interests are combined and connected.

Interest groups prime their negotiation efforts on influencing the local governments through political mechanisms such as lobbying for politicians or contributing to local government policy advocacy or political campaigns (Bickford, 1999). Public stakeholders engage in such means in the hopeful return of favor from local governments in supporting their interests in the specific negotiation of interest.

Establishing an Equitable Negotiation Space for Disadvantaged Stakeholders

Alternative negotiation theories, such as the feminist post-structuralist and radical pluralist theories, focus on stakeholder identity and equitable representation. Alternative views of negotiation give disadvantaged stakeholders a more influential voice. For example, feminists are generally skeptical of collective action and alliances because they think an entirely fair representation of every group at a negotiation table is difficult or impossible to achieve in actual negotiation practices. Radical pluralists are also wary of the outcome of negotiation processes influenced by Western rationalism (as seen in liberal pluralism above) because the negotiated consensus will likely overshadow the views of disadvantaged stakeholders.

Hence, proponents of these alternative theories suggest forming strategic and spontaneous alliances among disadvantaged stakeholders and their sympathizers to increase the volume of their collective voice in the negotiation process to achieve better outcomes and recognition.

Radical pluralists also argue that the cohesion of these disadvantaged groups is a complicated process of self-identification and representation, and they place increased significance on the differing access and influence over the policymaking processes of the local government. Thus, disadvantaged groups tend to politically contextualize the outcomes of negotiations while acknowledging the barriers to effective and fair negotiation communication.

Context of this Chapter and Research

In the context of this chapter on studying the best practices of local governments of various countries in negotiating the United Nations (UN) 2030 Agenda, these broad negotiation theories form the overarching principles to which local governments negotiate their policies with their respective public stakeholders.

Of course, no perfect negotiation theory can be considered "best practice," as each negotiation method has advantages and disadvantages. However, it is essential to recognize the category of the selected case studies because the negotiation tactics adopted by local governments in different countries will vary due to cultural, political, and social contexts.

The negotiation theories, backed by various political philosophies, enabled the team to identify and access the value creation and value distribution steps of the Newgotiation processes in the selected case studies. Following that, the team provided insight into the preparation process for the negotiation and the effective implementation of the negotiated outcomes based on the underlying negotiation theories and their surrounding assumptions. Again, the overall purpose was to use a common technique and language to promote the advancement of the negotiated SDGs.

Steps of a Negotiation Process

The following pages detail the four-step negotiation process applied to this research and case studies from our previous book. The four steps are (1) preparation, (2) value creation, (3) value distribution, and (4) implementation. The four steps provided a way to focus our research on the individual steps and create a theoretical foundation for examining local negotiations. Moreover, each step's theory and literature review created a mechanism to compare our selected cases in local negotiations.

Preparation

The first step of negotiation, preparation, includes all the preliminary and prospective work that negotiators must consider or complete before moving to value creation, value distribution, and implementation. Thus, a successful preparation step heavily relies on a thorough understanding of negotiating context/culture, communication, compliance, and time and the wise selection of analytical strategies and tools. In our Newgotiation paradigm, preparation is the first step in four steps, but it can determine the negotiation outcome. "Planning before the actual interaction process is the foundation for success in negotiating."

To be well prepared for a negotiation, context, communication, compliance, and time are vital elements. The context here refers to the environment where this negotiation takes place.The environment consists of the physical environment and the sociocultural environment. The latter counts more during the planning process, especially in the eye of a globalized and sustainable development agenda.

Along with many researchers, we have long argued the importance of culture in negotiation. Individual and organizational culture can influence how people perceive and rank critical elements in negotiating. Therefore, when preparing

TABLE 7.3 Relevant Table for Stakeholdership

Stakeholder Considerations	*Key Issues*
Stakeholder expectations: primary issue(s) (needs/wants)	
Knowledge of the issue	
Legitimacy of stakeholder representative(s)	
Assets and strengths to help with the initiative	
Willingness to engage	
Cultural context/awareness	
The geographic scale at which they operate	
Stakeholder engagement capacity	
Relationships of stakeholders with each other	

for a cross-cultural negotiation, identifying where cultural differences may arise is essential for every actor.

After laying out critical elements of preparation, negotiators must eventually consider using analytical strategies to synthesize information and then produce a list of interests and options of each party in the negotiation. Stakeholder analysis is one of the common strategies to sort out the power, standpoints, interests, and possible attitudes of each stakeholder in the upcoming negotiation. An excellent start to organize stakeholders in preparation for bargaining may begin by completing a table for stakeholdership (see Table 7.3).

Value Creation

Value creation refers to the second step in our Newgotiation framework, where the most creative and integrative processes can occur between stakeholders and policy negotiators. Unlike value-claiming/distribution, where value is divided among parties, the value creation step seeks to enlarge the overall value, creating additional worth for all stakeholders. Members must state their preferences and be honest and open to achieve a win–win scenario. However, this situation creates an environment where stakeholders can use asymmetric information to their advantage. Several best practices will increase value creation in SDG policy negotiations.

Social Motivations and Individual Behaviors of Negotiation

In "A Psychological Theory of Diplomacy," Rathbun attempts to diagram negotiation outcomes through negotiation styles. Negotiators with "different social motivations adopt different negotiating styles because they have unique framings of the same situation." For example, proself motivations are more self-centered, but prosocial motivations are more interested in not only one's interest but also in "maximizing joint benefits." In addition, proself individuals generally prefer value-claiming negotiation behaviors, and prosocial individuals prefer value-creating negotiation ones.

Moreover, traditional rationalist bargaining theories expected of stakeholders with power being more satisfied with the status quo do not hold in experimental research with prosocial motivations. Instead, a willingness of stakeholders to improve the overall social value will guide negotiations toward value creation if most members agree.

On the other hand, as quoted by Rathbun, there is epistemic motivation—"the need to develop a rich and accurate understanding of the world." Negotiators on the low end of epistemic motivation are characterized by cognitive impatience and looking for speedy closure because they are typically uncomfortable with uncertainty. High epistemic motivation describes individuals who are more open and likely to revisit and revise beliefs considering new information.

In the context of local negotiations for the 2030 Agenda, careful selection of negotiators (leaders who represent stakeholder groups in negotiations) will theoretically impact overall value creation. Value-creating negotiators for the 2030 Agenda are especially true for negotiators with prosocial and higher epistemic motivation.

Value Creation through Empirical Evidence

Various studies have examined the benefits of cross-sector collaborations—including businesses and NPOs. The results suggested that prior experience and alignment positively affect the factors for value creation. The study also showed that aligning mission and strategies is more important to value creation than aligning individual party values. Stakeholders may find value in creating solutions where goals are the same despite value differences after repeated experiences in the context of local 2030 Agenda policies.

The Institutional and Context Analysis (ICA) tool is a United Nations Development Program (UNDP) instrument that can help identify stakeholders with a genuine incentive to see a policy succeed. Recognizing those who enable or block policy interventions can help inform local government practitioners on strategies for engaging with stratified stakeholder interests.

The Public Institutions Context—Institutionalizing Effective Negotiation

The literature gathered previously has highlighted the skills of individual negotiators. However, promoting trust, even when government entities fully intend to be honest, may not depend on the socio-historical contexts in which the negotiation occurs.

Therefore, outside, unbiased negotiators (e.g., negotiators who possess the confidence of both private and public stakeholders) must be readily able to assist. Moreover, the institutional context in the United States is developing both in the private business and public policy spheres. As a result, awareness of mediation as a negotiating tool becomes universal, especially as society becomes more polarized. However, practitioners have indicated that some local governments interpret outside help as nefarious or self-interested. This conclusion is especially true for many less-developed or developing countries with a history of colonial interference. Therefore, practitioners may need to promote local skilled negotiators to engage first.

The next component is institutionalizing repeated negotiations with the same stakeholders and their representatives. Understanding negotiation as a long-term process that builds community engagement should be a necessary goal, and the negotiated outcomes create a forum where stakeholders can continuously reengage. This process builds relationships and trust that overcome many obstacles discussed in the preparation and value creation steps.

Value Distribution

Value distribution is the third step in our four-step project's core negotiation framework. Value distribution is mainly concerned with the balance of distributive and integrative tactics. These tactics refer to self and other concerns, respectively.

Research indicates that negotiations that lean too heavily in either direction do not yield the most remarkable outcome. Therefore, an intrapersonal and interpersonal framework is outlined, guiding negotiators to understand their motivations better and build a rapport with their counterparts.

After sufficiently preparing for a negotiation (Step 1) and then engaging in a collaborative process of value creation (Step 2), value distribution is the moment when the parties involved formally agree on the division of the resources under consideration (Step 3).

While there is a moment in the negotiation process where official ownership of resources is pronounced, the literature focusing on collaborative methods indicates that the value creation and value distribution phases will be nearly indistinguishable in an ideal negotiation scenario. Therefore, the literature defines distributive and integrative negotiation (see Figure 7.1).

Distributive negotiation fixedly conceives resources and their distribution as a matter of a win or loss; in other words, negotiation is a zero-sum game. This type of negotiation is inherently competitive, given that all parties involved could theoretically "lose" a stake in the resources under consideration. On the other end of the spectrum exists what is known as integrative negotiation.

In integrative negotiations, the parties work collaboratively to identify interests, increase the size of the project, and distribute it intelligently. Understandably, this framework may sound more pertinent to the concerns of value creation; however, by incorporating integrative negotiation strategies into practice, an understanding of the relationship between value creation and value

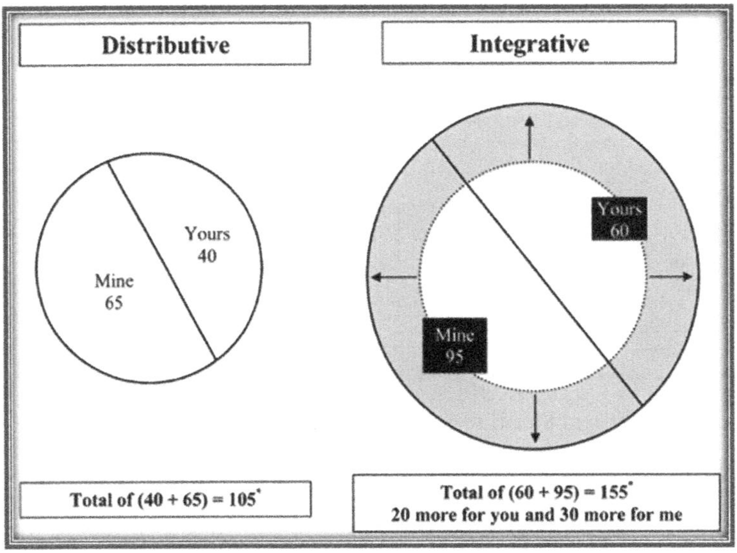

FIGURE 7.1 Distributive and Integrative Negotiation

distribution must transform. A pioneer of this concept of negotiation was Mary Parker Follett, a Harvard Business School scholar and change agent. She clearly described this integrative negotiation framework, starting with transparency and yielding critical parts of the deal (see Figure 7.2).

A fictional story in the literature describes a predicament between two individuals who clash over an orange. In a negotiation that solely utilizes distributive tactics, both individuals will be out to get as much of the orange as possible. Thus, the most egalitarian distributive outcome would seemingly be to split the

FIGURE 7.2 Negotiation Framework

Source Mattson, Rubio, Perex, Rouse, and Zollars

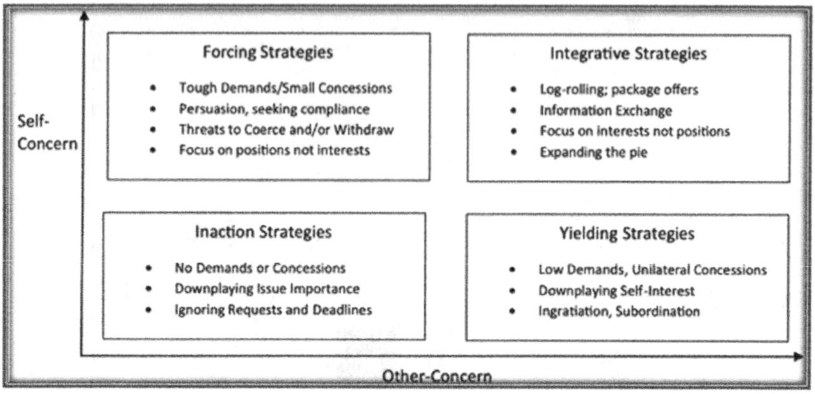

FIGURE 7.3 Dual Concern Model of Strategic Preferences

Source: De Dreu

orange into equal halves. However, in integrative negotiation, through benevolent inquiry for the "why" and relationship building, they would discover that one party needs the orange rinds and the other the fruit itself.

In this context, splitting the orange fifty/fifty is not the most intelligent way of using the available resource. In this light, integrative negotiations require the will of all parties to embrace transparency, build an understanding of one another's needs, and utilize the value creation process to arrive at an optimal value distribution scenario. Therefore, value distribution may be better understood as an extension of value creation.

Given our previous research on Sustainable Development Goals and their interconnectivity, our analysis will thoroughly explore the best tactics to ensure integration. That is not to say that distributive tactics are irrelevant to our consideration. For example, in De Dreu's research, a healthy balance between both "other-concern" and "self-concern," otherwise known as "dual concern," leads to more beneficial negotiation results (see Figure 7.3). Moreover, while self-concern may sound contrary to the interests of collaborative negotiation, it has been identified as a link to more ambitious self-goals, satisfying vital motivations, better outside alternatives, and stronger language that could overcome momentum deadlock.

Intrapersonal and Interpersonal Factors

The literature acknowledges that maintaining such a dual concern balance to create joint ambitions is problematic. Successful negotiations depend on the state of the individuals involved, as they do on the group's potential. Intrapersonal and interpersonal interests can frame the perfect balanced strategies.

In this frame, "intrapersonal" refers to "how an individual's sense of power influences his or her negotiation behavior, satisfaction, and outcomes." At the same time, "interpersonal" concerns "the ways that negotiators' behavior and outcomes depend upon the presence of the other party or parties." We uncovered a few critical intrapersonal characteristics: power, self-awareness, and regulation.

Power is a broad term and can be interpreted in many ways. However, according to Thompson et al. (2010), power may be best understood in negotiations as the leverage a party possesses based on their Best Alternative to a Negotiated Agreement (BATNA) because it gives a party the authority to make claims. Self-awareness is an emotional intelligence capacity that increases a party's emotional vocabulary consciousness and will help reign in excessive self-concern.

The key interpersonal characteristics include social awareness and trust. Social understanding is crucial to the equation. It improves a party's ability to have a general sense of the sentiment among the parties involved, gauge implicit concerns, or capitalize on opportunities for agreement. This sentiment helps build rapport and likeability with counterparts that are conducive to higher compliance and positive future negotiations.

Trust is essential in collaborative negotiation processes. In an integrative setting, parties must be willing to provide information regarding their interests, which could be sensitive, putting each party in a vulnerable position. Without trust, parties could engage excessively in self-interested tactics, throwing the dual concern off balance.

While this research does overlap significantly with value creation, it is essential to remember that the value creation process is supposed to be designed with value distribution in mind under the integrative negotiation model.

Implementation

Implementation is the last and the most crucial step in the Newgotiation paradigm. Public administrators must consider this step seriously and acknowledge the factors that may impede the implementation process, including legal and non-legal issues, lack of professional knowledge, and incorrect time settings. The implication for implementation includes the involvement of multi-stakeholders, the importance of monitoring, and the application of modern skills. In addition, it provides governments with insights into using the negotiation framework to promote the 2030 Agenda.

Survey Insight

Before discussing our case studies, our last section examines the insight we gained by reading our survey results. We discovered that practitioners at the local level were neither fully aware of the importance of negotiations nor capable of developing an effective negotiation process. They were generally "unprepared, not communicating effectively with donors, failing to implement a pro-active approach to deliver per deadlines," highlighting the leverage of negotiation in SDGs localization.

A closer inspection of the survey results shows that more than half of the respondents seldom engaged with stakeholders before the negotiation. Moreover, survey respondents did not have a backup plan prepared for possible negotiation impasse, indicating a lack of preparation for any SDG negotiation. Most respondents shared the common opinion that stakeholders were not very well-educated about the benefits of sustainable development and local governments were not effective enough in instilling an SDG mindset.

Understanding the SDGs is the foundation of the collaboration between local authorities and other stakeholders, directly contributing to successful value creation. Therefore, the problem here is that local governments still need human capital assistance to build value, which will lead to trust and mutual understanding.

The survey results also showed that people from different parties are concerned about the best interest of other stakeholders in negotiation. However, they are unsure if their interests can be equally reached, resulting from flawed value creation and distribution.

Case Studies

Overview

The following five cases were a nonrandom selection of local public policies advancing one or more SDGs that demonstrate segments of negotiation that inform the development of a working negotiation framework (see Table 7.4). Common negotiation elements observed across cases firmly announced the final framework on functional factors that lead to effective collaborative negotiations.

TABLE 7.4 Initiatives for Case Analysis

Initiative	*Country*	*Region*	*HDI Index*
Smart City Platform for Mayor	Republic of Korea (E)	Asia-Pacific	0.916
Decentralized Cooperation to Democratize Cities	Brazil and Mozambique (B)	South America and Africa	0.765 and 0.456
Careers by Design LA	United States (A)	North America	0.926
Shanghai "One Net Office"	People's Republic of China (D)	Asia-Pacific	0.761
Endearing Homes for Our Silver Generation	Singapore (C)	Asia-Pacific	0.938

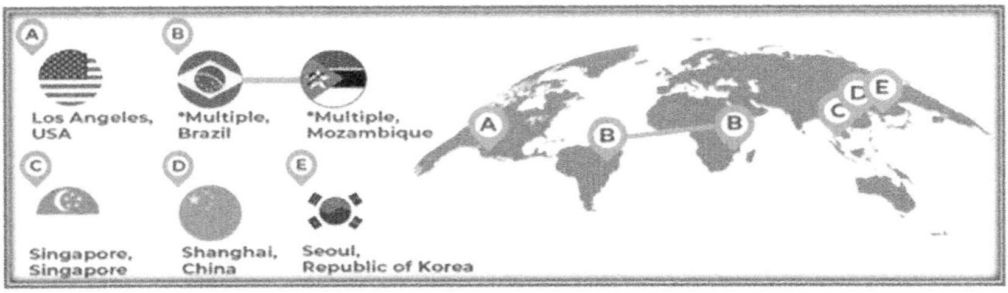

FIGURE 7.4 Selected Cases for Case Analysis

Case Study Insight Summary

The five case studies produced three critical elements. After listing essential negotiation elements from each task through the negotiation steps, it became apparent that they were categorized into one of three crucial elements. These three critical elements are (1) leadership, (2) trust, and (3) toolkits (see Figure 7.4). The following sections cover introductions to each case study, their negotiation elements, and critical insights for each case study that helped develop the three crucial factors.

For example, strong leadership fostered greater trust, and greater trust enhanced leadership capabilities and political and public will. However, without including one of the other elements, there are significant shortfalls in realizing more extensive value creation throughout the negotiation process.

Likewise, toolkits are a product of accumulated knowledge and other features in a local setting. Still, their existence does not equate to effective policymaking or negotiation outcomes and instead requires strong leaders to utilize the toolkits. Finally, some toolkits, such as past but interrelated policies and programs, rely on public trust in the systems because policy achievements predicate past achievements.

Leadership

Leadership is vital in sustainable development, influencing practitioner behavior and mindset during negotiations. Leaders with sustainable leadership share long-term visions, identify sustainability problems, strategize, and implement. Leaders maintain a high-quality relationship with different stakeholders. They scan and monitor potential variations in the external environment.

In addition, leadership is a critical element required in the negotiation process that involves the participation of interprofessional teams, which is a characteristic of many governmental programs. Establishing mutually beneficial collaboration in negotiation also requires balancing multiple interests.

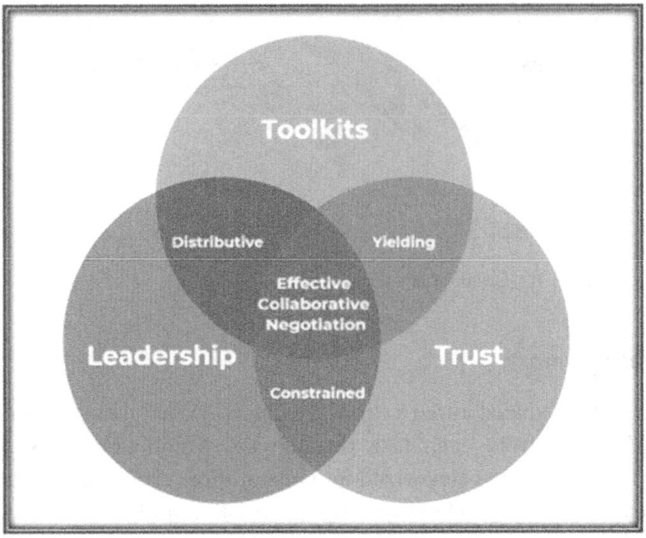

FIGURE 7.5 Effective Collaboration

Throughout the entire negotiation process, a standard feature found in the case studies was the leadership of individuals or parties to move projects forward to completion. Strong leadership had the characteristics of benevolence, foresight/foreplanning, and competency. Especially apparent were mayoral individuals fostering cross-city partnerships to advance SDGs globally, such as in the Republic of Korea, Mozambique, and Brazil, decentralized cooperation to democratize cities.

Moreover, mayors were essential leaders in moving the Careers by Design and Seoul Smart City Platform initiatives and visions forward in their local contexts. However, leadership alone or paired only with one other essential element will be characterized by constrained development of negotiated outcomes or characterized purely by distributive negotiation practices, limiting value creation.

Trust

The literature review on negotiation theory and practice heavily relied on trust as an element to forward value creation, and this was reiterated from the case studies. Moreover, trust was an element that permeated across all steps of the negotiation process, although not proportionally relevant across all stages. The essence of trust is not limited purely to the policy's negotiated outcomes, but it has implications for sustained engagement through the procedure or future related policy.

Trust has a significant impact on how the public perceives an organization. Trust is a relational and psychological state, referring to "an individual's belief in, and willingness to act based on, the words, actions, and decisions of another."

In policy negotiations, high public trust levels relate to promoting democratization and economic activities, superior performance of institutions, and low violence levels.

Public trust helps lower the transaction costs in any political, social, and economic system by improving compliance with rules and regulations, ensuring a more effective implementation process.

Trust also helps alleviate tensions arising from competing for organizational goals in the face of government and public administration constraints. While high public trust levels do not correlate to full accountability, it still results in government systems having greater administrative autonomy and more effective delegation with lower intrusion levels. High public trust levels allow government agencies to function effectively, facilitating amicable and workable negotiation outcomes. As a result, the negotiating parties will likely be more willing to accept government policy decisions voluntarily.

Some programs, such as the Seoul and Singapore cases, exhibited sustained policy engagement with primary stakeholders, establishing high trust. This trust also spills over into the leadership element and demonstrates the feedback loop observed with the three critical elements.

Toolkits

Local leaders cannot solely rely on leadership and trust for an idea to take root in the real world. They must have resources available to them that enable ideas to gain traction. Leadership is the motivation to fish and find allies, and trust can foster partnering relationships toward that end. Using this analogy, the toolkit is the rod, the fishing hook, and the worms. Ambitious and ethical processes carry their merit, but toolkits take ideas across the finish line.

Toolkits in the collaborative negotiation context may include funding, knowledge and skills, legal help, technical and expert assistance, logistical and administrative support, communication and information technology, relationships, and even power.

Both collaboration and SDGs are complex tasks independently and much more so when addressed simultaneously. Sharing resources can mitigate the burden of this challenging 2030 Agenda. Furthermore, by employing leadership and trust to manage available resources, local leaders will further the perceived fairness and legitimacy of the overall collaborative effort.

All our case studies used toolkits in some form or the other to steer their negotiation processes without significant inhibitions. However, to tap the full potential of those resources, leadership and trust were needed to rally help and have considerable buy-in from stakeholders.

Without leadership, negotiations are characterized by more soft demands, which inhibit the ambition of an initiative. Without trust, negotiations result in more distributive outcomes, which misses opportunities to create more value for the parties involved. Toolkits are elements tied to a country's development and historical contexts, much more so than the other two essential elements. A country may produce the necessary and effective tools in the short run, requiring an alternative set of frameworks to develop.

Introducing the Five Case Studies and What We Learned

Case 1: Smart City Platform for Mayor, Republic of Korea

Context

The Republic of Korea and Seoul have made considerable progress in the last few decades and improved citizens' quality of life. However, rapid urban and economic growth has challenged Seoul and cities alike. Like many sprawling metropolises worldwide, traffic congestion, air pollution, and other challenges hamper efficient and sustainable development.

Moreover, South Korea is one of the fastest-aging societies, with the elderly population 65 and above estimated to comprise 20% of the population in the city by 2026. The poverty rate of those citizens 65 and older is 44%, which is the highest in all 34 OECD nations. Significant challenges also arise from difficulty monitoring city policies and their progress. These challenges necessitated solutions for city policymakers and managers to improve city services and administration efficiency. As a hub for technological innovation, Seoul has invested deeply in transforming the city into a "Smart City," driven by goals of digital democracy and a "city-driven innovation ecosystem."

TABLE 7.5 Smart City Platform, Seoul, Republic of Korea

Member State	Republic of Korea
Institution Name	Seoul Metropolitan Government
Institution Type	Public Agency
Administrative Level	Local
Name of initiative	Smart City Platform
Project's Operational Years	4
Website of Institution	Seoul Metropolitan Government https://english.seoul.go.kr/?SSid=101_01&tr_code=foreign
Key Stakeholders & Partnerships	Seoul citizens, the Seoul Metropolitan Government, and Private ICT & IT companies
Relevant SDGs	5, 6, 7, 8, 9, 10, 11, 12, 13, 15, 16, and 17

In March 2019, the Seoul Metropolitan Government (SMG) unveiled a data-centric Smart City Master Plan and dedicated $1.2 billion to smart city initiatives until 2022 (Table 7.5). Still, the work began much earlier with other significant data initiatives on data collection. One such program is the Smart City Platform (SCP or the Platform). Since 2016, the Platform has been collecting big data from the technologies and initiatives employed earlier—and to be used—to understand and communicate meaningfully and efficiently with city agencies and citizens.

Digital media and technology have accelerated different forms of participatory democracy. An essential goal of the Platform is to increase and better connect citizens and government. The Open Data Plaza website is the participator hub for releasing public data. In addition, the public can engage in bottom-up civic engagement through complaints, notices, or opinions gathered from digital social media. These digital transformations of public-sector institutions have wide-ranging implications on citizen access to public services, economics, and political opportunity, creating fairer, more accountable, more efficient, and sustainable cities and communities. Keeping pace with technological growth, the Platform provides real-time updates to the mayor and public administrators through a graphical user interface.

The city information and indicators from the Platform enhanced city response times. In contrast, it used to take over a month for the mayor's initial request for information from city agencies to be prepared and reported. The Platform is the culmination of many smart city initiatives or smart city facilitating initiatives that began over a decade ago in Seoul, and it is ripe for analysis of the citizen–government negotiation dynamics before and during the Platform's implementation and operation. The idea of a smart city is continually growing, and citizen input is necessary for future initiatives in Seoul.

Solution

Seoul and the Republic of Korea (ROK) were quick and early adopters of mobile Information and Communication Technologies (ICTs) because of government ICT-driven economic policies in the 1990s. ROK's early investment in ICTs coincided with the global adoption of advanced ICTs, occupying a sizable portion of the annual export share.

The government's internet and mobile infrastructure investments laid the core Smart City and Smart Seoul initiatives and programs. Moreover, Seoul's 2012 second-hand device program and other ICT welfare services distributed mobile devices to elderly and low-income Seoul citizens to increase mobile smart device usage. The primary role of smart devices was to increase social interactions between citizens, citizens with private services, and citizens with government services. These structural and institutional communication linkages are the foundations of a Smart City Seoul vision.

The Application of Our Four Newgotiation Steps to the Seoul Case Study

Preparation was critical. The first phase of the project focused on transparency. Seoul citizens had access to the same information as the city's mayor. The Smart City plan bridged the citizens of Seoul, and the mayor before it even began. While the Seoul citizen stakeholder group is large and dilutes perceptions of trust among the entire group, trust is one of the most significant patterns recognized during effective negotiations, and repeated interactions build more vital trust.

The Seoul Open Data Plaza (SODP) and Seoul Information Communication Plaza (SICP), utilized in the Platform, grew out of Seoul citizens' frustration with the lack of information disclosures. The success of the Platform depended on the freedom of data and information in public disclosures. SMG made significant efforts to train city staff on the importance of open information disclosures, the process of disclosures, and disclosures with sensitive details. Buy-in from the team was necessary to create an institutional culture and an overall buy-in of open data projects and the quality of data information disclosures. The rate and quality of disclosures have made it easier and more efficient for citizens and journalists to obtain and digest this information.

The citizen–government bottom-up vision of former Mayor Park of Seoul had always considered a multi-stakeholder approach to policy buy-in and input from Seoul citizens and private businesses. Thus, the citizen suggestion platform for policies, called "Oasis of 10 million Imagination," was created to consider citizen input and governance. Moreover, the platform was released for public use after substantial private testing of public input.

Our interview responses also showed that project leaders emphasized expert consultations before any project's strategic planning could begin. These same outside experts continued to work on the Platform and are also involved with distributing smart technologies worldwide, which is vital for our value creation step.

Seoul's smart city knowledge base explicitly seeks to advance smart city technology and become an industry leader. Public–private partnerships work for industry-led leadership consortiums where smaller companies work with industry leaders on a segment of smart city-related technologies. For example, LG CNS, a subsidiary of LG Group, co-chairs the Smart City Synergy Alliance with over 100 companies. Larger companies, such as SK Telecom and Hyundai, along with multiple Small-to-Medium-sized Enterprises (SMEs) and start-ups, cover sectors of smart city initiatives, such as waste disposal, energy, education, and transportation. The public–private partnership also drafts and coordinates smart city policies.

Seoul participates and contributes to the World Government Organization of Cities and Local Governments (WeGO) to accomplish smart city technologies and knowledge delivery. This participation is a significant tool for the Seoul Mayor's office. WeGO consists of multiple foreign city and institution partners, and WeGO Seoul helps conduct feasibility studies, site visits, consulting, and knowledge sharing on e-government. Thus, Seoul's smart city efforts have cross-sectoral and cross-border impacts that make smart city initiatives resilient and valuable to large segments of the city's population and the world.

Finally, in implementation, the Platform's success depends on public support. The 2020–2022 phase of the Platform seeks user feedback and data logs on platform usage, among other technical aspects, to improve the user experience. Platform maintenance requires a high degree of discipline. In addition, since the Platform went live, the average number of users exceeds 27 million per month. With communication between city departments becoming more efficient, there has been an increased number of "decision-making cases for disasters, traffic, air quality, and water supply issues." Because the smart city vision is a journey, the Platform is evolving with Seoul's citizen engagement. Therefore, considerable effort is put into promoting the Platform across the city in high-density human traffic areas.

The SCP program demonstrates the need for strong leadership throughout the citizen–government contractual relationship of public policy. Much of the success of SCP and other smart city-related policies harkens back to former Mayor Park's vision of a citizen's role in governance. Without citizen complaints about former leadership's lack of public disclosures, his vision would not have been propelled to the local forefront. SGM created value from leadership and vision through a disciplined approach to making data accessible to the public. This effort also required synergistic and solid relationships between industry experts in the private sector to lead and create innovative technology that allows all components of SPC to come together. The private–public relationship is also essential for delivering knowledge and technology, from smart city programs to overseas initiatives.

Case 2: Decentralized Cooperation to Democratize Cities, Brazil and Mozambique

Context

The project is drawn from the UCLG database, a global network of cities and local, regional, and metropolitan governments and their associations, facilitating many international cooperation programs worldwide. The decentralized cities program was one of the symbolic programs of the city-to-city learning implementation (see Table 7.6).

As a South-South decentralized partnership puzzle, the Decentralized International Cooperation project aims to improve the management of local development in terms of effective governance, sustainability, and participation

TABLE 7.6 Cooperation of Brazil and Mozambique

Member State	Brazil and Mozambique
Institution Name	United Cities and Local Governments (UCLG), the National Association of Municipalities of Mozambique (ANAMM), and the National Front of Mayors of Brazil (FNP)
Institution Type	Public Agency
Administrative Level	Local
Name of initiative	Decentralized Cooperation to Democratize Cities
Project's Operational Years	4
Website of Institution	United Cities and Local Governmentshttps://learning.uclg.org/peer-learning/
Key Stakeholders and Partnerships	Local administrations and authorities, NGOs, Academia, Citizens, and Private and investment sectors
Relevant SDGs	11

to extend the population's rights to 14 cities in Brazil and Mozambique. This international project was officially launched in 2013 under the leadership of UCLG, the National Association of Municipalities of Mozambique (ANAMM), and the National Front of Mayors of Brazil (FNP). The triangle cooperation mode and city-to-city (C2C) learning methodology worked well in this project. In addition, the policy tools applied are highly compatible with the negotiation framework and elements.

Worldwide, cities are now home to more than 50% of the global population, which is bursting at the rate of 60 million people per year. The rapid growth of urbanization has a profound impact on human society. As a result, immense economic and social development opportunities occur in cities, which are also important political and cultural centers (see Table 7.7).

The decisive role that cities play in sustainable development highlights the significance of local government actions. In "Transforming Our World: the 2030 Agenda for Sustainable Development," UN practitioners emphasize the need to "work closely on implementation with regional and local authorities."

TABLE 7.7 Collaboration of Cities

Cities	*Countries*	*Basic Information*	
		Population	*Geographic Size*
Guarulhos	Brazil (the mentor)	1,312,197	341.00 km^2
Porto Alegre		1,409,351	496.68 km^2
Nampula	Mozambique (the mentee)	471,717	404.00 km^2
Inhambane		75,412	192.00 km^2

This bottom-up working pattern marks a shift from the top-down implementation paradigm widely used in MDGs. SDG 11, aiming to "Make cities and human settlements inclusive, safe, resilient and sustainable," also reflects a crucial first step toward integrating sustainable urban development into the global framework for action where local and regional governments can contribute to the 2030 Agenda. In other words, cities will be the fundamental fields and drivers of implementing the 2030 Agenda.

The most concerning questions at the local governance level have always been how to realize the improvement in a local government capacity, resident quality of life, and political participation. As cities grow, managing them becomes increasingly complex, especially for developing countries. Cities in less-developed countries were caught in the wave of industrial urbanization. Moreover, some cities went through an ill-developed urbanization process, which caused a series of urban diseases, such as traffic problems, housing and water scarcity, employment concerns, and other social service issues.

The biggest concern related to urban issues is the rapid growth in the numbers of urban poor due to the rapid population increase and the rural–urban migration. The distinct gap between urban and rural areas regarding social infrastructure investments and economic opportunities contributes to the belief that living in big cities is much better than living in small towns or villages. In Latin America, the concentration of population in large cities or metropolitan areas is extremely dramatic. There are 13 countries with over 20% of the national population living in the largest city. The situation in African cities is much more alarming. Africa's urban population is projected to more than double, from 295 million in 2000 to 748 million by 2030, accounting for over 70% of total population growth in this region. Africa will have the second-largest urban population behind Asia.

The unprecedented increase in urban population stresses the immediate and surrounding environment and poses significant challenges for sustainable development. The quality of city resident life fails to rise, falling sharply. Studies show that health care, education, and employment are widely underserved, as the early city-living advantages have declined since the 1970s and gradually disappeared by the 1990s. Meanwhile, an estimated 72% of the urban population of Africa now resides in slums, suffering poverty, pollution, and unsanitary conditions.

However, given a challenging future for city policymakers, a narrow perspective that urban issues can be addressed as the by-product of a single national concern in the economy, environment, and education still attracts advocates. More international efforts should occur between different partners to ensure local perspectives pursue urban policy in an integrated and collaborative manner.

This project involves local government leaders and their teams in target cities. Other vital stakeholders are nongovernmental organizations, including

TABLE 7.8 Collaboration among Sectoral Stakeholders

Stakeholders	*Means*	*Goals*
Local administrations and authorities	Policymaking decentralization	Delegate's planning, land management, and essential services Improve management capacity
NGOs	International collaboration	Fulfill the SDGs Gain support and recognition from local governments
Academia	Professional knowledge and skills sharing	Contribute to city development Analyze and address urban problems
Citizens	Democratic voting and dialogue processes	Demand public services and land use planning Expressing needs to local authorities
Private and investment sectors	Financial support to local government or NGOs and social responsibility	Need an environment to leverage Seek favorable conditions for sustainable investment and generate benefits

the UCLG and the EU (see Table 7.8). Technical experts and further academic research also engage in this project and offer professional suggestions. Citizens in these cities gain opportunities to participate in policymaking and help guide the investment and industry flow of the private sector.

Solution

This program approaches urban problems by encouraging cities from Brazil and Mozambique to form city-to-city learning partnerships. In this type of partnership, there are two roles—the mentor and the mentee. First, the mentor city shares the policy tools it used with the mentee city to learn from after a cooperation commitment. The mentor city also provides the mentee city with technical support to help it adapt these experiences to fit its municipalities. Second, the mentor city is responsible for program evaluation and summary after the mentee city implements the policy. In this case, the mentor cities were from Brazil. The mentee cities were from Mozambique because Brazil has a more extended history of dealing with excessive urbanization as a developing country and inspiring policy inventions that are worthwhile for other countries to learn and adopt.

In this C2C cooperation, cities in Brazil mainly promoted the most frequently used and well-executed policy tools to empower the citizens for a healthy domestic urbanization process: territorial management and registry and participatory budgeting. This territorial management and registry policy instrument focused on peer learning in Guarulhos, Brazil, and Nampula, Mozambique. The participatory budgeting tool was intensively discussed in Porto Alegre, Brazil, and Inhambane, Mozambique.

Territorial management and registry start with sorting out the current land use conditions of cities and relevant aims, challenges, policies, and development programs put forward by the government in an orderly fashion. After summarizing the existing land use policy, it promises to discover the potential use of specific land to guide the municipality's development. Lastly, base plans define the land's structure, labeling it as urban and suitable or unsuitable for urbanization and identifying the rights and responsibilities of the owners of each land class. In addition, an inclusive registry intends to build a digitized system, allowing users to collect, transfer, and analyze urban data. This database opens the possibilities to big data use and statistics for academic research and public service improvement related to urban planning, especially social inequality and resource stratification.

In addition to the political and technical strategies, financial tools always play an equal or more influential role in policy implementation. The participatory budget solution differs because it breaks with the convention that only government officials and experts can call for financial funding and public investment. Instead, the participatory budget opens the door for citizens to speak up. Thus, this tool represents the kernel of democratizing cities.

The Application of Our Four Newgotiation Steps to the Brazil–Mozambique Case Study

Preparation—External Broker

Before the cities from these two countries jumped into peer sharing and learning, the mentor and mentee cities needed to explore whether there was a potential for collaboration. Only appropriate matching can maximize the learning effect. Officials from each city have a chance to become familiar with each other and their respective municipal contexts. That is why there was a heavy reliance on an external broker or city "match-maker" in the preparation stage of the relationship.

In this case, UCLG and other local authority associations made the most of their experience in international cooperation with local authorities in Brazil and Mozambique. They organized the first meeting in the city of Nampula for politicians, technicians, and partners from the two countries to learn about each other and clarify their doubts and the goals of this cooperation in 2013. According to the participants of this project, this was very time-consuming. During the process, UCLG served as the bridge to each side and promoted the formation of the C2C relationship.

Value Creation—Reciprocity

After the cities establish one-to-one cooperation by mutual selection, the collaboration moves toward a higher level. The officials and technicians from both the mentor and mentee cities would pay visits in the following years to meet face to face. During these trips, the mentee cities are inspired by the work and the results of their mentor's strategic planning efforts. The mentors would share the story of their urban planning strategies and reveal all the difficulties faced, or achievements reached. At this point, both mentor and mentee cities would realize that what brought them together was a set of shared challenges and interests. Those common concerns are attributed to the healthy and reciprocal relationship between the mentor and the mentee cities. The win–win cooperation became a solid foundation of trust and mutual understanding between the officials of both cities.

Value Distribution—Creativity

Despite the city-to-city learning, cooperation allows cities from Brazil and Mozambique to achieve a win–win result. Inside each city, departments of local governments had to wrestle with the other municipal departments to agree on spending toward this cooperation with the limited budget and human resources available. In this case, the creative use of host city mayoral receptions, for example, is a concrete mechanism for augmenting limited project budgets to ensure more social interactions.

Implementation—Adaptability

The implementation of this project occurred in the mentee cities in Mozambique after learning the planning strategies being done in the mentor cities in Brazil. Although the cities that matched together have a great deal in common, the policy tools had to account for the need to fit within the local reality and meet the needs of local stakeholders, which required the policymakers and technicians to make the best of the local community's culture and wisdom. A smooth transition depends on distinguishing the subtle differences between the mentors and applying the policy tools to the practitioner's unique local context.

Critical Insights for Negotiating a 2030 Agenda

This case is unique because it sheds light on how the negotiation progress unfolds between cities from two developing countries through this project; meanwhile, cities on both sides endeavor to balance the input to the partnership from different internal actors. This cooperation can succeed because the common issues and goals tie those cities together. Moreover, a good and solid foundation of trust (the key to value creation) makes the negotiation unfold smoothly. Also, help from a third party, such as UCLG, played a critical role in promoting the negotiation because of their rich experiences implementing international cooperative solutions.

Case 3: Careers by Design LA, United States

Context

The city of Los Angeles (Los Angeles) covers 468 square miles. It is home to approximately 4 million people, making it one of the largest cities in the United States of America (US) in land area and the second-most populous after New York City (see Table 7.9).

Before the COVID-19 pandemic, Los Angeles appeared to thrive in aggregate economic terms. According to Bloomberg News, when measuring personal income, gross domestic product per capita, jobs, home prices, global trade and transportation, corporate equity, and municipal debt, Los Angeles was the most productive of the five biggest US cities in 2019.

Los Angeles outpaced New York City, Chicago, Houston, and Phoenix. Nevertheless, it becomes clear when factoring in equity that economic gains have not necessarily served those residents most in need. For example, the National Equity Atlas documented that since 1979, income for full-time workers at the 20th percentile decreased by 21%, while income for those at the 90th percentile grew by 15% (see Figure 7.6). In addition, prospects for disadvantaged communities are not favorable when considering higher education disparities among races in the city.

TABLE 7.9 Careers by Design in the City of Los Angeles

Member State	United States
Institution Name	Multi-stakeholder Partnership
Institution Type	Public Agency
Administrative Level	Local
Name of initiative	Careers by Design LA
Project's Operational Years	2016—ongoing
Website of Institution	Careers by Design Los Angeles (CDLA)https://sites.google.com/view/cdlacommunitybasedcurriculum/home?authuser=0
Key Stakeholders & Partnerships	City of Los Angeles Mayor's Office (LA Mayor's Office), Los Angeles Trade and Technical College (LATTC), Careers Excellence Academy (CEA), and Workforce Connections (WFC)
Relevant SDGs	4, 8, and 11

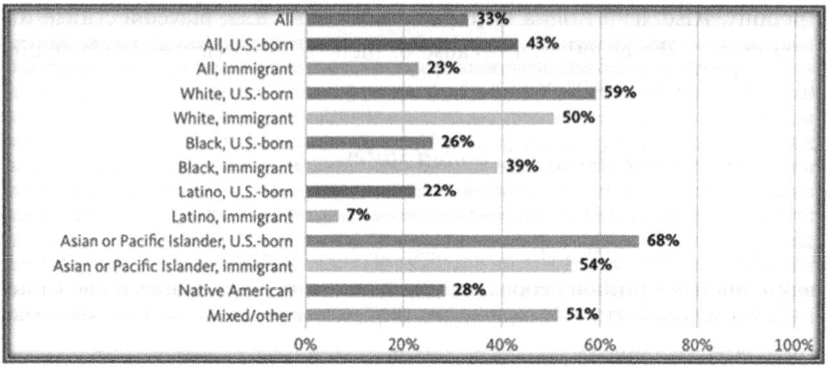

FIGURE 7.6 Los Angeles Demographic Breakdown; Diversity

Source LA City

Percent of Population with a Bachelor's Degree or Higher by Race/Ethnicity and Nativity

Sometimes, this disparity manifests in concentrated areas. Among such places is South Los Angeles. In 2016, South Los Angeles experienced an unemployment rate of 11.81%, while 46% of residents lived below the federal poverty line. The anthropological and economic history of the area is complex. However, in general terms, over the past half-century, South Los Angeles has dealt with social and economic struggles that have left it persistently disadvantaged relative to Los Angeles County (LAC) as a whole. By examining the green dotted line on the "Disparity Ratio" table, we see that the median wage parity in South Los Angeles has declined since 1960 and has recently settled at approximately 60% of the County's median salary (see Figure 7.7).

Disparity Ratio of South Los Angeles to Los Angeles County

> The disparity ratio indicates parity between South Los Angeles and the county. Each year, the ratio compares the rate of each variable in the county with that of South Los Angeles. In the case of earnings, the ratio is the median earnings of full-time, full-year individuals.
>
> **Note:** This figure defines South Los Angeles as a broader area relative to SLATE-Z. As such, the ratio for SLATE-Z would likely be different.

The condition of the area (see Figure 7.8) caught national attention after local entities led by the Los Angeles Trade Technical College advocated for the site to be granted "Promise Zone" status under the federal initiative created

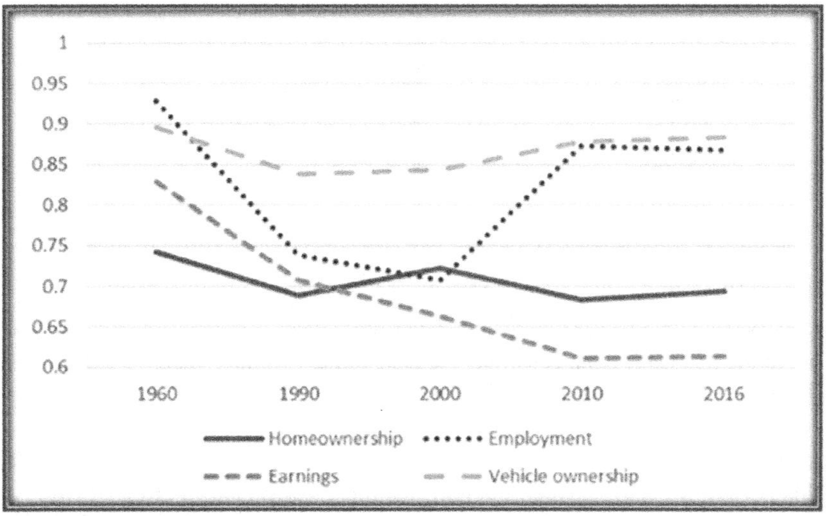

FIGURE 7.7 Ratio of Disparities in Los Angeles

Source: Ong & Comandom 2020

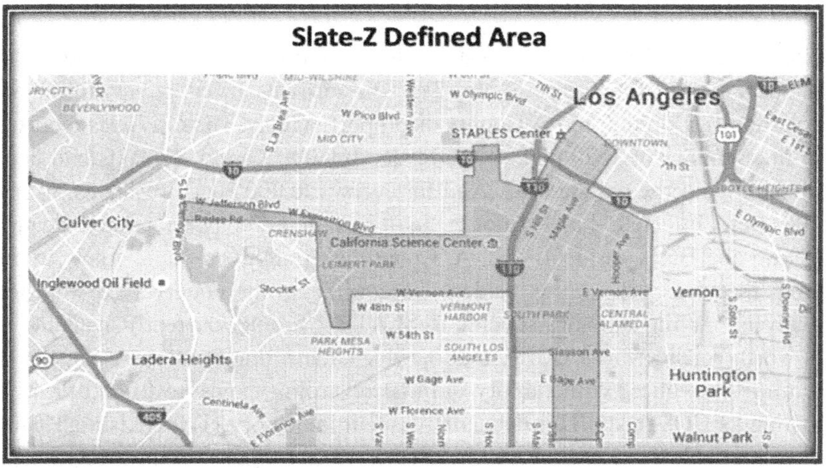

FIGURE 7.8 Map of South Los Angeles shown with SLATE-Z

by President Barack Obama (Clay, 2016). As a result, the initiative succeeded, and the South LA Transit Empowerment Zone (SLATE-Z) was formed within South Los Angeles.

Preliminary data from the most recent American Community Survey reinforces that SLATE-Z is economically disadvantaged relative to LAC. From 2015

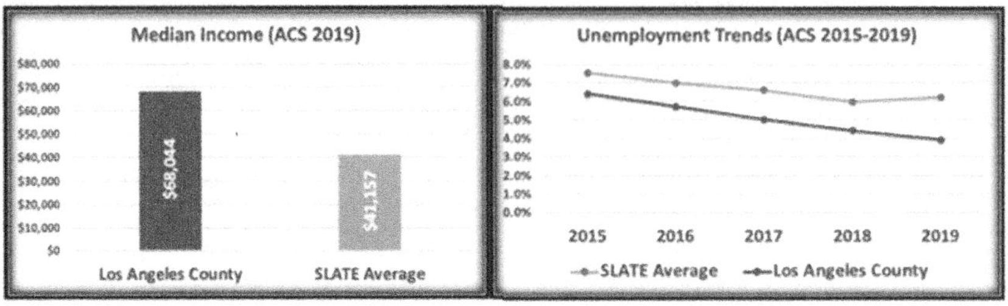

FIGURE 7.9 Los Angeles Census Statistics (2015–2019).

Note: SLATE-Z averages were calculated by averaging the statistics corresponding to the ZIP Codes that constitute the zone (90001, 90003, 90007, 90008, 90011, 90015, 90018, 90037, 90062, and 90089).

to 2019, SLATE-Z experienced higher unemployment trends than LAC. During this period, the gap between the two was most significant in 2019—SLATE-Z experienced 6.2% unemployment, while LAC experienced 4%. Additionally, data from the US Census reinforces the finding that SLATE-Z residents earn approximately half the median wage of LAC.

South LA US Census Statistics

Notably, the statistics mentioned above do not consider the economic and health impacts of COVID-19 (see Figure 7.9). The virus itself has proven to impact communities of color in LA County disproportionately. The *LA Times* reported in the Summer of 2020 that 700 for every 100,000 Latino residents had been infected with the coronavirus. And for every 100,000 Black residents, nearly 400 were infected. Furthermore, "In terms of coronavirus-related deaths, Latino and Black residents of L.A. County are roughly twice as likely to die from the virus than white residents, according to the county's age-adjusted analysis." While statistics specific to SLATE-Z are not currently available, it is worth considering a UCLA report, which states that South Los Angeles is within the highest vulnerability quintile regarding exposure to and positive testing for COVID-19. This data is across four indicators: (1) Preexisting Health Condition, (2) Barriers to Accessing Services, (3) Built Environment Risk, and (4) Social Vulnerability.

The racial and ethnic composition of South Los Angeles in 2016 was comprised of approximately 71% Latinos, 17% African Americans, and 43% immigrants. Thus, LAC has an elevated probability of disproportionate health impacts. Additionally, in a report released in 2021, the Los Angeles Economic Development Corporation found that of the Californians who filed unemployment insurance claims during the pandemic, 65% were people of color, and 57% had high school or lower education attainment. As a result, they hypothesized that higher education could provide some buffering effect against the labor market volatility (LAEDC, 2021).

To address this issue, four organizations partnered in 2016—the City of Los Angeles Mayor's Office (LA Mayor's Office), Los Angeles Trade and Technical College (LATTC), Careers Excellence Academy (CEA), and Workforce Connections (WFC). The initiative resulting from their collaboration is called Careers by Design LA (CDLA). CDLA is a program designed to create a pathway to professional services jobs within the Architecture, Engineering, and Construction (AEC) sectors for underserved residents of SLATE-Z. While there is some overlap in each organization's capacity, they all bring a unique skill set and resource pool to maximize the program's effectiveness.

The LA Mayor's Office is the host organization responsible for developing and implementing the program according to the City's Green New Deal objectives. The Mayor's Office assigned two employees to this program.

The Los Angeles Trade Technical College (LATTC) Architecture and Environmental Design Program is responsible for providing the technical knowledge necessary to excel in AEC fields. LATTC is a public community college, and 75% of LATTC's courses are in Career Technical Education (CTE). A professor of Architecture and Environmental Design at LATTC is leading the development and accreditation of the CDLA curriculum.

The Career Excellence Academy (CEA) provides professional development training seminars that prepare students to be qualified personnel in the construction industry. Their service includes technical and soft skills explicitly designed with the needs of construction industry employers in mind. Additionally, CEA exposes students to subject matter experts through in-class visits and field trips. Two CEA program facilitators work with CDLA.

Workforce Connections, Inc. (WFC) is a workforce intermediary that supports public and private organizations by connecting local workers' skills to meet employers' expressed needs. WFC partners with employers and community colleges to develop innovative training programs customized to specific employers and industry sectors, such as construction, architecture, engineering, automotive, transportation, logistics, and manufacturing. In addition, WFC plays a crucial role in connecting participants to on-the-job training in paid AEC internships, followed by placement support into permanent professional service jobs.

Solution

The program is part of the City of Los Angeles Mayor's Green New Deal, which aims to create 300,000 green jobs by 2035 and 400,000 green jobs by 2050 (LA Green New Deal 2019). Working toward the Sustainable Development Goals (SDG) is an explicit part of CDLA's mission.

The SDGs that are most relevant to this program are Goal 4 (Quality Education), Goal 8 (Decent Work and Economic Growth), Goal 9 (Industry, Innovation, and

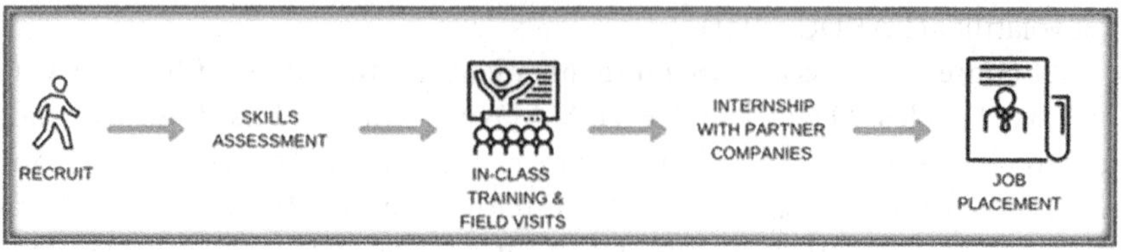

FIGURE 7.10 Careers by Design LA Program Model

Infrastructure), and Goal 11 (Sustainable Cities and Communities). Given the new challenges that COVID-19 has posed for SLATE-Z, which have exacerbated its already difficult conditions, CDLA has the potential to play a substantial role in recovery and future resiliency. Good-paying and stable jobs are vital to an area's overall prosperity. If CDLA is successful, the area could benefit from greater access to health resources, more purchasing power to support local businesses and reduce the rent burden, an enhanced tax base for community investments, etc.

CDLA's model to accomplish these goals is based on an intimate process beyond simply training students for careers in the AEC sector (see Figure 7.10). Instead, the program model creates a pathway for individuals of wide-ranging AEC backgrounds—from no experience to advanced accreditation—with skills that AEC industry recruiters seek so each participant can be placed in an internship or career after program completion. Student skills are assessed before classes and activities begin, and after that, the students are connected to CDLA's partners to secure paid internships or job placements. In addition, students in the program participate in a semester-long course on professional green jobs in the AEC industry.

This course provides:

- Essential green construction
- Sustainable architecture/engineering practices
- BIM/CAD digital knowledge
- Soft skills training

The Application of Our Four Newgotiation Steps to the CDLA Case Study

Preparation—Initiative

CDLA was not developed in the traditional sense of a public–private partnership where interested parties prepare to negotiate the terms of an agreement in silos and then proceed with the discussion. Instead, CDLA is collaborative from the onset. For example, CEA, a private enterprise that offers career development services, had the original idea for a career-oriented education service focused on the AEC industry. They took the concept to several relevant entities, including employers themselves. They received great feedback, but nobody knew how to apply it to their operation. That changed when the manager of the SLATE-Z program from the LA Mayor's Office caught wind of the idea. In short, CEA presented its program idea during a SLATE-Z event. The SLATE-Z manager seized the moment and connected with CEA leadership to follow up about collaborating. This action is a demonstration of an effective leader taking the initiative.

The SLATE-Z manager could leverage existing relationships with LATTC and Workforce Connections and eventually bring them on as project partners. The trust between SLATE-Z LATTC and Workforce Connections facilitated this alliance, and now, each organization is an integral part of CDLA. During interviews with the project leaders from each organization, it was evident that great rapport among the partners continues. It can be assumed that if a future opportunity to collaborate were to manifest, they could likely rely on these partners to aid in its development.

While the SLATE-Z manager was working to build the foundation of a program with CEA, it was brought to her that the LA Mayor's Office had recently conducted a labor study to identify potential economic industries of interest. Coincidentally, the findings indicated that CEA was on the right track—that worthwhile potential in the AEC sector was on the horizon. But again, the SLATE-Z manager had the leadership capacity to leverage this analysis in the program's favor, ultimately contributing to her supervisor's approval of the program and the mayor personally championing it.

Value Creation—Mission Driven

When local governments engage in collaborative partnerships, they must refer to guiding principles that detail their public mission. Without such a guide, their efforts may be aimless and thus not as productive as they could be. Developing a strategic plan that outlines the local government goals will prompt practical questions that ask how the goals can be achieved. Through this exercise, local governments create value and become more informed about the necessities of their vision.

CDLA is an example of this strategic method working. The LA Mayor's Office first developed the Los Angeles Green New Deal Sustainability Plan, which revealed the necessity of building a workforce capable of implementing the changes that the plan proposed. Then, merging the CDLA with the Los Angeles Mayor's Green New Deal Plan amplified the program's exposure while enhancing its mission's resolution. To successfully incorporate CDLA under the Green New Deal umbrella, leadership foresight, integration, and adaptability from each leading partner were critical.

Value Distribution—Common Cause

CDLA continues to be successful after completing several semesters. Each project partner works together to tackle the full range of complexity in imparting knowledge to students and transitioning them into a position where they can apply what they have learned and prosper. Each partner understands their duty and knows to do it well; however, they do not stop there.

In addition to their expertise, each participating organization shares similar skills and resource types. These skills could have led to disputes; however, the CDLA partners used this diversity of knowledge to their advantage. Instead of quarreling over who would do what, each partner took on a spirit of common cause and shared responsibilities to bolster program outcomes. This shared motivation manifests in curriculum development and employer networking. As a result, the program curriculum is more robust and focuses on making more employer connections for program participants.

Implementation

LATTC is a physical institution with a campus. This institution could be considered a part of CDLA's toolkit. It is a resource that is necessary to host the program participants. Of course, they could also create an online experience, and that is what they have done to adapt to the circumstances of the COVID-19 pandemic. But again, the ability to adjust shines as essential in a dynamic world.

Furthermore, the college's intangible infrastructure required that the CDLA course undergo the State of California community college audit process. This process ensures that the curriculum meets established standards. In addition to making the course more robust, it can be replicated in any community college in the state. The implementation of accepted standards makes the project easy to accomplish.

An essential step in the preparation phase of CDLA was organizing focus groups with potential AEC employers and participants from other workforce development programs to gauge what inputs would be necessary to create an effective program. This process was beneficial because it aided the partners in understanding the resources they would need to generate for the program. It also strengthened their relationship with potential employers of CDLA program participants. This relationship helped them secure paid internships and jobs for program participants completing the process, which is among the program's priority goals.

Leaders from each partnering organization continue meeting bi-weekly to provide updates and manage their partnership. This relationship is essential when considering implementation as an ongoing process instead of a fixed moment. Program durability and evaluation must be a part of program consideration when advancing the 2030 Agenda, which is long-term.

Critical Insights for Negotiating a 2030 Agenda

Countless factors contribute to a successful collaborative negotiation. While only a handful have been targeted in this qualitative analysis, each is a fragment of a more significant concerted effort that continues to employ leadership, trust, and toolkits to realize success. These elements allow each partner to bring their specialized assets while sharing responsibilities to maximize program effectiveness.

When assessing a collaborative initiative like CDLA, it is difficult to parse out the four negotiation steps because the boundaries are unclear. However, CDLA demonstrated that a negotiation process does not need to start in silos and that transparent and supportive negotiation can lead to positive outcomes for everyone involved.

Case 4: Shanghai "One Net Office," People's Republic of China

Context

Shanghai's "One Net Office," also known as Government Online–offline Shanghai, provides one-stop online–offline government services through an integrated online service platform (see Table 7.10). This local government project enables Shanghai residents to handle numerous matters that require the intervention of different public departments efficiently through one online platform, thereby providing Shanghai residents with greater convenience.

Previously, due to the lack of coordination and data sharing between government departments and their regional offices, most services were requested

TABLE 7.10 Shanghai "One Net Office" (People's Republic of China)

Member State	People's Republic of China
Institution Name	Shanghai Municipal Big Data Center
Institution Type	Public Agency
Administrative Level	Local
Name of initiative	Shanghai "One Net Office"
Project's Operational Years	8
Website of Institution	Shanghai Municipal Government http://english.shanghai.gov.cn/nw46669/index.html
Key Stakeholders & Partnerships	Shanghai residents, Shanghai government agencies, state-owned enterprises, national enterprises, private express delivery companies, and financial companies
Relevant SDGs	1, 3, and 16

and delivered in person. This method required many government office trips, wasting time and energy. Moreover, each city section's processing procedures and material requirements were not the same. Therefore, the public was forced to visit several locations dozens of kilometers away for processing. This situation has stimulated the Chinese government to explore new service models to integrate online and offline services and improve the disclosure mechanism of government departments.

Shanghai's "One Net Office" is a specific implementation plan formulated by the local government based on a national strategy decision (see Figure 7.11). As early as 2016, the State Council of China issued the Guiding Opinions on Accelerating the Work of "Internet + Government Services." Since then, local governments have begun to explore models suitable for their development. In 2018, the State Council of China made the "One Net Office" mandatory for internet-based government services. Shanghai's "One Net Office" has achieved remarkable results among many other places and has been a model case for digital government experience in the United Nations E-Government Survey 2020.

Influence on Society and SDGs

By the end of 2020, the cumulative number of users on Shanghai "One Net Office" had exceeded 2.07 billion, and the number of users had exceeded 43 million. Shanghai's "One Net Office" also has an evaluation system that allows companies and residents to provide feedback when using this portal to practically

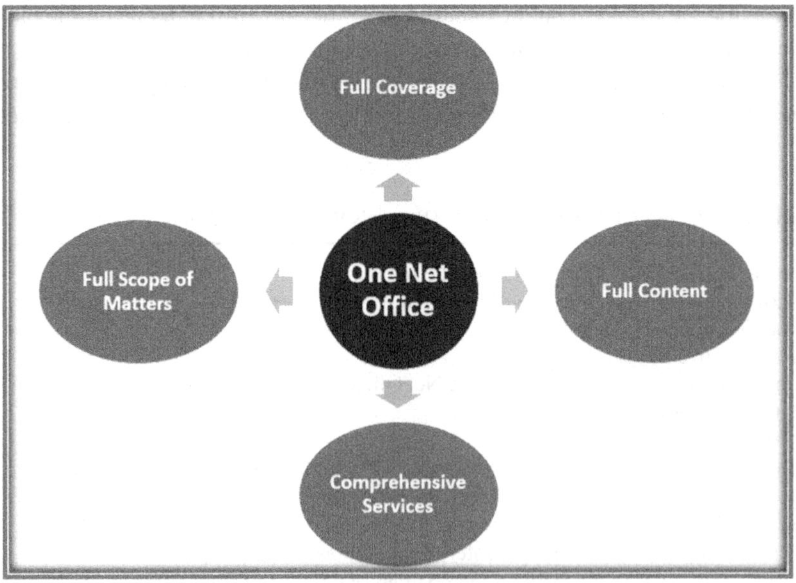

FIGURE 7.11 Shanghai "One Net Office" (People's Republic of China)

address inconveniences they encounter. From the online trial operation to April 9, 2020, the evaluation system received 1,297,200 public comments, including 4,928 negative comments, and all the related matters mentioned in the real-name negative review have been rectified.

By February 2021, Shanghai's "One Net Office" has already covered 1,541 government service items in more than 50 municipal departments, including education, public security, civil affairs, human resources, social security, health, and medical insurance. By 2020, the 15 most-used services, such as online registration for alternative fuel vehicles and online registration for newborns, have reduced the service time by 54%, the service materials by 75%, and the travel time by 70%, on average. By the end of 2020, the total usage of these 15 most-used services has exceeded 290,000.

On March 9, 2021, Shanghai's "One Net Office" launched 13 new services that require "zero operations" and "zero materials." This launch includes applying and activating the latest version of the social security card, reviewing individual housing provident funds, and signing and filing the Shanghai housing lease contract.

Problem

The critical innovation of Shanghai's "One Net Office" is to promote the transformation of government services from a traditional "department-centered" management model to a modern "user-centered" management model. However, the implementation challenges face internal and external constraints, such as

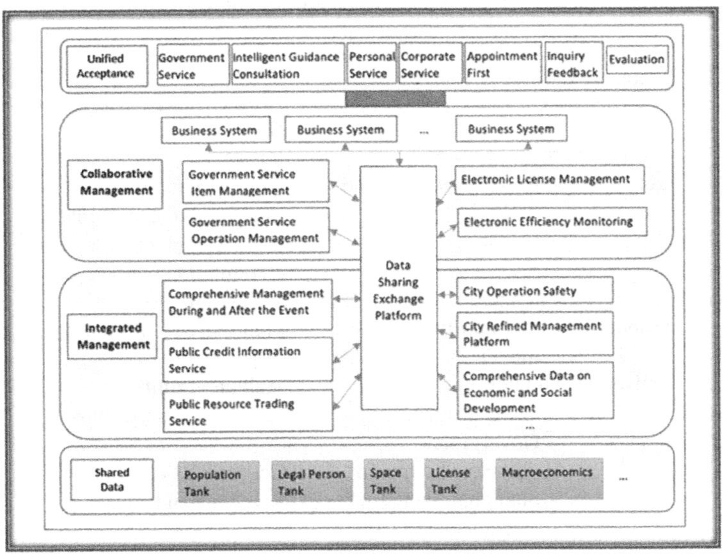

FIGURE 7.12 Shanghai's "One Net Office" System Framework

difficulties in cross-regional and cross-level information interconnection, conflicts between local practice and legal compliance, lack of long-term mechanism guarantees, and insufficient effective social participation.

The biggest implementation challenge for Shanghai's "One Net Office" comes down to integrating different organizations into one service platform. As shown in Figure 7.12, Shanghai's "One Net Office" system framework is "1+1+ X." The first "1" refers to the Shanghai Municipal Big Data Center, the data source and technical support platform. The second "1" refers to the web portal's entire process integrated online service platform. Finally, "X" refers to the multiple individual institutions that provide services through this portal, including public agencies and private companies.

The Shanghai Municipal Big Data Center is responsible for implementing the system framework. In addition, more than 50 municipal government departments and 16 district governments in the city have financial funds to support the project. All have personnel coordinating with more than 20,000 staff to provide offline services. This system framework has led to extensive, predictable cooperation and negotiation between institutions.

Stakeholders Analysis

As an overall project of the Shanghai Municipal Government, Shanghai's "One Net Office" is a large project involving several stakeholders. The stakeholders fall into three major categories: public institutions, private enterprises, and the residents in Shanghai (see Table 7.11).

The public institutions include governmental agencies, state-owned enterprises, and national enterprises. Governmental agencies most relevant in

TABLE 7.11 Stakeholder Analysis

Stakeholders	*Means*	*Goals*
Governmental agencies	Most relevant in people's daily lives	Increase efficiency Implement the sustainable development policy of the Central Government
State-owned enterprises, national enterprises	Run nationwide services, has a unified business model	Maintain profit Maintain decision-making power
Private express delivery companies and financial companies	All under the supervision of the Central Government	Maintain profit Maintain decision-making power
Residents	All people who live in Shanghai, including foreigners and Chinese citizens without the "Hukou" of Shanghai	Get access to services online Save time and energy

people's daily lives are the Shanghai Municipal Public Security Bureau, Human Resources and Social Security Bureau, Municipal Bureau of Justice and Municipal Tax Service, and State Taxation Administration.

State-owned enterprises include banking institutions and municipal hospitals. National enterprises include entities such as China Post, a leading logistics express enterprise in China. The private sector participants include Alipay and WeChat Pay, mainland China's leading payment platforms. They are part of the Alibaba Group and Tencent Holdings Ltd, respectively. Finally, SF Express is a privately owned express delivery company in China. Residents in Shanghai are the service targets of this project. Their experience and suggestions will be critical in measuring Shanghai's "One Net Office" success or failure. The evaluation mechanism is one of the crucial ways for this project to obtain feedback from the residents.

The Application of Our Four Newgotiation Steps to Shanghai's "One Net Office" Case Study

Preparation

In China, the fragmentation of public services, a key obstacle to implementing the online "One Net Office," is noteworthy for many reasons. One reason is the larger population and area in China. The "One Net Office" program heavily relies on sharing information and data. The ability to collect, process, and share data between institutions is essential for collaboration and negotiation success. Preparation for the negotiation involved a lengthy investigation process that explored the best way to integrate into a single platform and the research and development of the data collection, processing, sharing, and storage technology needed. Since "One Net Office" is reformative, the critical feature of the negotiations is to reach a final win–win situation. This preparation facilitates the value-creation step in the negotiation process by providing the same goal for both parties.

Value Creation

One manifestation of fragmentation includes the multiple supplies of public services. Public services with the nature of approval and resource allocation functions are often divided as scarce resources across many departments. Although the joint participation of multiple departments theoretically weakens the administrative power of each department, they all have the jurisdiction and ability to handle their departmental affairs. Also, departments calculate their performance. This process strengthens them at the departmental level but complicates integrating those public institutions into one system. The Central

Government plays a significant role here. The Central Government acts as a facilitator to support all departments. Based on this, ideology, power, and economic benefits have been combined and become the primary focus of negotiations between institutions.

Value Distribution

The negotiations are divided into two categories: government agencies versus government agencies and government agencies versus enterprises. Since the plan is under the guidance and support of the Central Government, government agencies play a leading role in the negotiations. Therefore, the negotiation between government agencies and enterprises is not as fierce as negotiating between government agencies and government agencies. However, all parties share an identical goal during the negotiation. For "One Net Office," the outcome is clearly stated at the beginning of the project—to create a one-stop, online–offline government services platform. Therefore, every stakeholder knows what they need to achieve during the negotiation. This process allows the negotiation to omit a lot of unnecessary maneuvers and speed up the process.

Implementation

Implementing the negotiation rests on the Shanghai Municipal Government's regulations on project integration. These known regulations dramatically reduce the delay in the implementation. However, the Central Government also plays a vital role in forcing implementation.

Critical Insights for Negotiating a 2030 Agenda

For countries with a centralized system, the results of a local program largely depend on the Central Government's emphasis on the project. For local projects, the Central Government's political will makes it easier for both parties to negotiate to reach an agreement quickly. The realistic common goal facilitates all four negotiation steps: preparation, value creation, value distribution, and implementation.

Shanghai's "One Net Office" is a program with significant meaning for sustainable development. This project makes its overall significance far greater than the value created by each organization (e.g., the whole is greater than the sum of its parts). Thus, the negotiation between each negotiator is under the same primary goal. The negotiation process is adaptable to other places that share the same political system as China. It is an excellent system for realizing the 2030 Agenda by improving efficiency and saving resources.

TABLE 7.12 Singapore Housing and Development Board

Member State	Singapore
Institution Name	Housing and Development Board
Institution Type	Public Agency
Administrative Level	Local
Name of initiative	Endearing Homes for Our Silver Generation
Project's Operational Years	6, since January 2015
Website of Institution	Singapore Housing Development https://www.hdb.gov.sg/cs/designedforlife/silvergeneration.html
Key Stakeholders & Partnerships	Housing and Development Board (HDB), Ministry of National Development (MND), Ministry of Health (MOH), National Parks Board, Ministry of Transport (MOT), private healthcare groups, public housing contractors
Relevant SDGs	11

Case 5: Endearing Homes for Our Silver Generation, Singapore

Context

Singapore's "Endearing Homes for our Silver Generation" initiative was nominated for the United Nations Public Service Awards (UNPSA) in 2019 under the category: "Ensuring integrated approaches in public-sector institutions." The nomination of this initiative for the UNPSA is the culmination of decades of public policy negotiations and tweaks to ensure that Singapore's overarching public housing policy remains adaptable to changing demographics and sociological trends. All this effort while not veering away from the foundational objectives and aims of public housing policy in Singapore: (1) to provide affordable public housing for residents and (2) to foster national unity and community spirit through public housing initiatives and neighborhood growth.

Overview of the Current Initiative

For almost six decades, Singapore's Housing Development Board (HDB), a Singapore government statutory board under the Ministry of National Development (MND), has been committed to providing affordable, inclusive, and equitable public housing for all Singapore citizens (Chua, 2014). This HDB initiative aims to tackle the challenges of an increasingly aging population (see Table 7.12). According to a United Nations projection in 2019, nearly half of Singapore's population would be above 65 years of age by 2050. Hence, there is a pressing need to create elderly friendly public housing apartments in readily convenient and conducive neighborhood environments so older adults can enjoy a comfortable and fulfilling retirement.

However, the target audience for this initiative is not just the vulnerable elderly but also their younger family members, who are usually their caregivers. A societal phenomenon in Singapore has seen most middle-aged Singaporeans being stretched, having to take care of their elderly parents or grandparents while simultaneously raising a young family; all these duties while they still contribute to the labor force. Hence, HDB's initiatives and policy innovations aim to integrate solutions to support the needs of many such Singaporean families shouldering these multigenerational duties and responsibilities.

Solution

In response to the challenges posed by Singapore's aging population, HDB's policies have prioritized physical housing needs for seniors and supported seniors who wish to tap into the value of their apartments to supplement their retirement income. HDB has constantly innovated its housing options regarding the physical design of individual flats and improving the creation of the surrounding neighborhood. For example, HDB has launched the "3Gen Flat" (larger apartments to accommodate elderly and young children) to encourage multigenerational living. The Enhancement for Active Seniors (EASE) scheme entails installing grab bars, wheelchair ramps, and other safety features to enhance safety for older adults, especially those living alone. These safety infrastructures can be installed at highly subsidized prices (up to 90% off the cost).

This year, HDB has launched new Community Care Apartments sold exclusively to older adults at affordable prices for a short-term lease. The cost of the apartment also includes access to essential healthcare services and round-the-clock emergency response, as well as access to communal spaces for social gatherings and affordable meals. In a typical HDB neighborhood, communal facilities such as senior citizen activity centers, food courts, and elevators that stop on every level increase convenience for seniors to socialize, even those who use wheelchairs. Childcare centers are also commonplace in the immediate vicinity, ensuring that both the young and elderly are well cared for while citizens go to work.

Furthermore, policies ensuring public housing prices remain fair and affordable have been innovated and tweaked with additional schemes and procedures in response to demographic and population changes and needs. For example, policies such as the Married Child Priority Scheme and the Proximity Housing Grant provide financial grants for families purchasing apartments near their parents' residences to encourage family members to live near one another.

Other policies, such as the Lease Buyback Scheme (LBS), allow HDB homeowners to unlock housing equity, granting them cash payouts to support their retirement expenses. Combining all these policies ensures a financially sustainable retirement for the Singapore elderly while strengthening family units and cohesiveness. In addition, social and emotional well-being is also being considered by providing amenities integrated within the HDB estate and surrounding neighborhood.

A Successful Blueprint: Kampung Admiralty

As part of the nomination of the "Endearing Homes for Our Silver Generation" initiative to UNPSA, MND, and HDB had highlighted a specific public housing project known as "Kampung Admiralty." This project would serve as the blueprint for further expanding this initiative to other neighborhoods in Singapore. A notable feature of Kampung Admiralty is that healthcare facilities are conveniently located in the same public housing apartment block to meet resident healthcare needs, primarily when a health emergency arises. Other features aimed at caring for senior citizens' social and emotional well-being include common spaces facilitating social interaction and activities for seniors. These spaces include community gardens and high-rise vertical farms where seniors can participate in gardening-related activities and grow more than 30 species of edible tropical plants and fruits. These activities enable seniors to remain active with a sense of purpose and fulfillment during retirement.

Consistent with HDB policy objectives to promote intergenerational bonding within families, Kampung Admiralty also features a childcare center, a community park, and a playground to facilitate interaction and bonding between older adults and grandchildren. Setting up a childcare center within the integrated living community also allows grandparents to care for their grandchildren and spend time with them more conveniently when their adult children are at work.

In the context of the successful negotiation of the Kampung Admiralty project, it must be noted that the success of this initiative is the fruit of the collective efforts of various government agencies and nongovernmental stakeholders. Integrative negotiations have always been a hallmark of policymaking in Singapore, including all public housing policy initiatives.

Hence, to find out more about the actual policy negotiation process behind the success of the Endearing Homes for Our Silver Generation initiative, particularly the Kampung Admiralty integrated living community project, we interviewed civil servants from HDB Singapore for additional insight.

The Application of Our Four Newgotiation Steps to the Singapore Case Study

Preparation

A key takeaway from the interview was the importance of meticulous policy planning, from goal setting to implementation. The need for detailed preparation of the implementation plan was highly emphasized by personnel at HDB. An essential element highlighted in the preparation process was establishing clear goals and policy objectives. In the context of HDB's policies, the explicit policy objective was to provide affordable housing for all seniors and a wide range of varying payment packages to suit the diverse needs of older adults.

For example, HDB explained that some seniors wish to age independently. In contrast, others preferred to move in with their children or to a smaller apartment near their children's homes to facilitate mutual care and support. The idea of seniors moving in or close to their children is an essential tenet of public housing policy options. Singapore is still a conservative society that places significant importance on filial piety.

However, the housing policies for seniors must be balanced against those of other demographics for fairness and recognition of limited resources, as public housing is heavily subsidized. Hence, a valuable element seen from this case study was the ability of HDB to anticipate the concerns of disadvantaged groups and produce proposed solutions for any problems expected to be brought to the negotiation table. This process would facilitate a faster and more effective public policy negotiation process.

Value Creation and Distribution

In terms of value creation, HDB emphasized that adopting a whole-of-government approach to the policy negotiation process was cardinal to its success. While the formulation, execution, and maintenance of this initiative are primarily under the purview of HDB and the MND, other ministries and government statutory boards were also involved in negotiating the initiative.

For example, given that the initiative aimed to create elderly friendly, accessible, and convenient neighborhoods for intergenerational living, the Ministry of Health (MOH) actively negotiated the health aspects and infrastructure. MND also had to enter inter-ministry negotiations with the Ministry of Transport (MOT) concerning transport link improvements, such as providing more wheelchair-accessible buses and subway stations.

Outside the government, facilitators brought contractors for infrastructure and NGOs to the negotiation table. To this end, steering committees, consisting of government and private stakeholders, were formed to facilitate effective negotiations and conversations regarding policy formulation and implementation, ensuring that all stakeholders involved had a fair voice in the policy negotiation process. However, the success of steering committees to facilitate policy negotiations has much to do with the higher level of public trust the incumbent People's Action Party government enjoys from its nongovernmental stakeholders.

According to the Edelman Trust Barometer, public confidence in the Singapore government ranks relatively high vis-à-vis other countries in Southeast Asia. Based on public policy literature, public trust encompasses the following elements: (1) competence, (2) benevolence, and (3) integrity. The

Singapore government has consistently displayed these three elements in governance and general policymaking.

HDB and MND have an outstanding record of accomplishing their previous public housing policy goals. This record reflects their competency, which increases trust between the nongovernmental public and private stakeholders, facilitating more effective negotiation processes.

The Singapore government has also proven to act in the public's interest, as seen by the commitment of elected parliamentarians to grassroots work. Committed to walking the ground and making frequent weekly visits to public housing apartments to reach out to residents personally. In addition, Singapore's Deputy Prime Minister, Mr Heng Swee Keat, recently crafted a slogan concerning governance, stating, "If it is not done with the heart, it is not worth doing." This statement truly encompasses the element of benevolence in Singapore's governing principles.

Lastly, Singapore is also known to be one of the least corrupt countries in the world. This culture also reflects an additional element of negotiation: resilient public institutions. Hence, stakeholders trust that negotiations will be more collaborative than competitive when entering policy negotiations with the government, contributing to good value distribution in the negotiation process.

Regarding the specific project in Kampung Admiralty, an integrative approach to policy negotiations was undertaken concerning this initiative, bringing together six other agencies and steering committees into the negotiation process. These agencies included:

- The Ministry of Health (Ageing Planning Office)
- Yishun Health Campus
- Early Childhood Development Agency/Ministry of Social and Family Development
- Ministry of Sustainability and Environment
- National Environment Agency
- National Parks Board

These government agencies also worked closely with grassroots organizations to gather public feedback. The development was envisioned as a one-stop hub that encourages social interaction and active aging through its innovative design and community spaces, which became the successful outcome of the negotiation process.

Implementation

Beyond policy design, an effective implementation plan was crucial to an effective negotiation process—this required collaboration with internal stakeholders, particularly operations and corporate communications departments. HDB relied on public relations teams to articulate their policy objectives and the rationales behind formulating these policies for the public. These are usually conducted through media briefings and press conferences, enabling the media to convey accurate information.

HDB also leveraged different media platforms, such as social media and blog posts, to gather more public feedback. Social media comments and reactions following policy announcements act as general feedback. Attaining feedback through such forms is extremely valuable because "on-the-ground" feedback is considered more genuine and not sugar-coated.

Hence, HDB's media and public relations team monitors social media posts and news reactions to identify areas of the policy that people are pleased with and, more importantly, areas where the public feels the need for further improvements. In addition, if opportunities arise, HDB will conduct real-life public engagement. For example, focus group discussions were conducted before working out HDB's two-room Flexi Scheme details. HDB also leveraged the findings from surveys from the different collaborating agencies within their integrated policy negotiation process.

Moreover, elected Members of Parliament (MP) also hold weekly "meet-the-people" sessions (MPS sessions) in their respective constituencies to understand resident concerns in their specific neighborhoods. The public often utilizes these MPS sessions to provide feedback to the MP representing their district's government policies. Elected MPs then relay resident input to relevant government agencies and statutory boards. HDB receives feedback on its policies through the elected MPs, particularly National Development and other government officeholders within MND.

For HDB (and the entire Singapore government, by extension), data and feedback are crucial drivers for future policy design. The data collected and feedback from implementing current policies are essential for the preparation phase of negotiations of future initiatives and policies. In addition, the feedback loop helps HDB and the government understand the ground-level issues and develop new or enhanced policies to meet these needs. Thus, the ability of HDB to be receptive to feedback and incorporate it in future policy tweaks was a factor in the successful implementation of policy negotiation.

Critical Insights for Negotiating a 2030 Agenda

The main takeaway from this case concerning policy negotiation is the importance of preparing a detailed implementation plan for the upcoming negotiation process before engaging the various nongovernmental public and private stakeholders. HBD's preparation for the negotiation process would entail a whole-of-government approach. HDB engaged the different government ministries and government-linked statutory boards to decide on a policy goal to present to external stakeholders. Intra-government negotiations leading to a consensus on the policy goals and implementation plans were part of the preparation phase of this negotiation process.

Steering committees receive a presentation on the comprehensive plan where other nongovernmental stakeholders add to the negotiation table. The ability of the government to present a united policy plan to external stakeholders is a display of good leadership in government, which in turn translates to an increased level of trust between the government and its stakeholders.

Moreover, the government's foresight in anticipating stakeholder concerns and resolving them before the negotiation and their receptiveness to feedback reinforces the importance of good leadership and higher levels of trust for successful policy negotiations for the 2030 Agenda.

8

FINAL NEWGOTIATION FRAMEWORK AND RECOMMENDATIONS

The Collaborative Negotiation Conceptual Framework is a culmination of all the insights gained in our research and practice (see Figure 8.1). The four steps to collaborative negotiation are oriented cyclically to exhibit that the goal of collaborative negotiations is to strive toward building lasting relationships. The interest of project leaders demands rapport building with stakeholders so that they may collaborate on future endeavors.

Preparation: A meticulous preparation phase is crucial to successfully negotiating the 2030 Agenda. Specifically, a key takeaway from the case studies and the project research is a well-prepared strategic (long view) and tactical (short and implementable) action plan. The project studied 167 cities worldwide and revealed that leading cities include SDGs in their urban plan. Cities are achieving their social, environmental, and economic goals through planning in the face of many contemporary challenges. The project revealed that most advanced cities succeed through a methodic approach to planned monitoring, engagement, good governance, and leadership.

Value creation negotiation steps create and expand the necessary value that makes SDGs valuable to governments and communities. Creative and integrative negotiation tactics increase the value of the negotiation for stakeholders, with trust being an essential element to realize the full potential of increasing value. Increasing value for all stakeholders reinforces a win–win mindset and greater attachment to a 2030 Agenda that can be sustainable and promising for all stakeholders. Moreover, critical success in expanding value for all stakeholders generates the necessary buy-in and future collaboration essential in the conceptual framework.

DOI: 10.4324/9781003497097-8

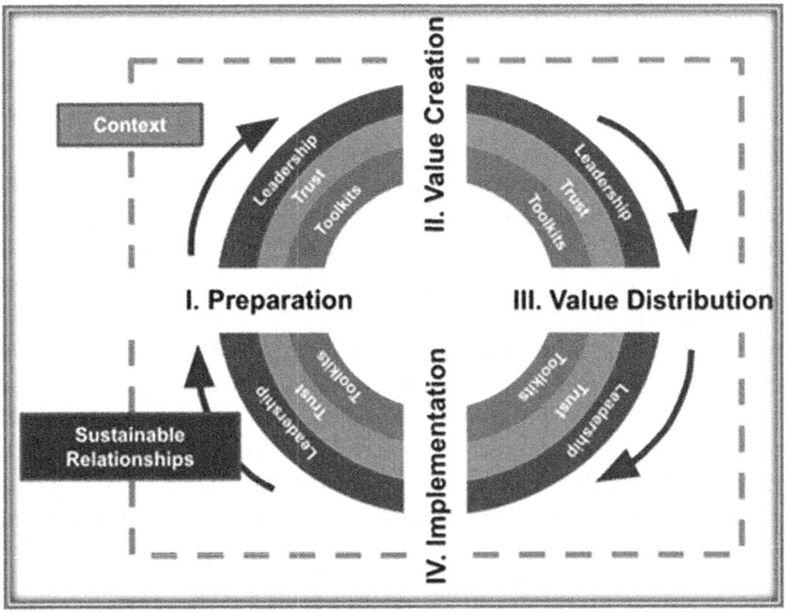

FIGURE 8.1 Newgotiation Framework

Value distribution in the negotiation process mainly concerns the balance of distributive and integrative tactics. It involves the integrative and complex act of balancing self-interest with the interests of other negotiators to achieve the optimal outcome of the negotiation. We also balance the intrapersonal and interpersonal framework to guide negotiators to understand their motivations better and build a stronger rapport with their counterparts.

Implementation is the last step in the negotiation framework, requiring the involvement of stakeholders in building actionable consensus. A policy cannot be of value if the agreed-upon terms cannot come to fruition because critical elements or consensus of the stakeholders may be missing. We believe in the adage that in public administration, implementation is everything.

Consensus-building in public administration involves balancing the executive policy with public engagement, participation, and expert input. The evolution of the negotiation technique consists of information, risk, values, ethics, and decision management rather than only politics with power mechanisms. The process of consensus-building can be taught with our four steps using the ten elements of any negotiation. This modern technique we call "Newgotiation" is an evolution of the mutual gains approach matched with the mindset of the contemporary negotiator. Newgotiation involves cognitive science, psychology, neuroscience, ethics, game theory, and management built into a common language that we describe here as the 4-10-10 technique. The culture of Newgotiation focuses on a new mechanism of governance to protect the reputation and prevent conflicts in building a civilization of empathy based on social responsibility.

As we indicated previously, the three critical elements identified in our research—leadership, trust, and toolkits—must be present in every step of the collaborative negotiation process to yield the most significant project value. A critical element without the other presents shortcomings that must motivate practitioners and SDG leaders to pursue all three essential requirements to produce lasting SDG policies that work toward the 2030 Agenda.

Leadership throughout the entire negotiation process and steps is essential. A standard feature found in the case studies was the leadership of individuals or parties to move projects forward to completion. Strong leadership had the characteristics of benevolence, foresight/foreplanning, and competency. Public management has always been a core concern and an essential subfield of public administration. But as governance increasingly occurs outside hierarchical silo-like structures, the skills of a traditional public manager using power and authority, motivation and delegation, performance measurement and evaluation, etc., become less important than the skills of a leader. Leaders initiate discussion, facilitate and articulate the organizational vision, and provide the trigger for action.

There is a concern for achieving significant organizational or societal goals in management and leadership while respecting human values. Leaders transcend structure. Steve Jobs eloquently described these skills, "Management is about persuading people to do things they do not want to do, while leadership is about inspiring people to do things they never thought they could." For the leader, this means starting with a process of personal transformation based on one's active imagination and then engaging the organization in a dialogue for potentialities and aspirations to provide the basis for change and development. The issues of leadership today are not technical but are instead issues of transformation that require leadership, which is more an art than a science.

Trust has a significant impact on how the public perceives an organization. Trust is a relational and psychological state, referring to "an individual's belief in, and willingness to act based on, the words, actions, and decisions of another." In policy negotiations, high public trust levels relate to promoting democratization and economic activities, reliable performance of institutions, and low violence levels.

High-quality governance, characterized by stakeholder collaboration, effective communication, higher levels of accountability and transparency, and strong human and institutional capacity, is critical to improving human development indicators for vulnerable populations around the globe. Research shows that an ethical organizational culture—free from personal self-interest—is necessary for high-performing governments, which are expected to make decisions that benefit the public. Furthermore, openness and transparency in government encourage valuable civic input and trust.

Openness and transparency are significant democratic values. They are the right thing to do and essential to accountability and trust. Transparency, for example, supports informed decision-making and gives all parties access to information critical to their interests and concerns, thereby leveling the playing field. Disclosure promotes full participation in the governance process. Corruption, which is private and concealed by nature, limits public engagement in the governance process, decreases public confidence in governance institutions, and increases the cost of public services.

In the collaborative negotiation context, toolkits may include resources like funding, knowledge and skills, legal help, technical and expert assistance, logistical and administrative support, communication and information technology, relationships, and even power (see Figure 8.2).

Both collaboration and SDGs are complex tasks independently and much more so when addressed simultaneously. Sharing resources can mitigate the burden of this challenging Agenda. Furthermore, local leaders further the perceived fairness and legitimacy of the overall collaborative effort by employing leadership and trust to manage available resources.

We suggested that the field of public administration is complex and already experiencing a paradigm shift in the "steering of society" from "government" to "governance." The latter term implies that the development and implementation

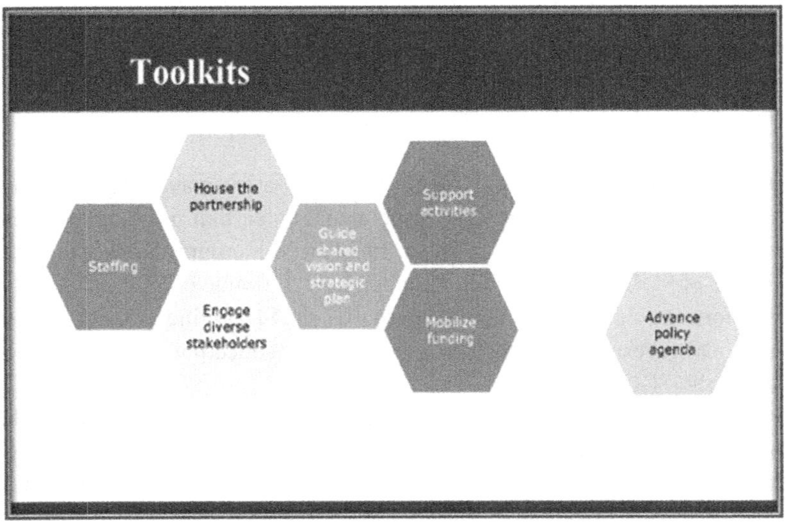

FIGURE 8.2 Toolkits for Success

of public policy are increasingly distributed or shared among a plurality of actors: public bodies, private groups, nonprofits and NGOs, and citizens in general, each with their interests, resources, and capabilities.

The global pandemic, constrictions of markets, international competition, growing fears of unemployment, and substantial infrastructure deficits present significant challenges for both the public and private sectors. On the other hand, such significant challenges represent leadership and investment opportunities of greater proportions for the public and private sectors. These sectors have never been so interdependent and predisposed, creating unprecedented opportunities for cross-sectoral and intrasectoral relationships and collaborations in delivering essential government functions, public goods, and infrastructures while addressing and solving socioeconomic problems.

With these complexities, the imperative for SDG implementation has gained priority among governments. Today, considerable number of governments refocuses on social good. While the pandemic forced people to work differently, it also re-emphasized the importance of effective collaborations for social good.

Recommendations for Practitioners

1. Continue educating stakeholders on the value of SDGs.
2. Create a knowledge base about the value of SDGs at the local level, curated for the specific needs of a locality. Include SDGs in urban plans. Share the plans.
3. Disseminate a common language for the four steps of Newgotiation.
4. Deliver toolkits to local officials—value human capital.
5. Promote best practices that enhance trust in government.
6. Inculcate leadership qualities in workshops practitioners conduct in localities.

(1) **Continue SDGs Education**: This recommendation comes directly from our survey result analysis. Our respondents noted that most stakeholders working closely with the local government are still unfamiliar with the substance of SDGs. They also fail to understand the value of SDGs to society. In short, the stakeholders do not internalize the SDG mindset daily. Hence, the local governments should be responsible for educating the communities about the SDGs.

(2) **Create a Knowledgebase**: A central repository for practitioners about the value of SDGs that tailors to regions and localities is essential. The repository should contain actionable items on SDG leadership and implementation concerning negotiations and other actions that help pass SDGs. The inventory of best practices and examples should come from similar cases either in the SDG goals they are achieving or in the regional contexts the

state occupies. A repository that is accessible and offers intuitive user experience designs will help broaden adoption. Member states that adopt the contents will gain valuable examples and next steps for their local SDG programs. As we discovered in our project, we discussed the thriving cities in SDGs leadership and implementation plan for them in Chapter 1. The project revealed that the most progressive cities ensure success through a methodic approach to monitoring progress, gaining public support, appointing a leader, and creating accountability measures—a potent recipe for effective public institutions, which we discussed in Chapter 3.

(3) **Disseminate a Common Language for the Four Steps**: Our research has revealed that policy negotiations succeeded because they each did well in the four steps. The local governments and project leaders exhibited exemplary leadership qualities and positive SDG-oriented mindsets within these four steps. They also undertook innovative negotiation methods and tactics to engage and understand their stakeholders, showing their competence and commitment to their policies in their own way. This innovation generated higher levels of trust between local governments and stakeholders, which was instrumental to successful negotiations. Hence, by creating a common language for negotiation, a standard, we suggested that the UN develop a common Newgotiation "vocabulary" and "manual" that all member states can easily use and understand. This common language would improve negotiation practices worldwide because member states can adapt negotiation tactics from other countries or cities to their context since a general audience better understands them.

(4) **Deliver Toolkits to Local Officials**: An initiative with leadership and trust but without toolkits leads to constrained negotiations and may result in simply being a great plan. Toolkits are crucial to collaborative negotiation processes. In the case studies, toolkits comprised strategic plans, expertise, steering committees, physical infrastructure, strong relationships/social infrastructure, and regulation. Equipping local government leaders striving to pioneer sustainable development with these tools will clarify and amplify their solution strategy, allowing them to take their ideas across the finish line. Again, in our project, we discovered the disparity between European, North American, and African cities in relation to people and prosperity. On average, 74% of cities in advanced economies progressed on SDGs compared to half that percentage in emerging markets. European and North American cities lead the way, while African cities trail behind relatively wide margins (e.g., Europe 77%, North America 71%, and Africa 33% on average). The UN, various NGOs, and the private sector can be influential in delivering the human capital necessary to provide these toolkits.

(5) **Promote Trust-building**: The analysis of the five cases suggests that trust-building plays a crucial role in governmental projects. There are three ways

for governments to promote trust-building through cooperation. First, they can create an inclusive decision-making environment before the project starts. Second, they can be transparent about decision-making throughout the entire process. Third, they can establish an internal mechanism to hold public officials accountable and be ethical. Lists of desired traits of ethical public servants and moral leaders are abundant and typically include honesty, integrity, credibility, fairness, equity, and inclusion. However, finding a specific moral code that applies in all or even most situations is challenging. Public servants have different ideas about ethical behavior depending on their position in society, their cultural background, or the accepted practices of their groups, organizations, or communities. The resolution of an ethical problem may not appeal to authority or even precedent but rather the interactive process of constructing a narrative that is not set at the beginning and only takes shape as the process continues.

(6) **Inculcate Leadership Qualities in Workshops Practitioners Conduct in Localities**: Leaders are invaluable in collaborative negotiation. In our case studies, with a particular emphasis on Careers by Design LA and the Seoul Smart City Platform, leaders helped spark and maintain the necessary energy to galvanize project resources and execute objectives. Inculcating leadership qualities, such as benevolence, foresight, and competency, does not happen overnight; however, in our professional experiences, workshops that reflect on these capacities through real-world applications, like creating a strategic city plan or business plan, can stimulate leadership growth. By guiding through developing a project with these qualities in mind, aspiring leaders or leaders looking to improve their performance will have the opportunity to consciously enhance their behavior and mindset, which will help formulate a foundation from which they can work in the future.

Governance and UN Principles of Effective Governance for Sustainable Development

We began by discussing the importance of governance and effective public institutions. We end as we began. If governments at all levels wish to achieve SDGs, we conclude that governments must have a practical governance framework through all the research and practice we cited in this book. Governance in the 21st century must be action-based on public processes and public values. The role of public administrators is to carry out the will of the people through democratic procedures and according to democratic norms. We also recognize that governance is increasingly complex, involving the government and various networks of public, private, and nonprofit organizations.

Also, the roles of organizations like the UN at national and international levels and metropolitan planning organizations like the Southern California Association of Governments (SCAG)[1] at the local levels cannot be understated.

Founded in 1965, SCAG is established as an association of local governments and agencies that voluntarily convene to address regional issues. One hundred ninety-one cities covering more than 38,000 square miles come together in Southern California to develop long-range regional transportation plans. These plans include Sustainable Communities' Strategy (SCS) and growth forecast components, regional transportation improvement programs, regional housing needs allocations, and a portion of the South Coast Air Quality Management District plans. Many of these policy arenas track SDGs, especially concerning persons and prosperity.

We end by citing the UN Committee of Experts on Public Administration's (CEPA) 11 Principles of Effective Governance for Sustainable Development (Appendix E). These voluntary principles provide practical, expert guidance to interested governments in a broad range of governance challenges associated with implementing the 2030 Agenda. The principles are organized into overarching categories: effectiveness, accountability, and inclusiveness. Effectiveness is composed of competence, sound policymaking, and collaboration. Accountability contemplates integrity, transparency, and independent oversight. Inclusiveness accounts for leaving no one behind, non-discrimination, participation, subsidiarity, and intergenerational equity.

CEPA's 11 Principles of Effective Governance for Sustainable Development have many overlapping characteristics but frame their solutions from a different angle that bolsters the recommendations presented in this book. Collaborative negotiations rely on effective governance, leadership, relationships, and trust. For this reason, we encourage our readers to consult the CEPA's principles to enhance their understanding of strategies that will effectuate greater collaborative negotiation to advance the 2030 Agenda.

Note

1 https://scag.ca.gov

APPENDIX A

Subject Matter Expert Interview Summaries

Janet Denhardt | "The best way to be trusted is to be trustworthy."

Dr Janet V. Denhardt was the Chester A. Newland Professor of Public Administration at the USC Sol Price School of Public Policy. She is a member of the prestigious National Academy of Public Administration and the 2013 recipient of Charles Levine Award given by the American Society of Public Administration and the National Association of Schools of Public Affairs and Administration (NASPAA). Dr Denhardt has published five books: *The Dance of Leadership, The New Public Service, Managing Human Behavior in Public and Nonprofit Organizations, Public Administration: An Action Orientation*, and *Street Level Leadership*. She earned a Ph.D. from the University of Southern California.

Dr Denhardt spoke to us about the values that drive organizational behavior, which are communicated through culture. An institution's organizational behavior is, in essence, its "personality," which is represented to its stakeholders. An effective public institution always seeks to build partnerships with its constituents based on mutual respect, trust, and transparency. Strong and supportive relationships with the public allow a public institution to effectively navigate challenging situations in which the institution's ability to work is inhibited by a lack of resources. Finally, the most important job of an effective public institution is to listen—listen to understand—and respond when its citizens speak.

Ray Rood | "Values are the soul of an institution."

Raymond Rood is the founder and senior consultant of The Genysys Group, a consulting firm that specializes in organizational and leadership development. The Genysys Group has worked with a variety of entities, including Fortune 500 companies (e.g., Amgen), state and local governments, nonprofit organizations, and universities. The firm's goal is to "sustain and safeguard transformational change" by teaching stakeholders about the visioning process and helping them develop an organizational strategic plan. Rood's expertise and work provide a foundation for our understanding of strategic planning as it relates to institutional effectiveness. In addition to his practice, Rood previously served as a professor at Azusa Pacific University, where he founded graduate programs in Student Development Education and Human Resource Leadership. Rood also previously served as a member of the Asuza Pacific University Board of Trustees, including four years as Vice Chairman.

Professor Rood emphasized two key areas relevant to our research: (1) institutional values and (2) transformational leadership. When directly asked to identify the requisite values of an effective public institution, Rood stated five values: (1) equity, (2) transparency, (3) accountability, (4) responsiveness, and (5) empathy. When executed properly, the outcome of these values is trust. When asked about leadership, Rood delineated three types of leadership: (1) catalytic, (2) transformational, and (3) generative. These categorizations represent phases of leadership in the creation of an effective public institution.

Carol Geffner | "Public institutions exist in a larger ecosystem."

Dr Carol J. Geffner was a Professor of the Practice of Governance, Management, and Policy at the USC Sol Price School of Public Policy and Director of the Executive Master of Leadership Program. She is known for her research on improving individual and institutional performance and the capacity for sustainable development. She also serves as Senior Vice President of Newpoint Healthcare Advisors and has worked on a broad range of strategy, growth, and performance issues related to the Affordable Care Act (ACA). Dr Geffner earned a Ph.D. from Claremont Graduate University and a Master of Public Administration from the University of Southern California.

Dr Geffner's interview focused on the practical elements of building effective institutions. Dr Geffner emphasized the need for institutional leaders to be aware of the positions of their organizations in relation to private sector partners, NGO partners, and community members. Public institutions can form partnerships, alliances, and affiliations with other members in their ecosystem to achieve their goals; this strategy is especially useful when public institutions lack resources. Dr Geffner also discussed best practices for defining values in behavioral terms and establishing criteria for measuring success. Dr Geffner also spoke on the importance of innovation as a driving force of institutional effectiveness.

Rick Culley | "The best leaders are the best learners."

Dr Rick Culley is the Associate Director of the Executive Master of Leadership Program at the USC Sol Price School of Public Policy. He teaches leadership in the Executive Master of Leadership Program and a graduate course in strategic planning. Dr Culley has more than thirty years of experience working as a corporate executive, university professor, and management consultant. He earned his Ph.D. and Master of Public Administration and Policy Analysis from the University of Southern California.

Dr Culley discussed strategic planning and transformational leadership as key elements of effective public institutions. Culley defined the seven prongs of a strategic plan: (1) comprehensive environmental assessment, (2) clear vision, (3) values, (4) mission, (5) goals to accomplish the mission, (6) strategies, and (7) tactics. Culley also spoke to the necessary characteristics of a transformational leader in executing a strategic plan, including delegation, empowerment, and effective listening.

APPENDIX B

Subject Matter Expert Interview Questions

Semi-Structured Expert Interview Questions

1. In your opinion, what qualities distinguish an effective public institution?
2. What values do effective public institutions have?
3. How do a public institution's values affect organizational behavior?
4. How do values affect partnerships?
5. How do effective public institutions build successful partnerships with stakeholders?
6. What is your understanding of transformational leadership?
7. What are its elements?
8. How is transformational leadership distinguished from leadership in general?
9. What is the role of a transformational leader in leading an effective public institution?
10. Do you have examples from your experience working with effective public institutions?
11. Do you have any literature recommendations for us as we continue our research on the characteristics of effective public institutions?
12. What qualities of public institutions are significant in achieving the SDGs?
13. Are some qualities more important than others?
14. Can you rank the qualities in hierarchical order?
15. How do you define leadership? To what extent is leadership needed … when you speak about leadership, tell me what you are thinking.

APPENDIX C

Selected Qualtrics Survey Results

Q1. Which Sustainable Development Goals have you worked on directly? [Select all that apply.]

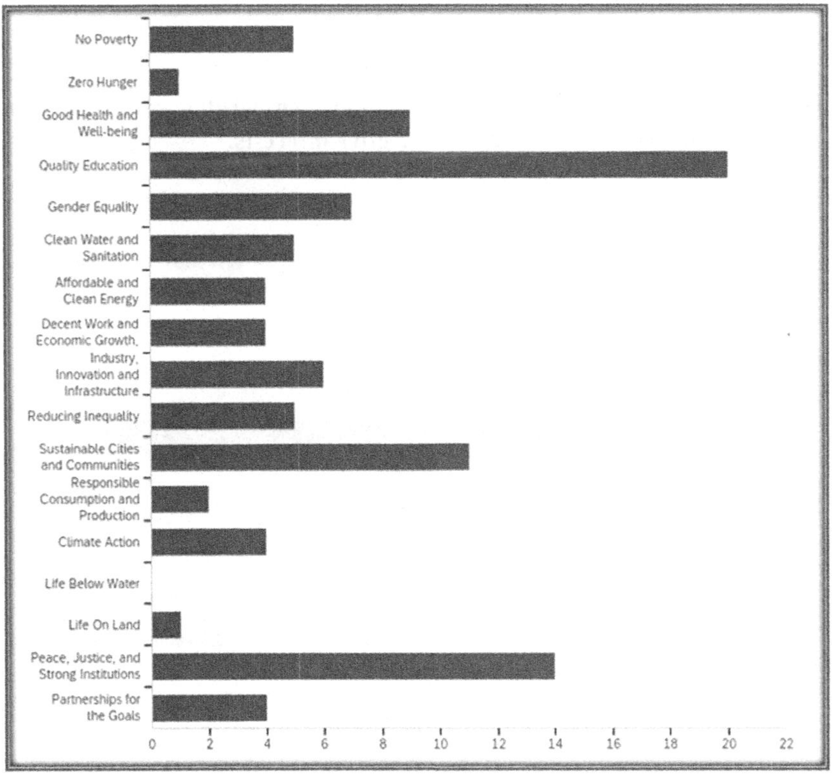

Q2. Please select the stakeholders that your work primarily involves.

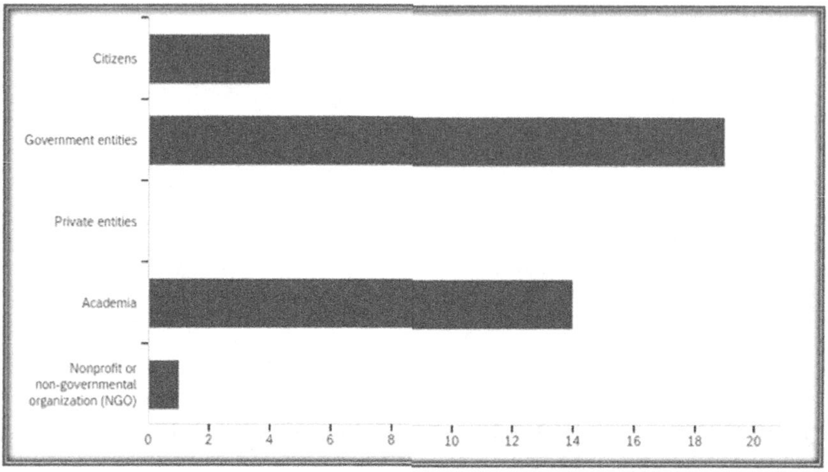

Q3. There is effective communication between local governments and stakeholders regarding their respective interests.

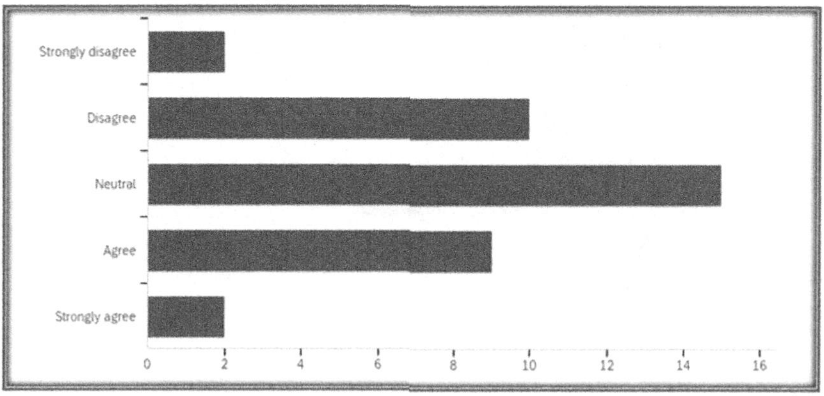

Q4. Local governments understand the interests of stakeholders.

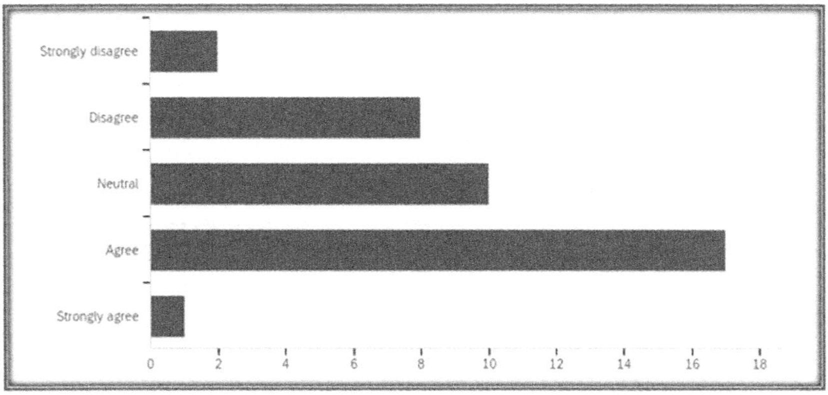

Q5. Local governments engage stakeholders before the negotiation process.

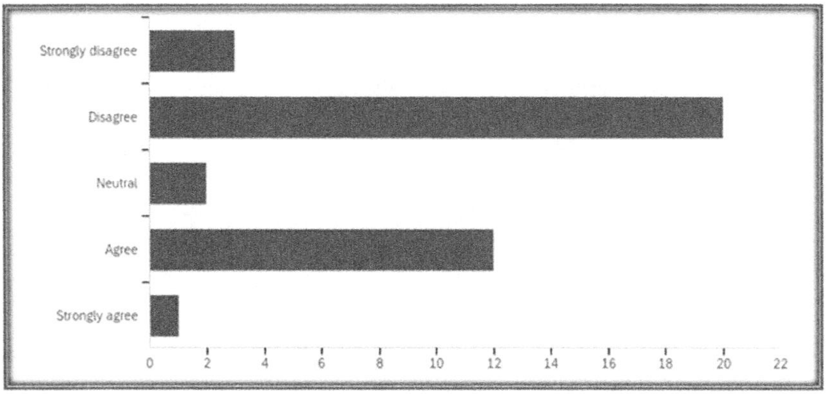

Q6. Local governments engage stakeholders during the negotiation process.

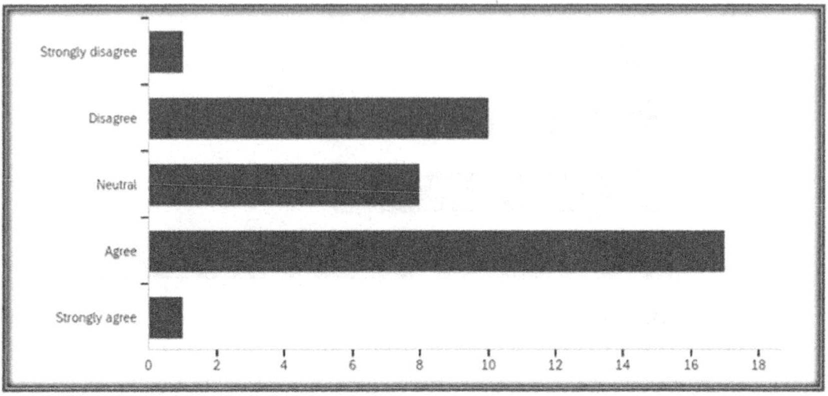

Q7. Local governments engage stakeholders after the negotiation process.

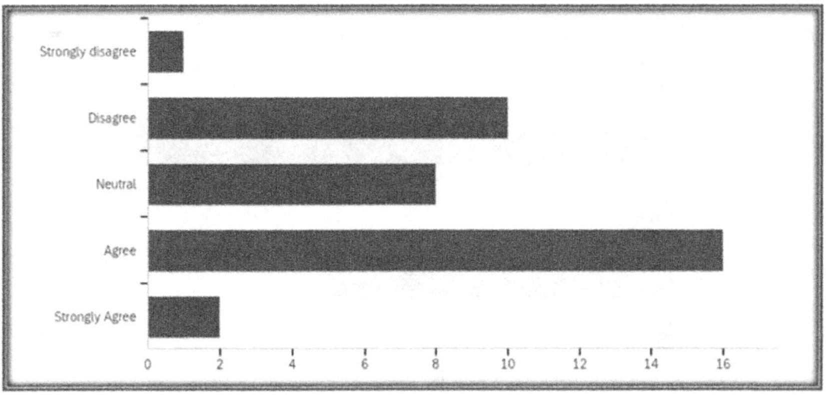

Q8. Local governments convey trustworthiness to stakeholders throughout the negotiation process.

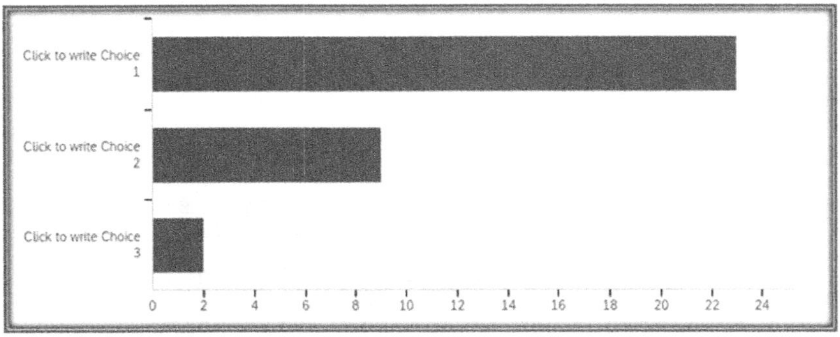

Q9. Incidents of government corruption are prominent factors in local-level negotiations.

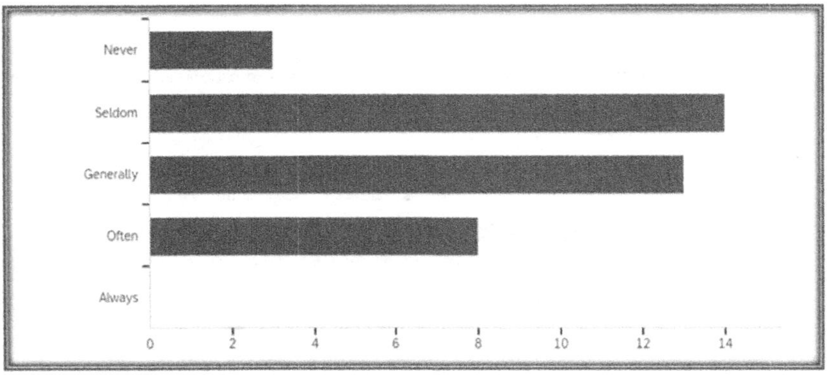

Q10. Parties involved in negotiations generally display concern for the best interest of other stakeholders.

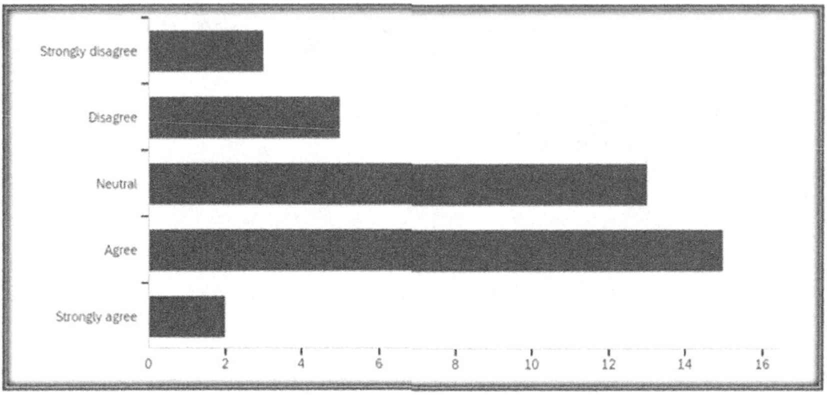

Q11. Negotiation agreements incorporate contingency terms in preparation for a failure in negotiated term(s).

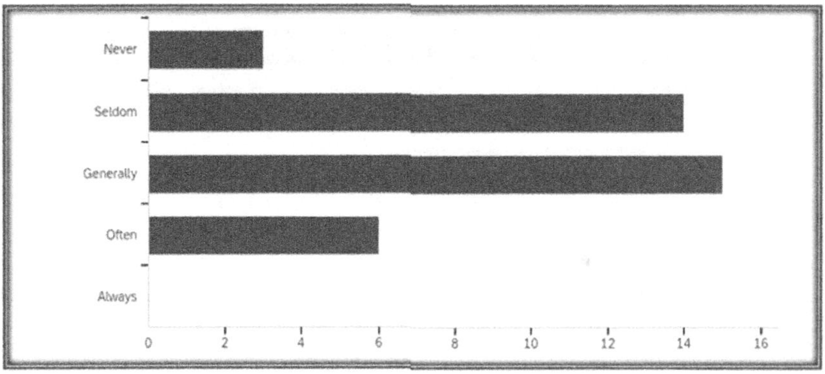

Q12. How often are alternatives or backup plans prepared in anticipation of a negotiation impasse?

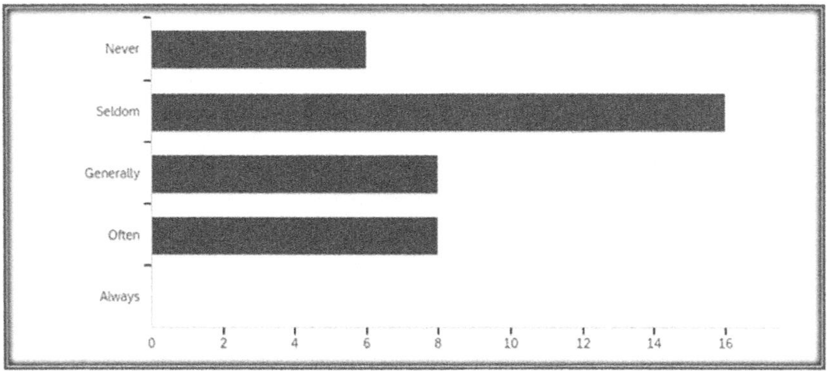

Q13. Implementation is successfully carried out after deals are negotiated.

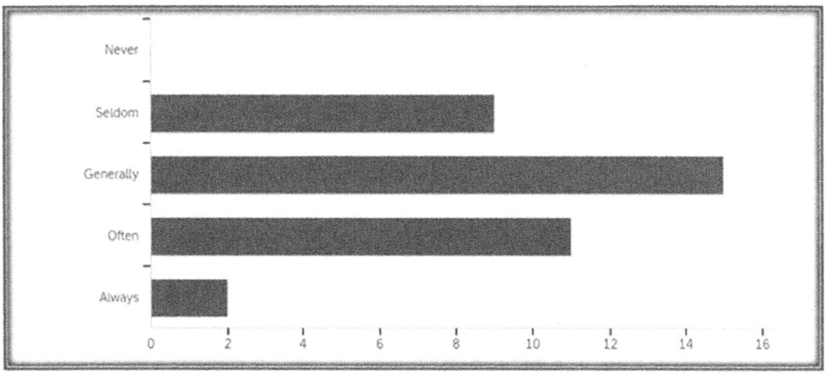

Q14. The stakeholders with which you work believe they will benefit from the advancement of the SDGs.

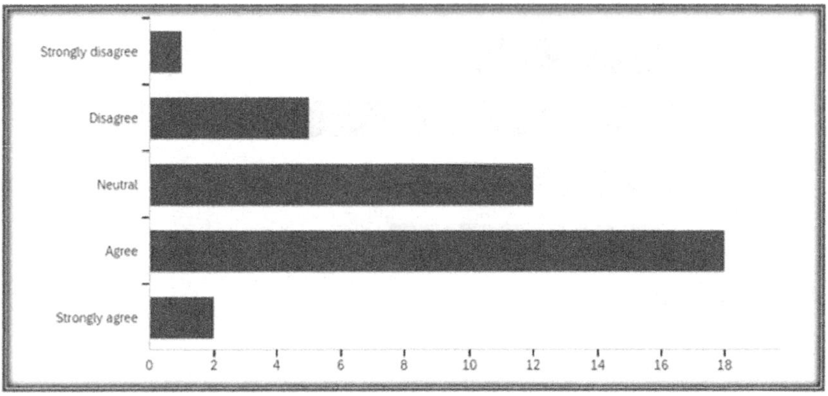

Q15. How well do you think stakeholders are educated about the benefits of sustainable development?

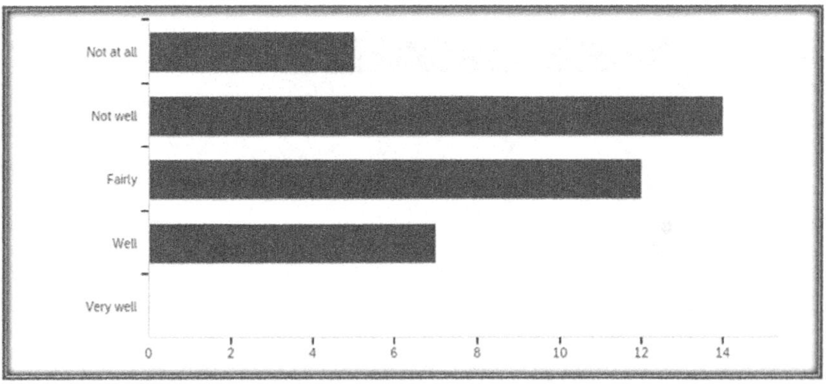

Q16. Partnerships and collaboration work well in the context in which I work.

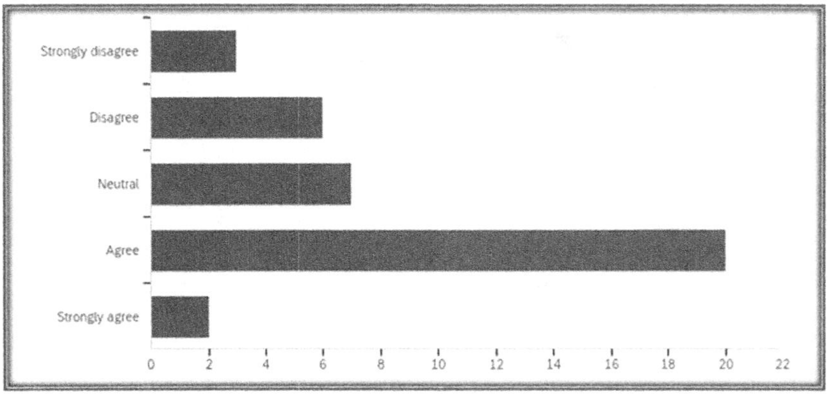

Q17. The context in which I work is well prepared to monitor the progress made on the SDGs.

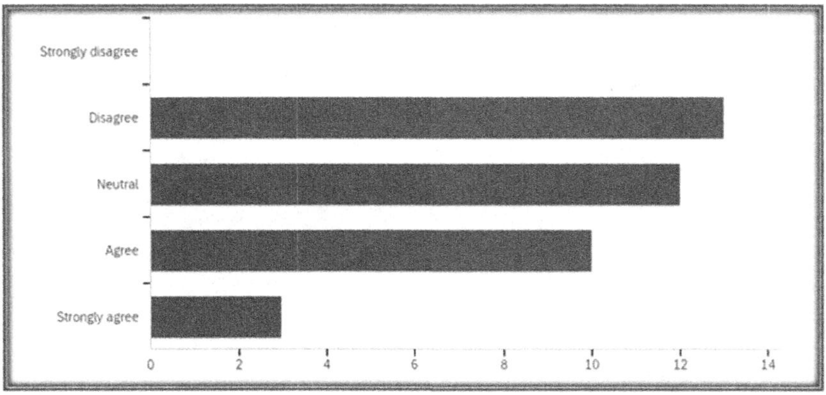

Q18. Local governments are effective in instilling an SDG mindset.

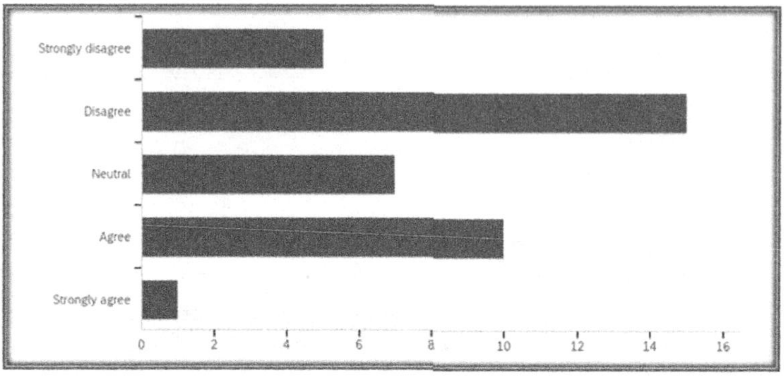

Q19. Rank the following negotiating tactics in order of importance that local governments must prioritize when normalizing the SDG mindset. (1= most important)

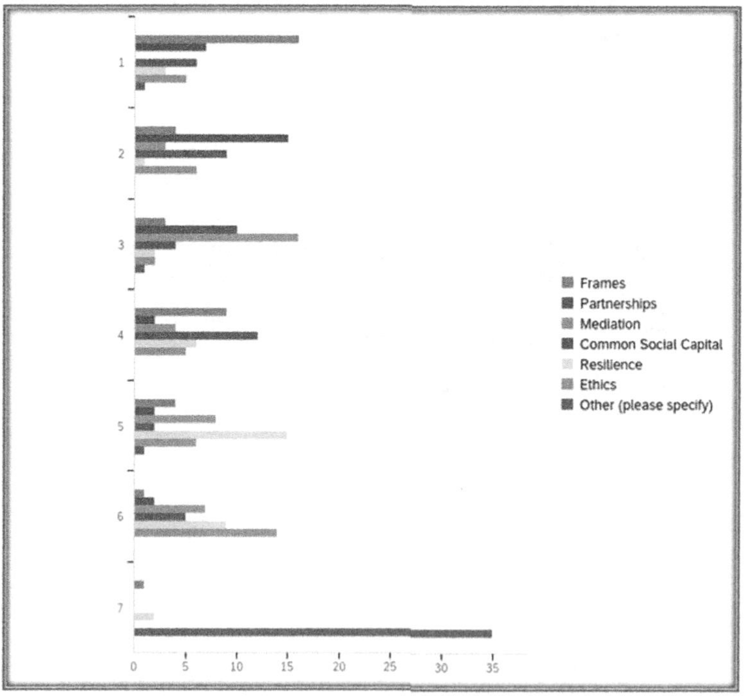

APPENDIX D

Official Interview Questions[1]

1. Could you briefly introduce your team and your program/project? What is it about? Where is your program located? Who are the stakeholders you work with? What inspired this program?
2. Were the 2030 SDGs explicitly thought of during the design phase and was the program itself tied to the UN 2030 Agenda when advertised or presented to the general public in XXX? If not, was the issue of sustainability involved with the presentation of the project?
3. What were your interests entering into the negotiation?
4. What were the main concerns of the other stakeholders?
5. Did anything go particularly well during the negotiation? What did you learn from this?
6. Talk us through the preparation process for the policy negotiation. What was the most important aspect of the preparation stage that contributed to an effective negotiation?
7. What were the main challenges to the negotiation process with regard to your initiative? What did you learn from this?
8. What would you have done if this negotiation didn't materialize?
9. Were the negotiated agreements finalized based on reaching the intended goal, or were efforts made to go beyond the goal and increase the size of the pie?
10. Collaborative vs competitive negotiation—pros and cons of each? Did either one incentivize success of the negotiation more?
11. Were there any instances in the negotiation process that encouraged the parties to have a collaborative relationship?

12. Were there any instances in the negotiation process that discouraged the parties from having a collaborative relationship?
13. What were you willing to compromise? What were the other parties willing to compromise?
14. What were you not willing to compromise? What were the other parties not willing to compromise?
15. Was there trust among the parties? Did you do anything to increase trust between the parties?
16. How did you ensure as many stakeholders were actively included in the negotiation process? Talk about your engagement style.
17. How did you make sure the agreement transitioned well into implementation?
18. How did going through the negotiation process affect your relationship with the other parties, specifically concerning future collaboration?

Note

1 These interview questions were modified to best compliment the specific case interviews. Team members also had discretion to add any questions they felt were necessary. The questions included here were to help team members create a genialized guideline to mention negotiation elements we felt necessary.

APPENDIX E

Principles of Effective Governance for Sustainable Development

https://publicadministration.un.org/Portals/1/Images/CEPA/Principles_of_effective_governance_english.pdf

Economic and Social Council
Official Records, 2018
Supplement No. 24

E/2018/44-E/C.16/2018/8, para. 31

Principles of effective governance for sustainable development

Preamble

The full realization of the Sustainable Development Goals and other internationally agreed development objectives will hinge in no small part on a common understanding of the basic principles of effective governance for sustainable development. The basic principles set out below are intended to clarify the governance agenda, taking into account different governance structures, national realities, capacities and levels of development and respecting national policies and priorities. They have been developed by the Committee of Experts on Public Administration to help interested countries, on a voluntary basis, build effective, accountable and inclusive institutions at all levels, with a view to achieving the shared vision for the people and the planet embodied in the 2030 Agenda for Sustainable Development. As basic principles, they apply to all public institutions, including the administration of executive and legislative organs, the security and justice sectors, independent constitutional bodies and State corporations. The principles are given depth and made operational through a selection of commonly used strategies and related practices, which are an integral and evolving part of this work.

Principle		*Commonly used strategies*
Effectiveness		
Competence	To perform their functions effectively, institutions are to have sufficient expertise, resources and tools to deal adequately with the mandates under their authority	• Promotion of a professional public sector workforce • Strategic human resources management • Leadership development and training of civil servants • Performance management • Results-based management • Financial management and control • Efficient and fair revenue administration • Investment in e-government
Sound policymaking	To achieve their intended results, public policies are to be coherent with one another and founded on true or well-established grounds, in full accordance with fact, reason and good sense	• Strategic planning and foresight • Regulatory impact analysis • Promotion of coherent policymaking • Strengthening national statistical systems • Monitoring and evaluation systems • Science-policy interface

Principle		*Commonly used strategies*
		• Risk management frameworks • Data sharing
Collaboration	To address problems of common interest, institutions at all levels of government and in all sectors should work together and jointly with non-State actors towards the same end, purpose and effect	• Centre of government coordination under the Head of State or Government • Collaboration, coordination, integration and dialogue across levels of government and functional areas • Raising awareness of the Sustainable Development Goals • Network-based governance • Multi-stakeholder partnerships
Accountability		
Integrity	To serve in the public interest, civil servants are to discharge their official duties honestly, fairly and in a manner consistent with soundness of moral principle	• Promotion of anti-corruption policies, practices and bodies • Codes of conduct for public officials • Competitive public procurement • Elimination of bribery and trading in influence • Conflict of interest policies • Whistle-blower protection • Provision of adequate remuneration and equitable pay scales for public servants
Transparency	To ensure accountability and enable public scrutiny, institutions are to be open and candid in the execution of their functions and promote access to information, subject only to the specific and limited exceptions as are provided by law	• Proactive disclosure of information • Budget transparency • Open government data • Registries of beneficial ownership • Lobby registries
Independent oversight	To retain trust in government, oversight agencies are to act according to strictly professional considerations and apart from and unaffected by others	• Promotion of the independence of regulatory agencies • Arrangements for review of administrative decisions by courts or other bodies • Independent audit • Respect for legality

Principle		*Commonly used strategies*
Inclusiveness		
Leaving no one behind	To ensure that all human beings can fulfil their potential in dignity and equality, public policies are to take into account the needs and aspirations of all segments of society, including the poorest and most vulnerable and those subject to discrimination	• Promotion of equitable fiscal and monetary policy • Promotion of social equity • Data disaggregation • Systematic follow-up and review
Non-discrimination	To respect, protect and promote human rights and fundamental freedoms for all, access to public service is to be provided on general terms of equality, without distinction of any kind as to race, colour, sex, language, religion, political or other opinion, national or social origin, property, birth, disability or other status	• Promotion of public sector workforce diversity • Prohibition of discrimination in public service delivery • Multilingual service delivery • Accessibility standards • Cultural audit of institutions • Universal birth registration • Gender-responsive budgeting
Participation	To have an effective State, all significant political groups should be actively involved in matters that directly affect them and have a chance to influence policy	• Free and fair elections • Regulatory process of public consultation • Multi-stakeholder forums • Participatory budgeting • Community-driven development
Subsidiarity	To promote government that is responsive to the needs and aspirations of all people, central authorities should perform only those tasks which cannot be performed effectively at a more intermediate or local level	• Fiscal federalism • Strengthening urban governance • Strengthening municipal finance and local finance systems • Enhancement of local capacity for prevention, adaptation and mitigation of external shocks • Multilevel governance
Intergenerational equity	To promote prosperity and quality of life for all, institutions should construct administrative acts that balance the short-term needs of today's generation with the longer-term needs of future generations	• Sustainable development impact assessment • Long-term public debt management • Long-term territorial planning and spatial development • Ecosystem management

BIBLIOGRAPHY

Bibliography for Effective Public Institutions Research and Chapters

About Sakala. (n.d.). Retrieved from http://www.sakala.gov.in/csr/about.html

Agbenorku, P. (2012). Corruption in Ghanaian healthcare system: The consequences. *Journal of Medicine and Medical Sciences*, *3*(10), 622–630.

Agrusa, E. D. (2010). Exploring the relationship of learning strategies and transformational leadership for business managers (Doctoral dissertation, University of Southern California).

Armstrong, E. (2005). Integrity, transparency, and accountability in public administration: Recent trends, regional and international developments, and emerging issues. United Nations, Department of Economic and Social Affairs, 1–10.

Bason, C. (2018). *Leading public sector innovation: Co-creating for a better society*. Policy Press.

Bass, B. M. (1985). *Leadership and performance beyond expectations*. Collier Macmillan.

Bass, B. M. (2000). The future of leadership in learning organizations. *Journal of Leadership Studies*, *7*(3), 18–40.

Bass, B. M., & Avolio, B. J. (Eds.). (1994). *Improving organizational effectiveness through transformational leadership*. Sage.

Boin, A., & Christensen, T. (2008). The development of public institutions: Reconsidering the role of leadership. *Administration & Society*, *40*(3), 271–297.

Boland, R. (2004). "I Think with My Hands": On balancing the analytical and intuitive in designing. In F. Collopy (Ed.).*Managing as designing* (pp. 164–168). Stanford University Press.

Brown, K., & Osborne, S. P. (2012). *Managing change and innovation in public service organizations*. Routledge.

Bunning, C. R. (1992). Effective strategic planning in the public sector: Some learnings. *The International Journal of Public Sector Management*, *5*(4), 54. Retrieved November 10, 2018, from http://libproxy.usc.edu/login?url=https://search-proquest-com.libproxy1.usc.edu/docview/234419537?accountid=14749.

Burns, J. M. (1998). Transactional and transforming leadership. *Leading Organizations*, 5(3), 133–134.

CPIA Criteria (Rep.). (2017). World Bank. Retrieved from http://pubdocs.worldbank.org/en/203511467141304327/CPIA-Criteria-2017v2.pdf

Cutright, P. R. (1985). *Theodore Roosevelt, the making of a conservationist*. University of Illinois Press.

Department of Economic and Social Affairs Division for Public Economics and Public Administration. (2000). Building partnerships for good governance: The spirit and the reality of south-south cooperation (Rep.). United Nations. Retrieved from https://publicadministration.un.org/publications/content/PDFs/E-Library%20Archives/2000%20Building%20Partnerships%20for%20Good%20Governance_the%20Spirit%20and%20the%20Reality%20of%20South-South%20Cooperation.pdf

Development in Practice Governance A World Bank's Experience (Rep.). (1994). World Bank. Retrieved from http://documents.worldbank.org/curated/en/711471468765285964/pdf/multi0page.pdf

Edler, J., & Fagerberg, J. (2017). Innovation policy: What, why, and how. *Oxford Review of Economic Policy*, *33*(1), 2–23.

Edlins, M., & Dolamore, S. (2018). Ready to serve the public? The role of empathy in public service education programs. *Journal of Public Affairs Education*, *24*(3), 300–320.

Eyler, J. (2009). *An exploration of principal self-efficacy beliefs about transformational leadership behaviors*. University of Southern California.

Falkow M. D. (2020). *A framework for good local governance: Achieving prosperity in an increasingly complex environment*. https://www.proquest.com/openview/0397506fa8af552ad8c9ba280681e420/1.pdf?pq-origsite=gscholar&cbl=18750&diss=y.

Fiol, C. M., Harris, D., & House, R. (1999). Charismatic leadership: Strategies for effecting social change. *The Leadership Quarterly*, *10*(3), 449–482.

Giguère, S. (2001). *Local governance and partnerships: A summary of the findings of the OECD study on local partnerships*. Co-operative Action Programme on Local Economic and Employment Development (LEED).

Helliwell, J. F., & Putnam, R. D. (1995). "Economic growth and social capital in Italy," *Eastern Economic Journal, Eastern Economic Association*, *21*(3), 295–307.

Hewitt, K. K., Davis, A. W., & Lashley, C. (2014). Transformational and transformative leadership in a research-informed leadership preparation program. *Journal of Research on Leadership Education*, *9*(3), 225–253.

Human Development Indices and Indicators 2018 Statistical Update (Rep.). (2018). United Nations. Retrieved from http://hdr.undp.org/sites/default/files/2018_human_development_statistical_update.pdf

Humphreys, J. H. (2005). Contextual implications for transformational and servant leadership: A historical investigation. *Management Decision*, *43*(10), 1410–1431.

Kazman, J. G., & Bonczek, S. J. (1999). *Ethics in Action*. ICCMA.

Kalantry, S. (2017). Women's Human Rights and Migration: Sex-Selective Abortion Laws in the United States and India (1st ed.). University of Pennsylvania Press, Inc. https://urldefense.com/v3/__https:/doi.org/10.9783/9780812294200__;!!LIr3w8kk_Xxm!q6S4Bf_FhJ3OccomwMAMnhO0trQAR0zcoNq1mAkv5agxQbQ_rG_mf_r n3O0BhAKa9fCUaNRWh5AOlDYZaz_vL-jK$"https://doi.org/10.9783/9780812294200

Khatri, N. (2005). An alternative model of transformational leadership. *Vision*, *9*(2), 19–26.

Khatri, N., Templer, K. J., & Budhwar, P. S. (2012). Great (transformational) leadership= charisma+ vision. *South Asian Journal of Global Business Research*, *1*(1), 38–62.

Kimeu, S. (2014). Corruption as a challenge to global ethics: The role of Transparency International. *Journal of Global Ethics*, *10*(2), 231–237.

LAEDC. (2021). *Pathways For Economic Resiliency: Los Angeles County 2021 – 2026*. https://laedc.org/wpcms/wp-content/uploads/2021/02/Pathways-report-Executive-Summary.pdf

Leithwood, K., & Jantzi, D. (2006). Transformational school leadership for large-scale reform: Effects on students, teachers, and their classroom practices. *School effectiveness and School Improvement*, *17*(2), 201–227.

Leithwood, K., & Sleegers, P. (2006). Transformational school leadership: Introduction. *School Effectiveness and School Improvement*, *17*(2), 143–144.

Leithwood, K., & Sun, J. (2012). The nature and effects of transformational school leadership: A meta-analytic review of unpublished research. *Educational Administration Quarterly*, *48*(3), 387–423.

Levine, K. J., Muenchen, R. A., & Brooks, A. M. (2010). Measuring transformational and charismatic leadership: Why isn't charisma measured? *Communication Monographs*, *77*(4), 576–591.

Lipsky, M. (1980). *Street-level bureaucracy: The dilemmas of the individual in public services*. Russell Sage Foundation.

Madlock, P. E. (2008). The link between leadership style, communicator competence, and employee satisfaction. *The Journal of Business Communication (1973)*, *45*(1), 61–78.

Manz, C. C., Anand, V., Joshi, M., & Manz, K. P. (2008). Emerging paradoxes in executive leadership: A theoretical interpretation of the tensions between corruption and virtuous values. *The Leadership Quarterly*, *19*(3), 385–392.

March, J. G. (1981). Footnotes to Organizational Change. *Administrative Science Quarterly*, *26*(4), 563–577. https://doi.org/10.2307/2392340

March, J. G., & Olsen, J. P. (1983). The new institutionalism: Organizational factors in political life. *American Political Science Review*, *78*(3), 734–749.

Mason, C., Griffin, M., & Parker, S. (2014). Transformational leadership development: Connecting psychological and behavioral change. *Leadership & Organization Development Journal*, *35*(3), 174–194.

Matveev, A., & Lvina, E. (2007). Effective transformational leadership across cultures: The role of cross-cultural communication competence. In *WCA Conference*, Brisbane, Australia.

McDonald, B. D., & Hatcher, W. S. (2019). Introduction to the issue. *Journal of Public Affairs Education*, *25*(1), 1–2.

Miller, J., & Dore, M. M. (1991). Innovations in child protective services in-service training: Commitment to excellence. *Child Welfare*, *70*(4), 437–449.

Milley, P., & Jiwani, F. (2014). Resilience and public administration: Implications for the "New Political Governance". Canada from person to society. In S. Ionescu, M. Tomita, & S. Cace (Eds.), *The Second World Congress on Resilience: From Person to Society* (803–808). Medimond.

Monkhouse, E., & Wilkinson, G. (1994). Strategic planning in public sector organizations. *Executive Development*, *7*(6), 16. Retrieved November 12, 2018, from http://libproxy.usc.edu/login?url=https://search-proquest-com.libproxy1.usc.edu/docview/205865035?accountid=14749.

Organisation for Economic Co-operation and Development. (2006). The challenge of capacity development working towards good practice (DAC guidelines and reference series, Rep.). Retrieved from http://www.fao.org/fileadmin/templates/capacitybuilding/pdf/DAC_paper_final.pdf

Organisation for Economic Co-operation and Development. (n.d.). Regulatory reform and innovation (Rep.).

Organization for Economic Cooperation and Development (OECD). (1996). *Ethics in Public Service*. OECD.

Owusu-Bempah, G., Amoako, D., Frempong, R., & Assampong, E. (2013). Preventing procurement corruption in the health sector of Ghana: A factor and principal component analysis. *European Journal of Business and Management*, *5*(1), 89.

Pelletier, K. L., & Bligh, M. C. (2006). Rebounding from corruption: Perceptions of ethics program effectiveness in a public sector organization. *Journal of Business Ethics*, *67*(4), 359–374.

Plant, T. (2009). Holistic strategic planning in the public sector. *Performance Improvement*, *48*(2), 38–43. Retrieved November 10, 2018, from http://libproxy.usc.edu/login?url=https://search-proquest-com.libproxy1.usc.edu/docview/237244315?accountid=14749.

Potter, J. (1999). *Best practices in local development*. OECD.

Prahalad, C. K., & Ramaswamy, V. (2004). Co-creation experiences: The next practice in value creation. *Journal of Interactive Marketing*, *18*(3), 5–14.

Rahimi, G., Damirch, Q. V., & Seyyedi, M. H. (2011). Job satisfaction levels and faculty members of Islamic Azad University. *Arabian Journal of Business and Management Review (OMAN Chapter)*, *1*(5), 87–95.

Redekop, B. (2012). The environmental leadership of Theodore Roosevelt. In *Environmental Leadership: A Reference Handbook* (pp. 95–104). SAGE Publications, Inc., https://doi.org/10.4135/9781452218601

Rood, R. (2016). *Strategic futuring™: A vision based approach to planning*. The Genysys Group.

Sanders, E. B. N., & Stappers, P. J. (2008). Co-creation and the new landscapes of design. *Co-design*, *4*(1), 5–18.

Sharbrough, W. C., Simmons, S. A., & Cantrill, D. A. (2006). Motivating language in industry: Its impact on job satisfaction and perceived supervisor effectiveness. *The Journal of Business Communication (1973)*, *43*(4), 322–343.

Sheng, Y. K. (2009). *What is good governance*. United Nations Economic and Social Commission for Asia and the Pacific. Disponível em: www. unescap. org/pdd. Acesso em, 21, 2012.

Shields, C. M. (2010). Transformative leadership: Working for equity in diverse contexts. *Educational Administration Quarterly*, *46*(4), 558–589.

SIGMA. (1999). *European principles for public administration*. Organisation for Economic Co-operation and Development.

Simonton, D. K. (1988). Presidential style: Personality, biography, and performance. *Journal of Personality and Social Psychology*, *55*(6), 928.

UN Women. (2010, October 31). Why is monitoring and evaluation important? Retrieved from http://www.endvawnow.org/en/articles/331-why-is-monitoring-and-evaluation-important.html

United Nations. (2015). Transforming our world: The 2030 agenda for sustainable development. Retrieved from https://sustainabledevelopment.un.org/content/documents/21252030%20Agenda%20for%20Sustainable%20Development%20web.pdf

United Nations Department of Economic and Social Affairs. (n.d.). Knowledge base of un public service awards initiatives. Retrieved from https://publicadministration.un.org/en/Research/Case-Studies/unpsacases

United Nations Development Programme. (2015). Towards SDG 16. Retrieved from https://sustainabledevelopment.un.org/sdg16

United Nations Sustainable Development Group. (n.d.). Results monitoring, reporting and evaluation. Retrieved from https://undg.org/programme/undaf-guidance/results-monitoring-reporting-and-evaluation/

Waheed, S. (1999). Capacity building in public sector organisations. *The Pakistan Development Review*, *38*(4), 913.

Williams, Jr, R., Raffo, D. M., & Clark, L. A. (2018). Charisma as an attribute of transformational leaders: What about credibility? *Journal of Management Development*, *37*(6), 512–524.

Yunus, M., & Sani, K. R. (2017). The capacity building of local government in Sanjai village, Sinjai regency. *Mimbar: Jurnal Sosial dan Pembangunan*, *33*(2), 243–250.

Bibliography for Collaborative Negotiation Research and Chapters

Ahmad, A., Weill, G., & Cleave, J. (2019). *Smart cities south Korea market intelligence report (Rep.)*. Department for International Trade.

Baarveld, M., Smit, M., & Dewulf, G. (2015). Negotiation processes in urban redevelopment projects: Dealing with conflicts by balancing integrative and distributive approaches. *Planning Theory & Practice*, *16*(3), 363–384. doi: 10.1080/14649357.2015.1058972

Behn, R. D. (2001). Discretion and Trust. In *Rethinking Democratic Accountability* (pp. 81–102). Brookings Institution Press. http://www.jstor.org/stable/10.7864/j.ctvdf03r8.8

Bellman, H. S., & Podziba, S. L. (2012). Public policy mediation. In *Dispute resolution magazine 18*(2), 14–18. American Bar Association.

Benhabib, S. (1992). Models of Public Space: Hannah Arendt, the Liberal Tradition and Jürgen Habermas. In *Situating the Self* (1st ed., pp. 89–120). Routledge. https://doi.org/10.4324/9781003059516-5

Bickford, S. (1999). Reconfiguring pluralism: Identity and institutions in the inegalitarian polity. *American Journal of Political Science*, *43*(1), 86–108.

Brockerhoff, M., & Brennan, E. (1998). The Poverty of Cities in Developing Regions. *Population and Development Review*, *24*(1), 75–114. https://doi.org/10.2307/2808123

Careers by Design Los Angeles (CDLA). (2016). MGBCE 202 CDLA presentation. Retrieved from https://sites.google.com/view/cdlacommunitybasedcurriculum/home/presentations?authuser=0

Carter, C. (2020). *Smartcitiesworld city profile February 2020 Seoul (publication)*. AVEVA.

Chatain, O., & Zemsky, P. B. (2011). Value creation and value capture with Frictions. *SSRN Electronic Journal*. doi: 10.2139/ssrn.1424950

Cho, I. S. (2017). Changing approaches to community participation for social sustainability: Neighbourhood planning in Singapore and Seoul. In F. Caprotti & L. Yu (Eds.), *Sustainable cities in Asia* (pp. 226–235). Routledge.

Chua, B. H. (2014). Navigating between limits: The future of public housing in Singapore. *Housing Studies*, *29*(4), 520–533.

Clay, J. (2016). South L.A. named a promise zone; goal is improving residents' lives. *USC News*. Retrieved from https://news.usc.edu/101608/south-l-a-named-a-promise-zone-with-goals-of-reducing-poverty-improving-residents-lives/

Cohen, B. (2006). Urbanization in developing countries: Current trends, future projections, and key challenges for sustainability. *Technology in Society*, *28*(1–2), 63–80.

Colglazier, W. (2015). Sustainable development agenda: 2030. *Science*, *349*(6252), 1048–1050.

De Dreu, C. K. W. (2014). Negotiating deals and settling conflict can create value for both sides. *Policy Insights from the Behavioral and Brain Sciences*, *1*(1), 156–163.

Draudt, D. (2016). South Korea's national identity crisis in the face of emerging multiculturalism. *Georgetown Journal of International Affairs*, *17*(1), 12–19. doi: 10.1353/gia.2016.0003

Duzert, Y., & Zerunyan, F. V. (2019). *Newgotiation for Public Administration Professionals*. Vandeplas Publishing.

Edmunds, D., & Wollenberg, E. (2002). A strategic approach to multistakeholder negotiations. *Development and Change*, *32*(2), 231–253.

Emerson, K., & Gerlak, A. K. (2014). Adaptation in collaborative governance regimes. *Environmental Management*, *54*, 768–781.

Flyvbjerg, B. (1998). Habermas and Foucault: Thinkers for civil society? *British Journal of Sociology*, *49*(2), 210–233.

Garcia-Castro, R., & Aguilera, R. V. (2014). Incremental value creation and appropriation in a world with multiple stakeholders. *Strategic Management Journal*, *36*(1), 137–147. doi: 10.1002/smj.2241

Glass, M. R., & Salvador, A. E. (2018). Remaking Singapore's heartland: Sustaining public housing through home and neighbourhood upgrade programmes. *International Journal of Housing Policy*, *18*(3), 479–490.

Gonzalez, I. (2020, January 3). Smart Seoul: A 4IR case study. Retrieved from https://www.smartnations.com/smart-seoul-a-4ir-case-study/

Habermas, J. (1992). Further reflections on the public sphere. In *Habermas and the Public Sphere* (pp. 421–461). MIT Press.

Habermas, J. (1995). Reconciliation through the public use of reason: Remarks on John Rawls's political liberalism. *The Journal of Philosophy*, *17*(3), 109–131.

Håkansson, P., & Witmer, H. (2015). Social media and trust — A systematic literature review. *Journal of Business and Economics*, *6*(3), 517–524. doi: 10.15341/jbe(2155-7950)/03.06.2015/010

Haraway, D. (1991). *Simians, cyborgs, and women: The reinvention of nature*. Routledge.

Harding, S. (1986). *The science question in feminism*. Cornell University Press.

Hawes, J. M., & Fleming, D. E. (2014). Recognizing distributive or integrative negotiation opportunities in marketing channels: The conceptualization of adaptive negotiations. *Journal of Marketing Channels*, *21*(4), 279–287. doi: 10.1080/1046669X.2014.905402

He, Y., & Qian, L. (2018). Departmental representative competition: An explanation of the fragmentation of public service supply 部门代表性竞争": 对公共服务供给碎片化的一种解释 - 中国知网. *Chinese Public Administration*, *10*, 90–97. Retrieved from https://kns.cnki.net/kcms/detail/detail.aspx?filename

=ZXGL201810018&dbcode=CJFQ&dbname=CJFDTEMP&v=xGSt3EhCmm9nOa1fmGC3ymjGAjWGx0eEpbDe8U3nQ9klC6zT8IEnnVn7RqaNcJXA

Hekman, S. (1997). Truth and method: Feminist standpoint theory revisited. *Signs: Journal of Women in Culture and Society, 22*(2), 341–365.

Housing and Development Board. (2021, February 17). *Community care apartments*. Housing and Development Board. Retrieved from https://www.hdb.gov.sg/cs/infoweb/residential/living-in-an-hdb-flat/for-our-seniors/Buying-a-New-Flat/community-care-apartments

Interview with SMG smart city division [E-mail interview]. (2021, April 30).

Jakobsen, J. R. (1998). *Working alliances and the politics of difference: Diversity and feminist ethics*. Indiana University Press.

Jiefang Daily. (2021). Shanghai "One Net Office" will launch a special edition for the elderly 上海"一网通办"将为老年人推专版_地方政务_中国政府网. Retrieved from http://www.gov.cn/xinwen/2021-01/06/content_5577386.htm

Jin, D. Y. (2017). *Smartland Korea mobile communication, culture, and society*. University of Michigan Press.

Jindal, A., & Choudhary, R. (2018). Ageing population in Singapore and government support. *International Journal of Advance Research and Development, 3*(1), 145–147. https://www.ijarnd.com/manuscripts/v3i1/V3I1-1185.pdf

Kang, M. (2020, January 23). How is Seoul, KOREA transforming into a smart city? Retrieved March 20, 2021, from https://blogs.worldbank.org/sustainablecities/how-seoul-korea-transforming-smart-city

Katz, N. H., and Sosa, A. (2015). The emotional advantage: The added value of the emotionally intelligent negotiator. *Conflict Resolution Quarterly, 33*(1), 57–74. https://doi.org/10.1002/crq.21127

Kim, S. (2005). The role of trust in the modern administrative state. *Administration & Society, 37*(5), 611–635. doi: 10.1177/0095399705278596

Kim, S. (2012). Transitioning from fast-follower to innovator: The institutional foundations of the Korean telecommunications sector. *Review of International Political Economy, 19*(1), 140–168. doi: 10.1080/09692290.2010.503125

Kwong, K.-S., Tse, Y.-K., & Chay, J. (2021). A hybrid equity release plan for retirement financing. *Asia-Pacific Journal of Risk and Insurance, De Gruyter, 15*(1), 1–24.

Lee. (2020). *WeGO 2020 Annual Report (Rep.)*. WeGO.

Levi, M., & Stoker, L. (2000). Political trust and trustworthiness. *Annual Review of Political Science, 3*(1), 475–507. doi: 10.1146/annurev.polisci.3.1.475

Lewicki, R. J., Mcallister, D. J., & Bies, R. J. (1998). Trust and distrust: New relationships and realities. *The Academy of Management Review, 23*(3), 438. doi: 10.2307/259288

Lim, S. (2020). Data as a public good: Creating open data platforms in Seoul, 2011–16. Global Delivery Initiative, November.

Lin (II), Rong-Gong. (2020). Latinos now twice as likely as whites to get coronavirus in L.A. County. *LA Times*. Retrieved from https://www.latimes.com/california/story/2020-07-10/l-a-countys-latino-residents-contracting-coronavirus-faster-than-other-groups

Los Angeles Economic Development Corporation (LAEDC). (2021). Pathways for economic resiliency: Los Angeles County 2021–2026. Retrieved from https://wdacs.lacounty.gov/wp-content/uploads/2021/02/Pathways-for-Economic-Resiliency-Executive-Summary-copy.pdf?utm_content=&utm_medium=email&utm_name=&utm_source=govdelivery&utm_term=

Los Angeles Green New Deal. (2019). https://plan.lamayor.org/

Lyakhov, A., & Gliedt, T. (2017). Understanding collaborative value creation by environmental nonprofit and renewable energy business partnerships. *Voluntas, 28*, 1448–1472. doi: 10.1007/s11266-016-9691-6

Montgomery, M. R., Stren, R., Cohen, B., & Reed, H. E. (2013). *Cities transformed: Demographic change and its implications in the developing world*. Routledge.

Moodley, S. (2020). Exploring the mechanics of city-to-city learning in urban strategic planning: Insights from southern Africa. *Social Sciences & Humanities Open, 2*(1), 100027.

Moomaw, W. R., Bhandary, R. R., Kuhl, L., & Verkooijen, P. (2017). Sustainable development diplomacy: Diagnostics for the negotiation and implementation of sustainable development. *Glob Policy, 8*(1), 73–81.

Morris, D. (1997). The feminist-postmodernist debate over a revitalized public philosophy. *Social Theory and Practice, 23*(3), 479–507.

Murphy, M., Arenas, D., & Batista, J. M. (2014). Value creation in cross-sector collaborations: The roles of experience and alignment. *Journal of Business Ethics, 130*(1), 145–162. doi: 10.1007/s10551-014-2204-x

Myeong, S., Kim, Y., & Ahn, M. J. (2020). Smart city strategies—Technology push or culture pull? A case study exploration of Gimpo And Namyangju, South Korea. *Smart Cities, 4*(1), 41–53. doi: 10.3390/smartcities4010003

National Equity at Last. (2017). Data summary: Los Angeles, CA. *National Equity Atlas*. Retrieved from https://nationalequityatlas.org/research/data_summary#/?geoSectionName=City&geo=07000000000644000

Ong, P. M., & Comandom, A. (2020). South Los Angeles since the 1960s: Race, place, and class. *The Review of Black Political Economy, 47*(1), 50–74.

Ong, P. M., Pech, C., Rios Gutierrez, N., & Mays, V. M. (2020). *Los Angeles neighborhoods and COVID-19 medical vulnerability indicators: A local data model for equity in public health decision-making*. UCLA Center for Neighborhood Knowledge. Retrieved from https://knowledge.luskin.ucla.edu/wp-content/uploads/2021/01/Los-Angeles-Neighborhoods-and-COVID-19-Medical-Vulnerability-Indicators_-A-Local-Data-Model-for-Equity-in-Public-Health-Decision-Making.pdf

Organisation for Economic Co-operation and Development. (2013). Trust in government, policy effectiveness and the governance agenda. Government at a Glance Government at a Glance 2013. doi: 10.1787/gov_glance-2013-6-en

Parajuli, P. (1998). Beyond capitalized nature: Ecological ethnicity as an arena of conflict in the regime of globalization. *Ecumene, 5*(2), 186–217.

Parkin, A. (1996). On the practical relevance of Habermas' theory of communicative action. *Social Theory and Practice, 22*(3), 417–441.

Pattberg, P. H., Biermann, F., Chan, S., & Mert, A. (2013). *Public-private partnerships for sustainable development emergence, influence and legitimacy*. Edward Elgar.

People's Daily. (2018). "One Net Office" need to be implemented 一网通办"通了还要能办_解读_中国政府网. Retrieved from http://www.gov.cn/zhengce/2018-04/26/content_5285973.htm

People's Daily. (2020). Shanghai "One Net Office" is moving towards "One net is easy to handle"上海"一网通办"迈向"一网好办"--陕西频道--人民网. Retrieved from http://sn.people.com.cn/n2/2020/0412/c186331-33942728.html

Phang, S.-Y. (2019). *Policy innovations for affordable housing in Singapore: From colony to global city*. Springer International Publishing.

Raith, M. G., & Starke, C. (2016). Negotiating the organizational effectiveness of social ventures among multiple stakeholders. *VOLUNTAS: International Journal of Voluntary and Nonprofit Organizations, 28*(4), 1473–1499. doi: 10.1007/s11266-016-9716-1

Ramirez, R. (1999). Stakeholder analysis and conflict management. In *Cultivating peace: Conflict and collaboration in natural resource management* (pp. 101–126). International Development Research Centre.

Rana, M. R. I., & Ha-Brookshire, J. (2019). New conceptual framework for fashion business ideation, negotiation, and implementation undergraduate curricula for sustainable development. *International Journal of Fashion Design, Technology and Education, 12*(2), 140–148.

Rathbun, B. C. (2014). *Diplomacy's Value: Creating Security in 1920s Europe and the Contemporary Middle East.* (1st ed.). Cornell University Press. https://doi.org/10.7591/9780801455063

Rescher, N. (1993). *Pluralism: Against the demand for consensus.* Oxford University Press.

Robertson, J. (2012). South Korean FTA negotiations: Patterns of negotiation outside a South Korean cultural context. *Asian Survey, 52*(3), 465–483. doi: 10.1525/as.2012.52.3.465

Roling, N. G., & Maarleveld, M. (1999). Facing strategic narratives: an argument for interactive effectiveness. *Agriculture and Human Values, 16*, 295–308.

Salto, K. S. (2020a, September 23). The success of Seoul as a leading smart city. Retrieved April 10, 2021, from https://saltoks.com/blog/the-success-of-seoul-as-a-leading-smart-city

Salto, K. S. (2020b, September 23). The success of Seoul as a leading smart city. Retrieved April 19, 2021, from https://saltoks.com/blog/the-success-of-seoul-as-a-leading-smart-city

Seoul Metropolitan Government (SMG). (2015). Seoul e-Government: Seoul, ready to share with the world! (Rep.). Information Planning Division, Seoul Metropolitan Government.

Seoul Metropolitan Government (SMG). (2019). Seoul smart city platform white paper smart city manual for citizens and mayor (Working paper).

Shanghai Municipal Big Data Center. (2020). 2020 UNPSA _上海政务服务一网通办_介绍PPT. Retrieved from https://publicadministration.un.org/unpsa/Portals/0/UNPSA_Submitted_Docs/2019/2c339aec-568f-4cb5-9afd-1ca1c82d0c77/2020 UNPSA _上海政务服务一网通办_介绍PPT_27112019_062819_f4a9da7f-b866-4044-86be-6d1380c815df.pdf?ver=2019-11-27-062819-210

Smith, L. (2018a, August 27). Seoul smart city portrait: The power of citizen participation. Retrieved April 10, 2021, from https://hub.beesmart.city/city-portraits/smart-city-seoul-part-1-the-power-of-citizen-participation

Smith, L. (2018b, August 29). Seoul smart city portrait: Collaboration and smart solutions. Retrieved April 10, 2021, from https://hub.beesmart.city/city-portraits/seoul-smart-city-part-2-collaboration-and-smart-solutions

Smith, L. (2021, February 22). Seoul smart city portrait: The power of citizen participation. Retrieved April 19, 2021, from https://hub.beesmart.city/city-portraits/smart-city-seoul-part-1-the-power-of-citizen-participation

Snyder, S. (1999). Patterns of negotiation in a South Korean cultural context. *Asian Survey, 39*(3), 394–417. doi: 10.1525/as.1999.39.3.01p0003h

Song, Y., Hale, C. L., & Rao, N. (2004). Success and failure of business negotiations for South Koreans. *Journal of International and Area Studies, 11*(2), 45–65.

Susskind, L., & Ali, S. H. (2015). *Environmental diplomacy: Negotiating more effective global agreements*. Oxford University Press.

Swartzendruber, A. (2016). Mediation in public administration. *Global Encyclopedia of Public Administration, Public Policy, and Governance*, 1–6. doi: 10.1007/978-3-319-31816-5_1044-1

Tao, Y., Zhang, W., Gou, Z., Jiang, B., & Qi, Y. (2021). Planning walkable neighborhoods for "aging in place": Lessons from five aging-friendly districts in Singapore. *Sustainability, 13*(1742), 1–25.

Tao, Z. (2019). How is it possible to provide government services through one network?——Taking Shanghai as an example 政务服务"一网通办"何以可能?——以上海为例 - 中国知网. *Lanzhou Academic Journal, 11*, 121–133. Retrieved from https://kns.cnki.net/kcms/detail/detail.aspx?dbcode=CJFD&dbname=CJFDLAST2019&filename=LZXK201911013&v=K2Vbejrh%25mmd2FBMQ9QArDkdR1nxe%25mmd2BT5nt2AgyE6YLUsgkaoRAQnBcCM2szDoYk9HbFiA

Thompson, L. L., Wang, J., & Gunia, B. C. (2010). Negotiation. *Annual Review of Psychology, 61*, 491–515.

U.S. Census Bureau. (2015–2019). Selected Economic Characteristics (ACS 5-Year Estimates Data Profiles).

UN-Habitat. (2004). The challenge of slums: global report on human settlements 2003. *Management of Environmental Quality: An International Journal, 15*(3), 337–338.

United Nations Department of Economics and Social Affairs. (2019). Endearing homes for our silver generation. United Nations Public Service Awards. Retrieved from https://publicadministration.un.org/unpsa/en/Home/Case-Details-Public?PreScreeningGUID=e376e2fd-5324-46a1-8f07-09b172e1eaf9&ReadOnly=Yes&ReturnURL=http://publicadministration.un.org/unpsa/innovation-hub/UNPSA-Initiatives-and-the-SDGs

United Nations E-Government SURVEY 2020. (2020). United Nations e-government survey. doi: 10.18356/8bdf045f-en

United Nations Habitat. (2004). The challenge of slums: global report on human settlements 2003. *Management of Environmental Quality: An International Journal, 15*(3), 337–338.

United Nations. (2015). United Nations transforming our world: The 2030 agenda for sustainable development. A/RES/70/1., 16301 United Nations §.

UNPSA. (2019). Case details (public). Retrieved March 25, 2021, from https://publicadministration.un.org/unpsa/en/Home/Case-Details-Public?PreScreeningGUID=4F4C5D55-C9E6-4E61-BC76-F8FC93BFDCDF&ReadOnly=Yes&ReturnURL=http%3A%2F%2Fpublicadministration.un.org%2Funpsa%2Fdatabase%2FHome%2FUNPSA-Initiatives-and-the-SDGs%2A%2F

UNPSA. (2020). Case details (Public). Retrieved from https://publicadministration.un.org/unpsa/en/Home/Case-Details-Public?PreScreeningGUID=2C339AEC-568F-4CB5-9AFD-1CA1C82D0C77&ReadOnly=Yes&ReturnURL=http://publicadministration.un.org/unpsa/database/Home/UNPSA-Initiatives-and-the-SDGs*/

Winkler, M. (2019). Los Angeles is having a loud economic boom. *Bloomberg News*. Retrieved from https://www.bloomberg.com/opinion/articles/2019-04-05/los-angeles-economic-boom-outpaces-u-s-cities#footnote-1

Xinhua News Agency. (2016). Guiding opinions on accelerating the work of "Internet + Government Services 国务院印发《关于加快推进"互联网+政务服务"工作的指导意见》. Retrieved from http://www.gov.cn/xinwen/2016-09/29/content_5113465.htm

Xinhua News Agency. (2020). Shanghai: "Two Networks" empowerment, digital governance has warmth 上海："两张网"赋能，数字治理有温度_滚动新闻_中国政府网. Retrieved from http://www.gov.cn/xinwen/2021-02/20/content_5587822.htm

Zweynert, A. (2016, October 17). Citizens are the mayor, will lead URBAN Sustainability drive, says Seoul's Mayor. Retrieved March 20, 2021, from https://www.reuters.com/article/us-southkorea-seoul-mayor/citizens-are-the-mayor-will-lead-urban-sustainability-drive-says-seouls-mayor-idUSKBN12H00D

INDEX

Note: Page locators in bold refer to tables.

3Gen Flat 138
4-10-10 technique 74; adaptability for post-settlement 97; communication 85–87; concessions 89–90; conformity to the rule of law 90–92; context 74–76; control and execution 97; emotions 96; environmental sustainability 96–97; ethics/fairness 96; interest 76–78; legal compliance 96; options 78; power 78–85; productivity 96; rationality of decision 95; relationships 87–89; satisfaction and optimization 95; social responsibility 96–97; standards 92–93; technical standards 97; time 93–95
2030 Agenda for Sustainable Development 1–4, 103, 119; Careers by Design LA, United States 131; Endearing Homes for Our silver Generation, Singapore 142–143; Shanghai "One Net Office," People's Republic of China 136–137

accountability 16, 38
accounting and management standards 92
adaptability, Brazil-Mozambique case study 123
adaptability for post-settlement, 4-10-10 technique 97
Adopt-a-Hydrant 12
Africa, urban population 120
AIDS, RED products 10
Alexa (Amazon) 12
APCS *see* Automated Passenger Clearance System
applied conceptual framework 19, 58–63, 98
Armenia: Elimination of mother-to-child transmission of HIV 24–25; strategic planning 51; transformational leadership 45–46
artificial intelligence (AI) 7
auctions 76
Australia: Cape York Region Project 26–27; innovation and co-creation 55–56
Automated Passenger Clearance System (APCS), Rwanda 31–32

bargaining, positional bargaining 90
Best Alternative to a Negotiated Agreement (BATNA) 78
best practices: applied conceptual framework 59–63; strategic planning 50–51
Blight Status, Code for America (CfA) 11
bluffs 80
Brazil, Decentralized Cooperation to Democratize Cities 118–123

capacity-building, applied conceptual framework 61
Cape York Region Project, Australia 26–27; innovation and co-creation 55–56
Careers by Design LA, United States 123–131
Careers Excellence Academy (CEA) 127
case analysis, institutional effectiveness 23; Newgotiation framework 99–100
case studies: Armenia: Elimination of mother-to-child transmission of HIV 24–25, 45–46, 51; Australia: Cape York Region Project 26–27, 55–56; Brazil: Decentralized Cooperation to Democratize Cities 118–123; Chile: Port Works Management 27–28, 40–41; India: SAKALA Mission 28–29, 46–47, 56–57; institutional effectiveness 20, 23–24; Mozambique: Decentralized Cooperation to Democratize Cities 118–123; Palestine: Establishment of the Palestine Public Finance Institute 29–30, 41–42, 52; People's Republic of China: Shanghai "One Net Office" 131–137; Republic of Korea: Smart City Platform 114–118; Rwanda: Automated Passenger Clearance System (APCS) 31–32, 47; Singapore: Endearing Homes for Our silver Generation 137–143; Spain: Decide Madrid 32–33, 52–53, 57–58; Thailand: Sa Kaeo Shelter for Children and Families 33–34; United States: Careers by Design LA 123–131
CCM *see* Country Coordination Mechanism
CDLA *see* Careers by Design LA, United States
CEA *see* Careers Excellence Academy
celebration, strategic planning, institutional effectiveness 50–51
census statistics, South Los Angeles 126–127
CEPA *see* Committee of Experts on Public Administration
CfA *see* Code for America
characteristics of negotiations 101–102
charisma 44–45
Child Health State Certificate, Armenia 25
Chile: Port Works Management 27–28; values and ethics 40–41
cities 2; mentee cities 120–121; mentor cities 120; New Orleans 11; Palo Alto 12; Sustainable Development Goals (SDGs) 5–7; *see also* Los Angeles (US)
Cities 4.0 7
City of New Orleans 11
City of Palo Alto 12
city-to-city learning partnerships 120, 122–123
civic innovation 12
Civic Insights 12
coaches, empathy 43
co-creation 11; Australia 55–56; India 56–57; institutional effectiveness 54–55; Spain 57–58
Code for America (CfA) 11
collaboration 9–11, 14, 17; civic innovation 12; communication 15; cross-sector partnerships 15; sectoral stakeholders **121**; stakeholder collaboration 15
collaborative governance 13–14, 17
Collaborative Negotiation Conceptual Framework 144
Colorado, Adopt-a-Hydrant 12
commitment to excellence: effective institutions 38; Palestine Public Finance Institute (PPFI) 41–42
Committee of Experts on Public Administration (CEPA) 150–151
common purpose 77
common spaces for negotiation 102
communication: 4-10-10 technique 85–87; collaboration 15
communicative rationality 102
Community Care Apartments, Singapore 138
community engagement, strategic planning, institutional effectiveness 50
community ownership 16
compassionate listening 84
competition, stakeholders 101
competitiveness of nations 83
compliance 73
comprehensive environmental assessment, strategic planning, institutional effectiveness 48–50
concessions 89–90
conformity to the rule of law 90–92
consensus, from individual interests 102–103
consensus-building 145

context, 4-10-10 technique 74–76
contextual assessment 58; applied conceptual framework 60
control, 4-10-10 technique 97
corporate social responsibility 81–82
corruption 146; addressing with values and ethics 36–40
Country Coordination Mechanism (CCM), Armenia 25
COVID-19 3, 6
cross-sector partnerships 15
crowdsourcing 11
Culley, Rick 155

DART Model (Dialogue, Access, Risk-benefit, Transparency) 55
Decentralized Cooperation to Democratize Cities, Brazil and Mozambique 118–123
Decide Madrid (2018) 20, 32–33; innovation and co-creation 57–58; strategic planning 52–53
Denhardt, Janet 153
direct talks 75
disadvantaged stakeholders, equitable negotiation spaces 103
disparity ratio, Los Angeles (US) 125–126
dispute resolution 75
distributive negotiation 107–108
distrust 16
dominance 14
dual concern model of strategic preferences 109

education 4
effective institutions *see* institutional effectiveness
efficiency 66
ego, power of 79
elimination of mother-to-child transmission of HIV, Armenia 24–25, 45–46, 51
emotions 77, 87; 4-10-10 technique 96
empathy 83–84; effective institutions 38–39; mentors or coaches 43; Sa Kaeo Shelter for Children and Families 42
empirical evidence, value creation through 106
Endearing Homes for Our silver Generation, Singapore 137–143; 2030 Agenda for Sustainable Development 142–143
energy use 12
Enhancement for Active Seniors, (EASE), Singapore 138
environmental sustainability, 4-10-10 technique 96–97
envy 79
equitable negotiation spaces, for disadvantaged stakeholders 103
equity: Chile 40–41; effective institutions 39; Sa Kaeo Shelter for Children and Families 42
ESI Thought Lab (ESI) research project 2, 17
ethics *see* values and ethics of institutional effectiveness
evaluation criteria, institutional effectiveness **21**
evolutionary continuum 16
Exxon-Mobil 97

facilitators 75
fairness, 4-10-10 technique 96
feminists 103
fire station negotiations 71–72
first impressions 85
five "Ps" 2

GAAP *see* generally accepted accounting principles
Geffner, Carol 154–155
generally accepted accounting principles (GAAP) 92–93, 97
geopolitical conflicts 3
global temperature 3
goals, strategic planning, institutional effectiveness 49
good cop/bad cop 81
good governance 14, 65–66
governance 9, 146, 150
governments, data business 93
Green New Deal, Los Angeles (US) 128, 130
gut instincts 84

haggling 89
Haiti, heat mapping 12
happiness 83
hard power 11
heat mapping 12
HIV, Armenia: Elimination of mother-to-child transmission of HIV 24–25, 45–46, 51
Home Kit 12

housing, Singapore: Endearing Homes for Our silver Generation 137–143
Housing Development Board (HDB), Singapore 137–138, 142
Human Development Index (HDI) 20; statistics of cases, institutional effectiveness 21–22
human rights violations; Kenya 12
human trafficking, Sa Kaeo Shelter for Children and Families 33–34
humor 85

ICTs *see* Information and Communication Technologies
idealized influence, transformational leadership 44–45
implementation 145; Decentralized Cooperation to Democratize Cities: Brazil and Mozambique 123; Careers by Design LA, United States 130–131; negotiation process 110; Shanghai “One Net Office,” People's Republic of China 136
India: Karnataka Guarantee of Services to Citizens Act of 2011 (SAKALA) 13, 28–29; innovation and co-creation 56–57; transformational leadership 46–47
individual behaviors, negotiation process 105–106
individual interests, workable consensus 102–103
influence, transformational leadership 44–45
Information and Communication Technologies (ICTs), Republic of Korea 115
information availability 64–65
innovation 53–54; Australia 55–56; co-creation 54–55; India 56–57; Spain 57–58
inspirational motivation, transformational leadership 44
Institutional Context Analysis (ICA) tool 106
institutional effectiveness 18–19; applied conceptual framework 58–63; case analysis 23; case studies *see* case studies; innovation 53–54; interviews 20; literature review 19–20; random selection 20–23; strategic planning 47–53; transformational leadership 42–47; values and ethics 35–42
institutionalizing effective negotiation, public institutions context 106–111
integrative negotiations 72, 107–108
intellectual stimulation, transformational leadership 43–44
intelligent governance systems 76
interest, 4-10-10 technique 76–78
interpersonal factors 109–110
Interrupted Time-Series Analysis (ITSA) 64
interviews: institutional effectiveness 20; Newgotiation framework 100–101; official interview questions 167–168
intrapersonal factors 109–110
intuition 84
Italy, social capital 82
ITSA *see* Interrupted Time-Series Analysis

jealousy 79–80
justice, 4-10-10 technique 96

Kampung Admirality, Singapore 139, 141
Karnataka Guarantee of Services to Citizens Act of 2011 (SAKALA) 13, 28–29
Kenya, human rights violations 12
Knowledge Base, of UN PSAI 20

Lakewood Plan of 1954 10
last bids 81
LATTC *see* Los Angeles Trade and Technical College
LDCs *see* Least Developed Countries
leadership 112–113, 146, 149–150; transformational leadership 42–47
learning retention rate 84
lease/leaseback 71
Least Developed Countries (LDCs) 15
legal compliance 91; 4-10-10 technique 96
LEGO 81–82
liberal pluralism 102–103
listening 84
literature review: institutional effectiveness 19–20; Newgotiation framework 99
local government 119
Los Angeles (US): Careers by Design 123–131; Green New Deal 128, 130; *see also* South Los Angeles
Los Angeles Trade and Technical College (LATTC) 127, 129

management 146
management standards 93
market standards 92
mayors 113
media, power of 81
mediation 107
mediators 75
mentee cities 120–121
mentor cities 120
mentors, empathy 43
mindful implementation, strategic planning, institutional effectiveness 50
Ministry of Public Works, Chile 27–28
mission, strategic planning 49
money, power 79
monitoring and evaluation: applied conceptual framework 63; effective institutions 39; strategic planning 50–51
motivation to negotiate 105–106
Mozambique, Decentralized Cooperation to Democratize Cities 118–123
multi-stakeholder dialogue 76

National AIDS Programme (NAP), Armenia 25
National Center for AIDS Prevention (NCAP), Armenia 25
Near East Relief Foundation 10
negotiation 68–70; characteristics of 101–102; common spaces for 102; defined 68; Newgotiation framework 5
negotiation process: implementation 110; preparation for 104–105; social motivations and individual behaviors 105–106; value creation 105; value distribution 107–109
negotiation spaces, for disadvantaged stakeholders 103
negotiators 71–72
negotiator's dilemma 94
Nest 12
neutral mediators 75
Newgotiation framework 5, 7, 11, 16, 67–73, 145; Brazil-Mozambique case study 122–123; case study analysis 99–100; communication 85–87; concessions 89–90; conformity to the rule of law 90–92; context 74–76; interest 76–78; interviews 100–101; literature review 99; options 78; power 78–85; qualitative method 99–101; relationships 87–89; standards 92–93; surveys 99; time 93–95; *see also* 4-10-10 technique
Newgotiators 69
Norwegian University of Science and Technology (NTNU) 6
not-for-profit/civil society organization/non-governmental (NFP/CSO/NGO) 14

Oasis of 10 Million Imagination 117
objective market standards 92
Obstetric Care State Certificate Program, Armenia 25
Open Data Plaza 115
Open Data Systems 12
Open Government movement 12
openness 146
optimization, 4-10-10 technique 95
options, 4-10-10 technique 78
organizational stakeholders 50
other-concern 109
outcome evaluation 63

Palestine: Establishment of the Public Finance Institute 29–30; strategic planning, institutional effectiveness 52; values and ethics 41–42
Palestine Public Finance Institute (PPFI) 29–30; strategic planning, institutional effectiveness 52; values and ethics 41–42
partnerships, applied conceptual framework, institutional effectiveness 61–62
pavement repair 7
Peninsula Development Road (PDR), Cape York Region Project 26
pension reform 91
People's Republic of China, Shanghai "One Net Office" 131–137
Philadelphia, pavement repair 7
PMTCT *see* preventive mother-to-child transmission of HIV
pollution 3
population, Singapore 137–138
population growth 119–120
Port Works Management, Chile 27–28; values and ethics 40–41
positional bargaining 90
power 78–79, 109–110; qualities that improve relationships 81–85; self-centered motivations 79–80; tactics

that misfire because they damage relationships 80–81
power-sharing 14
PPFI *see* Palestine Public Finance Institute
practitioners, recommendations for 148–150
predictability, effective institutions 39
preparation: Brazil-Mozambique case study 122; for negotiation process 104–105, 144; Newgotiation framework 70; People's Republic of China: Shanghai "One Net Office" 135; Singapore: Endearing Homes for Our silver Generation 139–140; United States: Careers by Design LA 129
preventive mother-to-child transmission of HIV (PMTCT) 24–25
principles of effective governance for sustainable development 169–172
private goods 9
private sector 9, 14
process innovation 53
productivity, 4-10-10 technique 96
program evaluation 63
public administration 147
public agencies 12
public confidence, Singapore 140–141; *see also* trust
public goods 9
public institutions, institutionalizing effective negotiation 106–111
public leaders, power of money and sex 79
public management 146
public participation 66
public-private partnership 71; Smart City Platform, Republic of Korea 117
public sector 9, 14
Public Service Innovation Branch of the Division of Public Institutions and Digital Governance (DPIDG) 2

qualitative method, Newgotiation framework 99–101
qualtrics survey results, selected 157–166
quiet corruption 36–37

radical pluralists 103
random selection, institutional effectiveness 20–23
rationality of decision, 4-10-10 technique 95
reciprocity, Brazil-Mozambique case study 122
RED 10
regulatory innovation 54
relationships: 4-10-10 technique 87–89; damaged by power 80–81; improving with power 81–85
Republic of Korea, Smart City Platform 114–118
Reputation Economy 81
reputation management 81
resilience 39, 66
responsiveness 40
rising sea levels 3
role models, transformational leadership 44–45
Rood, Ray 154
Roosevelt, Theodore 45
Rwanda: Automated Passenger Clearance System (APCS) 31–32; transformational leadership 47

Sa Kaeo Shelter for Children and Families, Thailand 33–34; values and ethics 42
SAKALA. *see* Karnataka Guarantee of Services to Citizens Act of 2011 (SAKALA)
SAKALA Mission (2017), India 20, 28–29; innovation and co-creation 56–57; transformational leadership 46–47
salami tactics 80
satisfaction 4-10-10 technique 95
SCS *see* Sustainable Communities' Strategy
sectoral stakeholders, collaboration **121**
self-awareness 109–110
self-centered motivations, power 79–80
self-concern 109
Seoul Metropolitan Government (SMG) 115–116
Seoul Open Data Plaza (SODP) 116
sex, power of 79
sexual harassment 91
Shanghai Municipal Big Data Center 134
Shanghai "One Net Office," People's Republic of China 131–137
shared value 83
Singapore: Endearing Homes for Our silver Generation 137–143
Siri 12
SLATE-Z *see* South LA Transit Empowerment Zone

Smart City Platform, Republic of Korea 114–118
smart power 11
SMG *see* Seoul Metropolitan Government
social capital 82–83
social motivations, negotiation process 105–106
social responsibility, 4-10-10 technique 96–97
SODP *see* Seoul Open Data Plaza
South LA Transit Empowerment Zone (SLATE-Z) 126, 129
South Los Angeles 125; census statistics 126–127
Southern California Association of Governments (SCAG) 150
Spain: Decide Madrid (2018) 32–33; innovation and co-creation 57–58; strategic planning 52–53
species extinction 3
stakeholder analysis 70, 105; Shanghai "One Net Office," People's Republic of China 134–135
stakeholders: collaboration 15; competition 101; multi-stakeholder dialogue 76; strategies to develop required relations and data for negotiations 88–89
stakeholdership **105**
standards: 4-10-10 technique 92–93, 97; management standards 93; market standards 92
Standby Taskforce 12
state-owned enterprises, People's Republic of China 135
storytelling 85
strategic planning 47–48; Armenia 51; community engagement 50; components of plans 48; comprehensive environmental assessment 48–50; mindful implementation 50; Palestine 52; Spain 52–53
strategies: to develop required relations and data for negotiations 88–89; for strategic planning 49–50
support from mentors/coaches 43
surveys 110–111; Newgotiation framework 99; qualtrics survey results, selected 157–166
Sustainable Communities' Strategy (SCS) 150
Sustainable Development Goals (SDGs) 1–2, 101; Goal 4 128; Goal 11 119, 128; Goal 16 4–7

tactics, strategic planning 50
Team UN 2019 4
Team UN 2021 4–5, 18, 99; Newgotiation framework 67–73
technical standards, 4-10-10 technique 97
technology, communication 86
territorial management and registry 121
Thailand: Sa Kaeo Shelter for Children and Families 33–34; values and ethics 42
threats 80–81
time, 4-10-10 technique 93–95
TMR *see* Transport and Main Roads
toolkits 112, 114, 147, 149
transformational leadership: Armenia 45–46; India 46–47; Rwanda 47
transparency 16, 40, 146
Transport and Main Roads (TMR), Australia 26–27, 56
trust 37–38, 66, 82–83, 110, 113, 146
trust-building 149

UN Region, statistics of cases 21–22
United Nations (UN) 150; Committee of Experts on Public Administration (CEPA) 150–151; Department of Economic and Social Affairs (DESA) 2, 99–100; Development Program (UNDP) 106; Institutional Context Analysis (ICA) tool 106; Public Service Award Initiatives (PSAI) 4; Public Service Awards (UNPSA) 99–100; Sustainable Development Goals (SDGs) Progress Report 2023 3; Team UN 2019 4; Team UN 2021 4–5
University of Southern California Sol Price School of Public Policy (USC Price) 6–7
urban population 119–120
urbanization 119

validity 63–64
value creation 77, 87, 90, 144; Brazil-Mozambique case study 122; from empirical evidence 106; negotiation process 105; Newgotiation framework 71; People's Republic of China: Shanghai "One Net Office" 135–136; Singapore: Endearing Homes for Our

silver Generation 140–141; United States: Careers by Design LA 130
value distribution 90, 107–109, 145; Brazil-Mozambique case study 123; Newgotiation framework 72; People's Republic of China: Shanghai "One Net Office" 136; Singapore: Endearing Homes for Our silver Generation 140–141; United States: Careers by Design LA 130
values and ethics of institutional effectiveness 35–42; addressing corruption 36–40; Chile: Port Works Management 40–41; Palestine: Establishment of the Palestine Public Finance Institute 41–42; strategic planning, institutional effectiveness 49; Thailand: Sa Kaeo Shelter for Children and Families 42
vision 44; strategic planning 49

Walt Disney Company 82
Waste Management 10
Waze for Cities 12
Workforce Connections (WFC) 127–128

Made in the USA
Monee, IL
13 September 2026

62977457R20125